George William Ross

The Universities of Canada

Their history and organization

George William Ross

The Universities of Canada
Their history and organization

ISBN/EAN: 9783337035983

Printed in Europe, USA, Canada, Australia, Japan

Cover: Foto ©ninafisch / pixelio.de

More available books at **www.hansebooks.com**

The Universities of Canada

THEIR HISTORY AND ORGANIZATION

WITH AN OUTLINE OF

British and American University Systems.

APPENDIX TO THE REPORT OF THE MINISTER OF EDUCA-
TION, 1896.

TORONTO:
PRINTED BY WARWICK BROS. & RUTTER, 68 AND 70 FRONT STREET WEST.
1896

TABLE OF CONTENTS.

Part I. Universities of Canada.

	Page.
Chapter I. Introductory	3
Chapter II. The University of King's College, Toronto	7
Chapter III. The University of Toronto	49
Chapter IV. Victoria University	84
Chapter V. Queen's University	108
Chapter VI. Trinity University	119
Chapter VII. McMaster University	127
Chapter VIII. The Western University of London	136
Chapter IX. Roman Catholic Universities of Ontario	140
Chapter X. Protestant Universities of Quebec	147
Chapter XI. Roman Catholic Colleges of Quebec	159
Chapter XII. Nova Scotia Universities	170
Chapter XIII. New Brunswick Universities	192
Chapter XIV. The University of Manitoba	204

Part II. Universities of Great Britain.

Chapter XV. The University of Oxford	213
Chapter XVI. The Universities of Scotland	247

Part III. Universities of the United States.

Chapter XVII. Harvard University	281
Chapter XVIII. Yale University	294
Chapter XIX. The College of New Jersey	302
Chapter XX. Columbia University	308
Chapter XXI. The University of Michigan	318
Chapter XXII. Cornell University	330
Chapter XXIII. Johns Hopkins University	341
Chapter XXIV. Clark University	349
Chapter XXV. The University of Chicago	352

APPENDIXES.

A. King's College Charter and Land Grant . . . 363
B. Upper Canada College 374
C. Inauguration of King's College 378
D. King's College Commissions 383
E. Toronto University Commissions 387
F. Basis of University Federation 390
G. Victoria College Charter 396
H. Queen's College Charter . . . 405
I. Trinity College Charter 414
J. McGill College and Bishop's College Charters . . 418
K. Laval University Charter 434

PREFACE.

For several years the desirability of revising and consolidating the laws with respect to the University of Toronto has pressed itself upon my attention. Owing to the amendments made by the Legislature during the last twenty years, the Statutes under which the University is administered have become somewhat obscure. As it is an exceedingly difficult matter to incorporate amendments into an Act of Parliament without affecting the arrangement and symmetry of existing sections, a complete revision of the Act was therefore necessary.

More important, however, than the symmetrical arrangement of the Statutes, was the introduction of such amendments as would increase the efficiency of the University, and prevent confusion in its government or collision between the different bodies having authority in its administration. The investigation held last year before a Royal Commission showed very clearly that, at least as far as discipline is concerned, there was great difficulty in determining the jurisdiction of those concerned in the management of University affairs.

The growth of the University and the place which it fills in our educational system have also increased the responsibility of the Legislature in dealing with it. In the brief period of ten years, the attendance of students has increased from 348 to 875. The Senate of the University, in the exercise of its right to fix the standard for matriculation, practically determines the course of study in all our High Schools, now attended by over 23,000 pupils. The teachers in training at the Ontario Normal College, the Provincial Normal Schools, and the County Model Schools, numbering over 2,000 annually, receive the greater part of their professional and non-professional instruction from graduates of the University of Toronto. Its influence, therefore, as the centre of educational activity for the Province upon its own students and upon the educational forces of the country cannot be overestimated.

In considering what should be done to increase the usefulness of the University of Toronto, a study of the organization of other Universities cannot fail to be helpful. While it is true that the educational as well as the political institutions of a people must be adapted to the local conditions which call them into existence, it is equally true that the experience of those concerned in the administration of other institutions of a similar kind is worthy of consideration. Owing to our colonial relationship it will be observed, particularly in reading the history of the University of Toronto, that an effort was made to transplant from the Mother Country a University organization adapted to conditions of society which did not prevail in this country. Many of the difficulties with which the Legislature has to contend, and indeed some of the anomalies which the Legislature has now to consider, grew out of this circumstance. By the Act of 1853 it was intended that the University of Toronto should be a transcript of the University of London (England). The idea of a great University surrounded by a group of affiliated colleges appealed very strongly to the popular imagination, and for a time appeared, both in England and here, to work well. It was found by experience, however, that this ideal did not meet the educational wants of the Province, and so in 1887, on the federation of Victoria University, a radical change was made in the constitution of the University. From the report of a Royal Commission laid before the House of Commons last year, it is altogether likely the British Parliament will take a similar course with regard to the London University, making it a teaching as well as an examining body, as the University of Toronto was made by the Act of 1887.

In the report which follows, I have endeavored to set forth, somewhat fully, the history of all the Universities of Canada. Although the Legislature of the Province has mainly to deal with education as directed by the Provincial University, still for the last twenty years it has very properly recognized the Degree of any University in the British Dominions for all purposes of higher education. The ties which politically bind the various Provinces of Confederation and the most distant colonies of the Empire together are thus duplicated educationally and so far with the most satisfactory results. The graduates of the Universities of Ontario and the rest of Canada, as well as the graduates of the great seats of learning at the heart of the Empire, vie with each other in contributing to the intellectual development of the Provinces. On this account it will be the more interesting to know how such Universities are organized and the courses of study required of their alumni.

In the report which follows, the resumè of the organization of Oxford and of the Scottish Universities will, I hope, be found interesting and instructive.

In order to compare older methods of organization with methods of a more modern character, I have included in my report an outline of the history of eight of the more advanced Universities in the United States. In this list will be found the names of some operating under private charters and therefore more dependent upon popular support, and of others maintained largely by State aid, such as the University of Michigan. For simplicity of organization and government, the charter of the University of Michigan is worthy of careful study, and were it not for our traditions and associations, it might be taken as a model for the re-organization of University of Toronto.

I am indebted to William Houston, M.A., Toronto University, for the report on the Universities of Canada; to F. J. A. Morris, M.A., Oxford University, for a report on English Universities; to Alexander Fraser, M.A., Glasgow University, for a report on the Universities of Scotland; to J. Pelham Edgar, B.A., Toronto University, now of Johns Hopkins University, for a report on the Universities of the United States.

GEO. W. ROSS,

EDUCATION DEPARTMENT,
TORONTO. 24th February, 1896.

PART I.

UNIVERSITIES OF CANADA.

CHAPTER I.

INTRODUCTORY.

Higher education was in Canada a plant of late origin, and it was for a long time a plant of slow growth. This country, with the exception of small portions of Quebec and Acadia, was not occupied by a white population until after the close of the American Revolutionary War. The conclusion in 1783 of the Treaty of Paris, by which the independence of the United States was recognized, was the signal for the exodus from that country of the United Empire Loyalists, who settled in various parts of the Dominion of Canada. Their struggle for life in what was virtually an unbroken wilderness was extremely severe and protracted. They had to hew homes out of the forest, and after they were in a position to grow produce for export there was little to be had in exchange for it, while the means of transportation was extremely defective and its cost very great. It is not at all surprising, therefore, that nothing like a system of education, higher or lower, was organized in any of the Provinces during the first half century after their colonization. The population was small; the settlements were isolated; there was no municipal machinery; and the attention of the legislatures was chiefly occupied with providing for the administration of justice, developing means of communication between different parts of the country, and devising systems of exchange to facilitate a growing commerce.

During all this period of strenuous effort to better their material condition, however, the colonists never lost sight of the desirability, if not necessity, of establishing universities. The United Empire Loyalists came largely from New England and New York, where the idea of higher education was quite familiar to the people. Harvard College had then been in active existence for over a hundred and fifty years, Yale College for over eighty, and Columbia College for a generation. Not a few of the immigrants were themselves men of culture, which had been acquired in some cases by actual attendance at seats of higher learning, in others at secondary schools taught by university alumni. Of the early immigrants into Canada from Great Britain some had actually received a university education, and others were in a position to appreciate the civilizing effect of academical culture on a community. It was natural that these two classes should deeply regret the want of such educational advantages as would have been afforded to their families in the countries they had left, and should earnestly strive to create similar educational opportunities in the country to which they had come.

Their efforts were probably stimulated by what had been done for the education of the French people already in the country. From an early period in the colonization of New France, the higher as well as the lower culture had been a feature in the ideal of those who promoted its settlement, and development, and liberal endowments were granted by the French King to religious societies to enable them to perform this important work—endowments which play a prominent part at the present day in securing for Quebec efficient and well-equipped colleges and universities. There never was a time in the history of that Province when it had not creditable and valuable facilities for imparting higher education to those who desired it, and the existence of such facilities, and the use made of them, could not fail to intensify the zeal of the English speaking colonists in all the provinces and keep alive their determination to provide educational opportunities equally good for the youth of their own race and language.

Though the progress of higher education was for the first half century after the influx of the United Empire Loyalists very slow, it has during the past half century, and especially the last generation, been very rapid. The gradual expansion of settlement, the development of agriculture, the improvement of transportation facilities by the construction of canals and railways, the growing efficiency of elementary and secondary schools, and the widening of the political horizon of the people by the confederation of the Provinces in 1867, have all operated as causes to produce this effect. So have the stimulating examples set by the academical institutions of Great Britain and the United States. The liberalization of the Universities of Oxford and Cambridge and the establishment of the University of London offered increased inducements to students from the colonies, while the valuable endowments, efficient organizations, and greater proximity of such institutions as Harvard, Yale, Columbia, Cornell, and Princeton, enabled them to hold out quite as strong incentives to young Canadians to expatriate themselves. The only way to keep them at home was to provide similar facilities in Canada. To this task the authorities of Canadian universities were constrained to address themselves, and this they have done with a fair degree of success.

The enterprise in the field of higher education, which has long characterized both the French and the British people of Canada, was sure to find practical expression in the North-West Territories. In the Province of Manitoba there are three teaching colleges, all in close connection with the non-teaching Provincial University. The energy of the great religious denominations has there, as in the older provinces, been enlisted in the work, and they have never wavered in their determination or their efforts to provide facilities which will keep the youngest members of the Confederation abreast of educational progress in all other parts of Canada.

CHAPTER II.

THE UNIVERSITY OF KING'S COLLEGE.

One of the most eminent of the United Empire Loyalist immigrants into that part of Quebec which afterwards became "Upper Canada" was Mr. Richard Cartwright. He was born at Albany, in New York, where his father had settled as an emigrant from England. He was educated at a school in his native city, and there he became acquainted with Latin, Greek, and other subjects usually included in a higher education. Mr. Cartwright was in training for the Christian ministry when his preparatory work was interrupted by the outbreak of the Revolutionary War, in which he took an active part on behalf of the Crown. At its conclusion he settled in Kingston, where he became prominent in mercantile pursuits, and also in the public life of the young colony. As early as 1789 he addressed a memorial to Lord Dorchester, then Governor-General, suggesting that an appropriation of public lands should be devoted to the establishment of a "decent Seminary of Education," and this with a view rather to future than to present advantage. Lord Dorchester's response was favorable, but before anything could be done the Constitutional Act* was passed by the Imperial Parliament.

---

*The Constitutional Act (31 Geo. III, cap 31) was passed in 1791. The King having intimated to Parliament his intention to divide the Province of Quebec into two Provinces, Upper Canada and Lower Canada, this statute created for each of them a Legislature of two chambers.

Governor Simcoe's Policy.—The first Lieutenant-Governor of Upper Canada was John Graves Simcoe, who had distinguished himself as a British officer during the Revolutionary War. He had been educated as a boy at Eton, and before entering the army had spent some time as a student at Merton College, Oxford. In 1790, he was elected a Member of the British House of Commons, and in that capacity took an active interest in the progress of the Constitutional Act during its passage through its various stages. Before leaving England to fill the position of Lieutenant-Governor he indicated in a letter to Sir Joseph Banks, then President of the Royal Society, the importance he attached to a system of higher education in a community such as that to which he was commissioned : " In a literary way I should be glad to lay the foundation stone of some society that I trust might hereafter conduce to the extension of science. Schools have been shamefully neglected ; a college of a higher class would be eminently useful, and would give a tone of principle and manners that would be of infinite support to Government."* After his arrival in Canada, Governor Simcoe wrote from Quebec to the Right Honourable Henry Dundas, then Secretary of State for the Colonies, pointing out that while "lower education" might be provided for out of the resources of the Province " the higher must be indebted to the liberality of the British Government, as owing to the cheapness of education in the United States, the gentlemen of Upper Canada will send their children there, which would tend to pervert their

---

* Hodgins' Documentary History of Education in Upper Canada, vol. I, p. 11.

British principles." Mr. Dundas in his reply gave his opinion that "schools" would be sufficient for some time, adding that whenever steps should be taken by the Province to establish "a higher seminary" he would have great pleasure in forwarding the project. In 1795 the Governor wrote to the Bishop of Quebec, of whose diocese Upper Canada then formed a part, stating that his views respecting a University were "totally unchanged," that they were "on a solid basis," and that whether they were or were not complied with by his superiors, they would certainly appear as his system to the "judgment of posterity." In the following year he again wrote to the Bishop admitting that he had "no idea" that a University would be established, though he was daily confirmed of its necessity. A few months afterwards he ventured to press the matter once more on the attention of the Imperial authorities in a letter,* from which the following is an extract: "In the meantime the sevenths† of the Crown will become gradually productive as lands which have been granted shall be cultivated, or withdrawn from the market, and appropriations may be made agreeably to the opinion of the Council, to be sold hereafter for public purposes, the first and chief of which, I beg to offer

---

*Written to the then Colonial Secretary, the Duke of Portland, from York (now Toronto), on the 20th of July, 1796, a month before his final departure from Upper Canada.

†From the first settlement of the Province two sevenths of all the lands in the settled townships were reserved—one for the maintenance of a "Protestant Clergy," under the authority of section 36 of the Constitutional Act of 1791, the other for such special purposes as might be designated by the Crown. These were known as "Clergy Reserves" and "Crown Reserves" respectively, the rest of the surveyed territory being described as "Waste Lands of the Crown."

with all respect and deference to Your Grace, must be the erection and endowment of a University, from which, more than any other source or circumstance whatever, a grateful attachment to His Majesty, morality, and religion, will be fostered and take root throughout the whole Province."

The First University Appropriation.—The interregnum between the *regime* of Lieutenant-Governor Simcoe and that of his successor Lieutenant-Governor Hunter, was filled up by the administration of the Hon. Peter Russell, President of the Executive Council. During this period a most important step was taken toward the carrying out of Gov. Simcoe's long cherished plan. On the 3rd of July, 1797, the following address* to His Majesty George III., was adopted by both Houses of the Legislature of Upper Canada :—

Most Gracious Sovereign—" We your most dutiful and loyal subjects, the members of the Legislative Council, and the Commons House of Assembly of Upper Canada, in Parliament assembled, being deeply persuaded of the great benefits that the Province must necessarily derive from the establishment of a respectable Grammar School in each district thereof, and also of a College or University, where the youth of the country may be enabled to perfect themselves in the different branches of liberal knowledge, and being truly sensible of the paternal regard your Majesty entertains for every description of your subjects, do most humbly implore your Majesty to appropriate a certain portion of the waste lands of the Crown as a fund for the establishment and support of such useful institutions."

This address was transmitted by acting Governor Russell, and before the close of the year the Duke of Portland

---

* It would be interesting to trace the progress of this address through the two Houses, but unfortunately the journals of both for that session have been irrecoverably lost.

informed the Legislature that its prayer would be granted after consultation with the Executive Council, the judges, and the law officers of the Crown in the Province as to the manner in which and the extent to which the Crown lands should be appropriated. After hearing from the judges and law officers the Executive Council discussed the whole question very fully in a report* which was submitted to and approved by President Russell. It recommended (1) the immediate establishment of one grammar school at Kingston and one at Newark (Niagara); (2) the establishment of one each at Cornwall and Sandwich, as soon as the state of the fund would permit; (3) the establishment of a university in the town of York, (Toronto); (4) the appropriation of 500,000 acres of "waste lands of the Crown" for the establishment and maintenance of the four schools and the university; and (5) the reservation of at least one-half of the whole grant for the purposes of the university.†

The Advent of Dr. Strachan.—As the proceedings connected with the organization of the Provincial University are closely connected with the personal work of the late Bishop Strachan of the Anglican Diocese of Toronto, it may be useful to note the circumstances which brought

---

*Dated December 1st, 1798. For the full text of this Report see Hodgins' "Documentary History," vol. I, pp. 20-23. See also Appendix to the Journals of the Legislative Assembly of Upper Canada for 1831, pp. 105-8.

†The amount of land actually appropriated in consequence of this report was 550,274 acres, of which there were set apart 190,573 acres in 1823 for "District Grammar Schools," and 63,996 acres in 1831 for Upper Canada College, leaving for the University 295,705 acres. See report of a special committee of Toronto University Senate on "Claims respecting the assets and endowment of the University." (Ont. Sess. Paper for 1895, No. 74.)

him from Scotland to Canada and made him the prominent figure he afterwards became in the development of educational work in this Province. He has himself recorded* that after concluding his university course in Aberdeen he settled down at the age of nineteen as a parish schoolmaster in Fifeshire, where he had for pupils Sir David Wilkie, the famous painter, and Commodore Barclay, who afterward figured in Canadian History. Disappointed in his expectation of a subordinate position on the staff of the University of Glasgow, he accepted an offer to come to Canada. This had been conveyed to him through the Hon. Richard Cartwright from Governor Simcoe. The object in view was the organization of a "college or university," and had Governor Simcoe remained in office this might have been attempted after the lapse of no long interval. Mr. Strachan found, however, on his arrival at Kingston on the last day of the year 1799, that the Governor had for reasons of state been transferred to another position, and that the university project had been indefinitely postponed. After spending three years at private tuition in Kingston he entered the ministry of the Church of England, and in 1803 removed to Cornwall, where, in addition to discharging his duties as clergyman of the parish, he conducted for nearly ten years the noted "Grammar School" of which several young men, who afterwards became distinguished politicians and jurists, were pupils. Among these were Sir John Beverley Robinson, Sir James Macaulay, Sir Allan MacNab, and the brothers, Sir James and Andrew Stuart. In 1812 he

---

* In an autobiographical address delivered to the clergy of his diocese in 1860. See Hodgins' "Documentary History," vol. I., pp. 9, and 41-42.

removed to York, where he became rector of the parish and headmaster of the "Home District School," which had at that time been over five years in operation. The increasing efficiency of this institution under his management enhanced the scholastic reputation of its Principal, and the active part taken by him in the controversies of a rather stirring time brought him into both political and ecclesiastical prominence. Dr. Strachan remained at the head of the School till 1823, and the School itself continued in active work until the establishment of Upper Canada College in 1830. His elevation to the Bishopric of Toronto took place in 1839, and he filled this office till his death in 1867.

University Representation.—In 1819 the then Lieutenant-Governor, Sir Peregrine Maitland, called the attention of his Executive Council to the state of the university scheme, and that body reported,* on the advice of Attorney-General Robinson, that, as no answer to the Report of the Executive Council to President Russell in 1798, advising the allotment of half a million acres for grammar schools and a university, could be found in the Executive Council Office, the appropriation of that quantity of land was "not sufficiently sanctioned to authorize a grant in other portions than as limited by His Majesty's Commissioner," and recommended that "formal sanction under the Royal Sign Manual, or the signature of His Majesty's Principal Secretary of State for the Colonies," be obtained "to sell, lease, grant, and dispose of the said five hundred thousand acres of land, for the pur-

---

* The full text of the Council's report is given in Hodgins' " Documentary History," vol. I, pp. 151-152.

pose of establishing a university in this Province." The Council also expressed the opinion that it would "conduce much to the importance and utility of the projected university if the constitution should be by royal charter." In the same year Lieutenant-Governor Maitland suggested in a message to the Legislature " the propriety of providing for a distinct representation of the contemplated university, when founded, in conformity to the established practice in the Mother Country." This suggestion was acted on in 1820, when the following clause was inserted in the "Act* to provide for increasing the Representation of the Commons of this Province in the House of Assembly":—

And be it further enacted by the authority aforesaid,† that whenever any university shall be organized and in operation as a seminary in this Province, and in conformity to the rules and statutes of similar institutions in Great Britain, it shall and may be lawful for the Governor, Lieutenant-Governor, or person administering the Government of this Province, for the time being, to declare by proclamation‡ the tract of land appendant to such university, and whereupon the same is situated, to be a town or township, by such name as to him may seem meet, and that such town or township so constituted shall be represented by one member. Provided always, nevertheless, that no person shall be permitted to vote at any such election for a member to represent the said university in Parliament who, besides the qualifications now by law required, shall not also be entitled to vote in the Convocation of the said university."

---

*1 Geo. IV, cap. 2, sec. 4. The date of this statute is the 7th of March, 1820. George IV had become King on the 29th of January, previous. Owing to a confusion of dates the Act is often cited as 60 George III.

† The Constitutional Act of 1791.

‡ As no proclamation was ever issued this provision never became operative. It was finally repealed when the Statutes of Canada, Upper Canada, and Lower Canada were consolidated in 1859. (C. S. U. C., pp. 1044 and 1113.)

The Land Endowment.—Not till 1822 were any further steps taken to give practical effect to the intention of the Imperial and Provincial Governments to provide Upper Canada with a seat of higher learning. In that year* Sir Peregrine Maitland "invited the attention of His Majesty's Government to the unproductive state of the school lands, and obtained leave to establish a Board for the general superintendence of education throughout the Province, and to place at its disposal, for the support of new grammar schools where they might be wanted, a portion of the reserved lands, retaining a sufficient endowment for the university." During the following two years the subject continued to occupy the anxious attention of the Lieutenant-Governor and his Executive Council, of which Dr. Strachan had been appointed a member† in 1817. In 1825 it was suggested to Sir Peregrine Maitland that, as the school lands continued practically unsalable, a portion of them might be resumed by the Crown in exchange for an equal amount of the "Crown Reserves," which in the older townships had become by this time comparatively valuable under the influence of settlement and cultivation. The Lieutenant-Governor approved of the suggestion, and toward the close of that year forwarded it for the consideration of "His Majesty's Government." Early in 1826, in a statement‡ prepared at

---

* Inaugural address delivered by Bishop Strachan, as President, at the opening of the University of King's College, June 8, 1843.

† He was created a member of the Legislative Council in 1820. He resigned his seat in the Executive Council in 1836, and his seat in the Legislative Council in 1840.

‡ The text is given in full in Hodgins' "Documentary History," Vol. I., pp. 211-215 ; and in the "Report of the Commissioners of Inquiry into the Affairs of King's College and Upper Canada College " (1848-1850), pp. 78-83.

the request of Sir Peregrine Maitland, Dr. Strachan laid before the latter the reasons which made the establishment of a university a matter of urgency, gave a sketch of the curriculum of studies which he deemed advisable, and indicated the procedure that should be adopted in order to procure the necessary ways and means. He estimated that the annual outlay for salaries and other expenses would be over $8,000, which might be met by the exchange of lands in the way above mentioned. In order to press on the attention of the Imperial Government both the expediency of this plan and the advisability of granting a royal charter as the constitution of the university, Dr. Strachan was sent the same year by the Lieutenant-Governor to England, where he remained for nearly twelve months in the active prosecution of the task assigned him. He brought back with him in March 1827, to use his own words,* " the charter and authority for the endowment, and, Sir Peregrine Maitland lost no time in forming the Council. Schedules of the lands were prepared, and in obedience to his Majesty's commands they were secured by patent† to the corporation of the University of King's College."

---

* Inaugural address, 1843.

† The amount of " Crown Reserves " actually patented to King's College was 225,944 acres. See " Report " of King's College Commissioners, pp. 16-19. The original parchment M.S. of the grant by George IV. to the " Chancellor, President, and Scholars " of King's College is still on file in the office of the Bursar of the University of Toronto, with the Great Seal of the Province appended, and Sir Peregrine Maitland's signature to the document. The date of the grant was January 3, 1828, and that of the registration of the instrument January 11 of the same year. For the text of the conveyance see Appendix A.

King's College Charter.—A reference to the text of this interesting charter* will show that King's College was intended to be strictly sectarian in its control and management, in fact a university of the Church of England in Canada. The Bishop of the diocese was made *ex officio* Visitor of the College; the Archdeacon of York was made *ex officio* its President; each of the seven professors who were to be members of its Council was required to be also a member of the "Established United Church of England and Ireland," and, before his admission into the College, "to sign and subscribe to the Thirty-nine Articles of Religion as declared and set forth in the Book of Common Prayer." Provision was made for the recognition of Divinity as one of the faculties, though no religious test or qualification was to be required of, or appointed for, any matriculant into any faculty except that of Divinity. In explanation of the fact that so liberal a public endowment should have been placed under the control of a single religious denomination, and of the still more singular fact that such a charter should have been put forward as " not only the most open charter for a university that had ever been granted, but the most liberal that could be framed on constitutional principles,"† it should be borne in mind that the Church of England

---

* See Appendix A. The date of the issue of the charter is March 15th, 1827, the eighth year of the reign of George IV. The original parchment, with the Great Seal of the Realm attached, was in 1891 delivered to the Bursar of the University of Toronto by the Anglican Bishop of Toronto, by whom it had been retained after the retirement of Bishop Strachan from the Presidency of the institution. It is endorsed as having been registered in the office of the Registrar of Upper Canada on the 22nd of November, 1827.

† Dr. Strachan's Inaugural address, 1843.

was then virtually, though not legally, the established church of Upper Canada, and that subscription to the Thirty-nine Articles was then required, not merely of all who had any share in the control of the Universities of Oxford and Cambridge, but of all who proposed to take in them any degree in any faculty. The standpoint from which this subject was viewed by those who obtained control of the charter and the endowment was lucidly set forth by Chief Justice (afterward Sir John Beverley) Robinson, in his address at the opening of King's College in 1843 :

"I feel a satisfaction (melancholy indeed it is, because my humble efforts were unavailing) that I was never led by any motive to concur in these alterations* which deprived this University of its distinct religious character. To have excluded from instruction in literature and the sciences all who belonged not to a particular church, might justly have been considered as illiberal as unwise ; and to have allowed only those to impart instruction in these departments, who professed their adherence to a particular creed, might have seemed a course as little suitable to this time and country. The charter as it originally stood, did neither : but it did contain some provisions plainly intended to ensure consistency in the government and harmony in the working of the institution, and intended moreover to proclaim openly to all what was the form of worship, and what the doctrine which alone they might expect to be maintained and inculcated in King's College. * * * * It was, we know, contended at the time that to endow an university in connection with one church from funds in which people of all persuasions might claim an interest, was contrary to justice. But the church mentioned in the royal charter was that church which the Sovereign swears at his coronation to support in all parts of his Dominion, except in Scotland ; and the spirit which denied to the Sovereign the right to endow from resources, which the constitution had vested in the Crown, an university in communion with the great Protestant Church of the Empire might, as it seemed to me, have been justly discountenanced as an unreasonable spirit."

---

*Made by the University Act of 1837. See below, p. 32.

Sectarian Controversy.—The return of Dr. Strachan was the signal for the outbreak of a controversy both protracted and acrimonious. It lasted for twenty years almost without cessation either in or out of Parliament, and it had the effect of completely paralyzing all effort to put the University into operation. Those who controlled the charter were able for a decade to prevent all proposed modifications of or alternatives for it, and those who proposed these modifications and alternatives were able to prevent the application of the endowment to the academic purpose for which it had been originally appropriated. The granting of the charter and the improvement of the endowment by an exchange of lands were announced by the Colonial Secretary, Lord Bathurst, to the Lieutenant-Governor, and the latter promptly conveyed the announcement to Parliament. The Legislative Council, of which Dr. Strachan was a leading spirit, took no exception to what had been done; the Legislative Assembly replied with a caution which foreboded trouble: "We shall be highly gratified to find that His Majesty has very graciously provided for the establishment and endowment of an university in this Province, if the principles upon which it has been founded shall, upon enquiry, prove to be conducive to the advancement of true learning and piety, and friendly to the civil and religious liberty of the people." Many petitions were, during the session of 1828, sent to the Legislative Assembly asking that body to enquire into the principles on which the proposed university was to be established, and urging that steps be taken to prevent "any ecclesiastical or literary body corporate, at whose hands danger could or might be apprehended to the constitution, or to their religious liberties," from holding lands and other property, and also from being represented by an additional member of Parliament.* These petitions, together with the charter itself, and all other information obtainable by an address to the Lieutenant-Governor, were referred to a special committee, with power to take evidence and to send for persons and papers. Of this committee, Marshall Spring Bidwell was Chairman, and its efforts to ventilate the whole subject were actively supported by John Rolph. The report† of this committee, after giving a brief analysis of the charter, mentions the fact that 225,944 acres of "Crown Reserves" had been appropriated as an endowment for the university, and that £1,000 a year for sixteen years had been appropriated‡ as a building fund; it also denounces the sectarian character given to the proposed university, and defines the principles on which it should have been founded. The following passage gives a good idea of the spirit of the report, and of many subsequent utterances from the same quarter :—

"An university adapted to the character and circumstances of the people would be the means of inestimable benefits to this Province. But to be of real service, the principles upon which it is established must be in unison with the general sentiments of the people. It should not be a school of politics or of sectarian views. It should have about it no appearance of partiality or exclusion.

---

*See the university representation clause of 1 Geo. IV., Cap. 2, quoted above, p. 14.

† See Hodgins' "Documentary History," Vol. I., pp. 240-242.

‡ Out of payments made to the Crown by the Canada Company. See Report of King's College Commission, pp 114-117; Ont. Sess. Paper No. 74, of 1895; Hodgins' "Documentary History," pp. 225-226.

Its portals should be thrown open to all, and upon none who enter should any influence be exerted to attach them to a particular creed or church. It should be a source of intellectual and moral light and animation, from which the glorious irradiations of liteiature and science may descend upon all with equal lustre and power. Such an institution would be a blessing to a country, its pride and glory. Most deeply, therefore, it is to be lamented that the principles of the charter are calculated to defeat its usefulness, and to confine to a favored few all its advantages."

Attitude of the Imperial Government.—The Legislative Assembly followed up this report with an address to the King, representing that the charter contained " provisions calculated to render the institution subservient to the particular interests of the Church of England,' and " to exclude from its offices and honors" all who did not belong to it, and praying that he would cause it to be " cancelled," and would grant another free from the objections specified in the report. This address was brought shortly afterward before a special committee* of the British House of Commons, from whose report the following is an extract:—

"It cannot be doubted, as the guidance and government of the College is to be vested in the hands of the membe·s of the Church of England, that in the election of professors a preference would inevitably be shown to persons of that persuasion; and in a country where only a small proportion of the inhabitants adhere to that church a suspicion and jealousy of religious interference would necessarily be created. For these and other reasons the committee are desirous of stating their opinion, that great benefit would

---

* This was a Committee on Canadian affairs. It was appointed on the motion of Mr. William Huskisson, and included such prominent statesmen as Mr. (afterwards Lord) Stanley, and Sir James Mackintosh.

accrue to the Province by changing the constitution of this body.* They think, that two theological professors should be established, one of the Church of England and another of the Church of Scotland, whose lectures the respective candidates for holy orders should be required to attend, but that with respect to the President, professors, and all others connected with the College, no religious test whatever should be required ; that in the selection of professors no rule should be followed, and no other object sought, than the nomination of the most learned and discreet persons, and that (with the exception of the theological professors) they should be required to sign a declaration that, as far as it is necessary for them to advert in their lectures to religious subjects, they would distinctly recognize the truth of the Christian revelation, but would abstain altogether from inculcating particular doctrines."

A little later in the same year the Colonial Secretary, Sir George Murray, in a despatch to Sir John Colborne,† acknowledged the receipt of the address of the Legislative Assembly. In the course of this letter he says:—

"It would be deservedly a subject of regret to His Majesty's Government, if the university recently established at York should prove to have been founded upon principles which cannot be made to accord with the general feelings and opinions of those for whose advantage it was intended. Your Excellency will acquaint the House of Assembly that I have laid the address before the king, and that I have in command to convey, through you, to the House of Assembly the expression of His Majesty's desire to receive with the most serious attention any representation which may be made to him by the representatives of his faithful subjects in Upper Canada. I have observed that your predecessor in the Government of Upper Canada differs from the House of Assembly as to the

---

* The College Council, which, according to the charter, was to be composed of the Chancellor, the President, and seven of the professors. The Anglican Archdeacon of York was to be *ex officio* President, and the seven professors were to be members of the English Church. See Charter, Appendix A.

† He had been appointed Lieutenant-Governor on the recall of Sir Peregrine Maitland in November, 1828. See Hodgins' "Documentary History," Vol. I., pp. 257-258.

general prevalence of objections to the university, founded upon the degree of exclusive connection which it has with the Church of England. It seems reasonable to conclude, however, that on such a subject as this an address adopted by a full House of Assembly, with scarcely any dissentient voices, must be considered to express the prevailing opinion in the Province upon this subject. In the event, therefore, of its appearing to you to be proper to invite the Legislative Council and House of Assembly to resume consideration of this question, you will apprise them that their representations on the existing charter have attracted the serious attention of His Majes'y's Government, and that the opinions which may be expressed by the Legislative Council and House of Assembly on that subject will not fail to receive the most prompt and serious attention.

This despatch has been held to authorize the Parliament of Upper Canada to amend the royal charter, and accordingly Sir John Colborne, in his capacity of Chancellor of the University, suspended its operation almost immediately* after his accession to office. When the Legislature met in 1829, he brought the question before both Houses by messages, in which he recommended that the "Royal Grammar School" of the Home District† should be connected with the University "in such a manner that its exhibitions, scholarships, and chief sup-

---

* Dr. Strachan in his "Inaugural Address" in 1843 says that, a few days after he assumed the administration, Sir John Colborne "convened King's College Council, and acting, it is supposed, under special instructions, stated that no further steps should be taken towards bringing the University into operation."

† Under the Public School Act of 1807, a "Public" (afterward "Grammar," and now "High") School was established in each of the eight "Districts" of the Province. A Parliamentary appropriation of £100 per annum was made for the maintenance of each school, and besides this sum a Royal Grant of £250 was made to each of four out of the eight, namely, those of York (Toronto), Cornwall, Kingston, and Niagara. These were known as "Royal Grammar Schools."

port may depend on the funds of that endowment." His message to the Legislative Council further expressed his personal opinion that the Archdeacon of York should not be President of King's College *ex officio*, and that religious tests should not in the case of professors be made a condition of membership in the College Council. The Legislative Council concurred in the latter of these views but dissented from the former, and approved of the proposal to connect the Royal Grammar School as a "Minor College" with the University, but not at the latter's expense. The Legislative Assembly favored the idea of using part of the University endowment to improve the Grammar School, but preferred to keep it independent of King's College Council. The attitude of the Assembly toward the University was expressed in a series of resolutions* to the tenor of which that body adhered steadily during the subsequent controversies between the two Houses. The "Royal Grammar School" was replaced later in the same year by "Upper Canada College," and was endowed with land amounting to 63,268† acres, besides the site in Russell Square on which the new buildings were erected, and the old Grammar School site which was sold to provide funds for their erection.‡

---

* Hodgins' "Documentary History," Vol. I., pp. 274-275. Their purport may be summed up in the *ipsissima verba* of one of them: "That whatever in the said charter in any degree gives a sectarian character to the said University, ought to be done wholly away."

† Afterwards increased to 63,996 acres. See Note, p. 11, above.

‡ Upper Canada College was both founded and endowed by Order of the Lieutenant-Governor in Council, not by any Act of the Provincial Parliament. The land endowment came out of what remained of the half million acres originally set apart as an endowment for "Grammar Schools" and a "University." On this point see the Report of the King's College Commissioners, p. 339, and

Opposing Policies in the Legislature.—In the session of 1830 the two Houses of Parliament drifted still further apart in their treatment of the question of higher education. The Assembly, acting apparently on the belief that it was useless to expect to secure any amendment of the royal charter of King's College, passed a bill* expressly sanctioning the establishment of Upper Canada College, creating a " College Council " as a "body politic and corporate " for its administration, and constituting the institution a university with power to confer "the degrees of Bachelor, Master, and Doctor, in the several arts and faculties." This bill was not agreed to by the Legislative Council, which placed its views on record in a series of resolutions† that reaffirmed the expediency of proceeding with the organization of a university proper under the royal charter, but at the same time approved of the establishment of " a great public school," and expressed the opinion that, " so far from injuriously interfering with the University of King's College, this institution will eminently conduce to its utility, and was necessary to prepare the way for its beneficial intention."

---

the "Report of a Special Committee of the Senate of the University of Toronto," printed as Sessional Paper No. 74 of the Ontario Legislature for 1895. The administration of the College was vested in "a president, directors, and trustees," and so remained till 1833, when it was transferred to the Council of King's College. The relations between Upper Canada College and the University of Toronto subsequently varied from time to time until the former was, in 1887, placed by the Legislature under the control of trustees appointed by the Crown. See Appendix B.

* Hodgins' "Documentary History," Vol. 1., pp. 301-304.
† Hodgins' "Documentary History," Vol. I., pp. 310-311.

In November, 1831, the then Colonial Secretary, Lord Goderich, in a despatch* to Lieutenant-Governor Colborne, adopted a very peremptory tone in dealing with the question of securing amendments to the King's College charter. Quoting the resolutions passed by the Legislative Assembly in 1829, he requested that the College Council " at the earnest recommendation and advice of His Majesty's Government, do forthwith surrender to His Majesty the charter of King's College of Upper Canada, with any lands that may have been granted them." The object aimed at was not the issue of a new charter by the King, but the amendment of the existing one by the Legislature under the instructions of his predecessor.† Later in the same year the Legislative Assembly, unaware of the receipt of the despatch from Lord Goderich, passed another address to the King asking for the cancellation of the charter. The Lieutenant-Governor promised to forward the address, but at the same time informed the House that, while " a charter solemnly given cannot be revoked, or its surrender obtained, without much delay and circumspection," he had reason‡ to believe either that " the exclusive provisions considered exceptionable in the charter" had been cancelled, or that " such arrangements had been decided upon by His Majesty's Government as would render further applications on this subject unnecessary." His belief proved to be not well founded, for the College Council refused to surrender either the charter or the endowment, alleging as

---

* See Hodgins' "Documentary History," Vol. II., pp. 55-56; and Report of King's College Commission, pp. 111-114.

† Sir George Murray. See above, p. 22.

‡ Probably from Lord Goderich's despatch.

a reason* the absence of any assurance that, if the charter was surrendered, the Legislature would be able to provide for the University another constitution which "would equally secure to the inhabitants of the Colony, through successive generations, the possession of a seat of learning, in which sound religious instruction should be dispensed." The College Council further intimated its willingness to concur in some modifications of the charter, which would make it less exclusively sectarian, but the Legislative Council refused for some years to accept any proposal emanating from the Legislative Assembly with this end in view. In opening the session of 1833 Sir John Colborne again invited the attention of the Legislature to the subject, and the Assembly responded in a series of resolutions,† one of which suggested the erection of Upper Canada College into a Provincial University and its endowment out of "the general funds arising from the sale of school lands," but nothing came of the suggestion.

The session of the Legislature held in 1835 was the first of a new Parliament, and the Legislative Assembly was even more radical in its educational policy than any of its predecessors had been. It was quite natural, therefore, that the King's College charter should be assailed with unabated hostility. As the expression of its opinion on

---

* Bishop Strachan's "Inaugural Address, 1843." The introductory part of the report of King's College Council on the surrendering of the charter is extant in MS. among the archives of the University of Toronto, in the handwriting of Sir John Beverley Robinson. The whole of it is printed in Appendix D.D. to the Journals of the Legislative Assembly for the Session of 1846. See Hodgins' "Documentary History," Vol. III., pp. 32-37.

Hodgins' "Documentary History," Vol. II., pp. 133-136.

the subject the Assembly passed a bill* which nominally
" amended " the charter, but really furnished the University with a new constitution. This measure provided
inter alia, that the Archdeacon of York should not be
ex officio President of the University ; that the professors
should not be required to be members of the Church of
England, or to subscribe to its " thirty-nine articles ;" that
the members of the Council constituting the corporation
should, to the number of twelve, be elected quadrennially
by the Legislature, each House separately electing six ;
that the Council so elected should have authority (1) to
appoint all members of the teaching staff, (2) to enact
rules and ordinances for the Government of the College
and the definition of the duties to be performed by its
appointees, (3) to suspend from office for cause assigned
any officer of the University (including the President) or
any of its own members, and (4) to control the property
and manage the funds of the institution ; that no " religious test or qualification " should be required of candidates for standing or degrees in " any art or faculty;"
that there should be no professorship of " doctrinal divinity " in the University ; and that the Visitor at once, and
the President after Dr. Strachan's vacation of the office,
should be appointed by the Council. Practically all that
was left unrepealed of the royal charter was the provision that the Lieutenant-Governor should be *ex officio*
the Chancellor of the University.

---

* The full text of this measure will be found in Hodgins' " Documentary History," Vol. II., pp. 210-213, and in Appendix No.
13 to the Journals of the Legislative Assembly of Upper Canada for
the Session of 1835.

Sir John Colborne's Scheme.—This measure was killed in the Legislative Council, as a matter of course, but it was also repugnant to the Lieutenant-Governor. The latter embodied his views in an "amended charter,"* which he probably transmitted for the consideration and approval of the Imperial Government, along with the Assembly's bill for which he intended it to be a substitute.† Sir John's scheme contemplated the organization of King's College as a university, with Upper Canada College attached to it and under the Council's management and control as a preparatory school. Under it the Lieutenant-Governor would have been *ex officio* Chancellor and the "Court of King's Bench" would have been *ex officio* Visitor; Dr. Strachan, would have retained the Presidency, but not *ex officio* as Archdeacon of York. The Council, as the governing body of the University, was to be composed of the Chancellor, the President, the Speaker of the Legislative Assembly, and five professors who should be "members of the Established United Church of England and Ireland." The faculty of Divinity was to be retained, but, with the exception of candidates for degrees therein, no "scholar" in the University should be required to submit to any religious test, and divinity students only to such as the College Council should "think fit." Sir John Colborne's despatch, enclosing these documents, elicited from the Colonial Secretary, then Lord Glenelg, a reply‡ which shows that the policy suggested by Sir George Murray in 1828, and empha-

---
* Hodgins' "Documentary History," Vol. II., pp. 217-220.
† See quotation from Lord Glenelg's despatch below, p. 30.
‡ Hodgins' "Documentary History," Vol. II., pp. 213-214.

sized by Lord Goderich in 1831, was still to be maintained, namely, that of allowing the two Houses of the Parliament of Upper Canada to say what amendments should be made in the King's College charter, before it should be put in operation. Sir John had admitted to the Colonial Secretary his conviction that the Assembly and Council would not agree in the adoption of amendments to the charter, but had expressed his belief that it might be "so modified by the interposition of His Majesty's Government as to leave, in essential points, no grounds for dissatisfaction on the part of either House," adding that he had informed the Legislature that he would, in the hope of obtaining such amendments, strongly urge the Imperial Government to sanction the immediate opening of the College. This advice had little weight with the Colonial office, which refused to interfere in the matter, alleging as reasons (1) that Sir John Colborne's plan departed in "every essential particular" from the one just adopted by the Legislative Assembly; (2) that Lord Goderich had "referred the matter to the discretion of the Provincial Legislature, which would be displeased with "the retraction of His Lordship's order;" and (3) that the decision of such a question by the Imperial Ministers "would be condemned with plausibility, and not indeed without justice, as a needless interference in the internal affairs of the Province." Lord Glenelg added:—

"The supposed amendments, even if they had not been preceded by any controversy or debate on the subject, could hardly fail to give umbrage to the House of Assembly. * * * * * I should think it impossible that the scheme which you have proposed could ever be carried into execution. It is contrary to the whole tenor of the recent resolutions of the representatives of the people to suppose that they would acquiesce in giving to the Church of England permanently, so many as five members in the governing body of the College. * * * I cannot hesitate to express my opinion that this plan claims for the Established Church of England privileges which those who best understand and most deeply prize her real interests would not think it prudent to assert for her in any British Province on the North American Continent. * * * * It is with the most lively regret that I have heard of the dissensions on this subject between the Legislative Council and the House of Assembly. I would respectfully and earnestly impress upon the members of both of those bodies, the expediency of endeavouring by mutual concessions, to meet on some common ground. Especially wou'd I beg the Legislative Councillors to remember that if there be any subject on which, more than others, it is vain and dangerous to oppose the deliberate wishes of the great mass of the people, the system of national instruction to be pursued in the moral and religious education of youth is emphatically that subject."

The despatch concluded with an intimation that the charter was again referred to the two Houses of Parliament; that, if both Houses should concur in asking him to do so, His Majesty would be "most happy to interpose as a mediator for the adjustment of the question;" but that "except in compliance with such a joint application," His Majesty "would not think it expedient to resume the decision of a question which, by His Majesty's commands, Lord Ripon* referred to the judgment of the Provincial Legislature."

Partial Secularization of the Charter.—Sir Francis Bond Head, who had meanwhile† succeeded Sir John Colborne as Lieutenant-Governor of Upper Canada, called the attention of the two Houses to the University question in his speech at the opening of the first session of the new Parliament in 1836, and early in the following

---
* Formerly Lord Goderich.
† In November, 1835.

year they agreed on a policy of secularization of the institution. Each House referred the matter to a special committee*, and the result of this and subsequent proceedings was the enactment of a statute†, which, after reciting the royal charter in the preamble, provides: (1) that the judges of the Court of King's Bench shall, instead of the English Church Bishop, be the Visitors of King's College; (2) that when the office of President becomes vacant it may be filled by Crown appointment without requiring that the appointee shall be "the incumbent of any ecclesiastical office;" (3) that the members of the College Council shall, exclusive of the Chancellor and President, be ten in number, of whom the Speakers of the two Houses and the Attorney-general and Solicitor-general shall be four, the remaining members being the five senior professors in arts in King's College, and the Principal of Upper Canada College; and (4) that "it shall not be necessary that any member of the College Council, or any professor to be at any time appointed, shall be a member of the Church of England, or subscribe to any articles of religion other than a declaration that they believe in the authenticity and Divine inspiration of the Old and New testaments, and the doctrine of the Trinity, and that no religious test or qualification be required or appointed for any person admitted or matriculated as scholars within the said college, or of persons admitted to any degree or faculty." The remaining sections of the

---

*The Members of the Assembly Committee, by which the bill subsequently passed was drawn up, were Messrs. W. H. Draper, Malcolm Cameron, Mahlon Burwell, Michael Aikman, and Henry Sherwood.

† 7. William IV. cap. 16.

Act (four in number) have reference to Upper Canada College and the relation in which it should stand to the University of King's College. This statute was passed unanimously by both Houses, and it received the Royal assent on the 4th March, 1837. Apart from the purely academic interest attaching to it as an incident in the evolution of the Provincial University, it is important as a proof of the right of a Provincial Legislature to amend a royal charter, a right that was subsequently exercised in a similar case by the Legislature of New Brunswick.* Though the Legislative Council assented to the amendments proposed by the Assembly, it did so with avowed reluctance, and its special committee† on the question embodied its opinions in a report which undoubtedly expressed the views of the Council, though these were not pressed lest they might endanger the passage of a statute so moderate, and leave the way open to a more drastic enactment.

Inauguration of the University.—At the instance of the College Council Sir Francis Bond Head at once took steps to put the amended charter in operation. Under it the Council was reconstituted with a somewhat changed *personnel*, each member of it making the required sub-

---

* For an opinion from the Imperial Government on this aspect of the New Brunswick case, see a letter from Lord Stanley, Colonial Secretary, under date Nov. 12th, 1845, printed in Appendix D. D. to the Journals of the Legislative Assembly of Upper Canada, for 1846. For opinions of Canadian constitutional authorities on the point, see Hodgins' "Documentary History," Vol. III., pp. 201-210.

† The Committee of the Council was composed of Dr. Strachan, Hon. Geo. Crookshank, Hon. William Morris, and Hon. John S. Macaulay. Its report is printed in full in Hodgins' "Documentary History," Vol. III. pp. 61-70.

scription to a declaration of his religious belief. Preparations were made for the erection of a university building on a site* that had been chosen in what is now called the Queen's Park. The Council authorized the President and Bursar to borrow £20,000 for the purpose, and adopted a plan† of instruction and organization which had been drawn up by Dr. Strachan. Before anything could be accomplished, however, the political agitations of the previous ten years culminated in the Rebellion of 1837, which interrupted for a time the execution of the plan.‡ Sir Francis Bond Head was recalled from the Lieutenant-Governorship, and was replaced by Sir George Arthur. Lord Durham was sent out in 1838 as Governor of British America, and as " High Commissioner " to investigate the political condition of Upper and Lower Canada. His "Report" was laid before the House of Lords early in 1839, and later in the same year Charles Poulett Thomson was sent out as Governor of both Provinces. When the Union Act of 1840, which was based on Lord Durham's " Report," came into operation,§ Mr. Thomson, as Lord Sydenham, filled the position of first Governor-General of Canada, but he was too much preoccupied with the work of political and municipal organization of the new Province to be able to give continuous attention to the duties of the Chancellorship of the University, however much he may have desired to do so. Before the close of 1841 he was succeeded by Sir Charles Bagot, who was an

---

* Almost coincident with the one on which the Provincial Building now stands, facing the College Avenue to Queen St.

† See Appendix C.

‡ Dr. Strachan's "Inaugural Address," 1843.

§ The date fixed by Proclamation was the 10th of February, 1841.

alumnus of Christ Church, Oxford, and a Master of Arts of that university. His previous training no doubt made it comparatively easy to interest him in the projected College, and on the 23rd of April, 1842, he laid the foundation stone of a new academic building.* Pending the completion of so much of it as might be found necessary to accommodate the College in actual operation, the latter obtained leave to occupy for a time the Parliament Building, which had not been used after the Union of the Provinces.† There on the 8th of June in the following year took place the opening services under the Presidency‡ of Dr. Strachan, who had four years before been created the first Bishop of the Diocese of Toronto. In his "Inaugural Address" he gave a very valuable outline of the history of the university scheme, took credit for liberality in assenting to the changes made by the University Act of six years before, and defended the policy of leaving higher education to the care of the different religious denominations. Addresses were delivered also by two of the Visitors—Chief Justice Robinson, from whose speech a characteristic quotation has already been made,§ and the Hon. Justice Hagerman,

---

* Only the eastern wing of this edifice was completed. Under authority of an Act passed in 1853 (16 Vict., cap. 161) this building and the land around it were expropriated from the University, and the latter was appropriated as a site for the erection of a Provincial Parliamentary building. See Ont. Sess. Paper No. 74 of 1895.

† The seat of Government of the new Province of Canada was fixed at Kingston, and the administrative services were withdrawn from Quebec and Toronto to be consolidated there.

‡ Dr. Strachan was President of King's College from 1827 to 1848, when he was succeeded by the Rev. Dr. McCaul. For an account of the opening proceedings, and of those connected with the laying of the corner stone, see Appendix C.

§ See above, p. 18.

who expressed his sense of the great importance of the provision made for the study of divinity, and a hope that King's College might, " year after year send forth from its halls an abundant supply of persons worthy to become the ordained Ministers of our Church."

Parliamentary Action of 1843-45.—It was quite natural that, after the controversies of fifteen years, public feeling should fail to re-echo such aspirations, and therefore it is not surprising that in the Canadian Parliament the effort to completely secularize the chartered University was continued with unabated energy. Mr. Robert Baldwin in the session of 1843 introduced into the Legislative Assembly a bill which, as its title* and preamble show, was intended not merely to make King's College non-denominational, but also to draw into incorporation with it the Colleges of Regiopolis, Queen's, and Victoria. These had by this time been established by the Roman Catholics, the Presbyterians, and the Methodists respectively, the first two at Kingston, and the third at Cobourg. The protest of the Council of King's College against the measure was presented at the bar of the Assembly by Mr. W. H. Draper. He attempted to show, may perhaps be said to have succeeded in

---

* The bill was entitled : "An Act to provide for the separate exercise of the Collegiate University functions of the College established at the City of Toronto in Upper Canada, for incorporating certain other Colleges and Collegiate Institutions of that division of the Province with the University, and for the more efficient establishment and satisfactory Government of the same." The text of the bill is given in Hodgins' "Documentary History," Vol. IV. A strong defence of it will be found in a speech delivered by Mr. (afterwards Sir) Francis Hincks in 1843, and inserted in his "Reminiscences," pp. 178-184.

showing, that the proposed measure was crude, and that it would be found unworkable; but he was less successful in his contention that it was unconstitutional, if not *ultra vires* of the Provincial Legislature, which, according to him, could have no power to amend a royal charter without the consent of those to whom it had been granted. He met the embarrassing fact that he had been instrumental in securing the amendments made in the charter by the University Act of 1837,* with the plea that to those amendments the Council of King's College had been a consenting party, while it was protesting against the changes proposed in the bill then before the House. In spite of his learned and skilful presentation of the case of his clients, the measure would probably have passed the Legislative Assembly, had the session not been brought to an untimely close† by a sharp quarrel between Governor Metcalfe‡ and the majority of his Ministerial advisers over the interpretation and application of the principle of "Responsible Government."§ Mr. Baldwin and those who agreed with him retired *from* the Executive Council, and at the general election, which was held a few months afterward, the control of the Legislative Assembly passed into the hands of Mr. Draper, who became Premier and Attorney-General.

---

* See above, p. 32.
† On the 9th of December, 1843.
‡ Sir Charles Metcalfe became Governor-General in March, 1843.
§ Recommended in Lord Durham's Report, 1839; ordered by Lord John Russell's letter of instructions to Governor Thomson in the same year; and formulated and adopted by the Legislative Assembly during the first session of the first Parliament of Canada, 1841.

Either because he really favored a further measure of university reform, or because he saw that the popular demand for it could not be much longer withstood, Mr. Draper himself, during the session of 1845, introduced three bills into the Legislative Assembly, one* to create "The University of Upper Canada," one to vest in it the endowment of King's College, and one to repeal the University Act of 1837 and make certain amendments in the royal charter. While these measures were in progress the despatches† of Lord Goderich and Lord Glenelg on the University question were brought down and printed for the use of the members. King's College was again heard by counsel at the bar of the House. A petition against the bills was sent to the Assembly by the Visitors‡ of the University. The Council of the College passed resolutions protesting against the proposed legislation. Bishop Strachan wrote to Governor Metcalfe, who was still Chancellor of the University, an indignant denunciation of the threatened interference with the charter and endowment, as he had previously denounced the University bill of 1843. In spite of this strenuous opposition the motion for the second reading of the bills was carried by a fair majority,§ but they were then dropped for the session.

---

*See Hodgins' "Documentary History," Vol. IV.

† These despatches were both addressed to Sir John Colborne. The former was dated Nov. 2, 1831; the latter, June 17, 1835. See pp. 26 and 29-31, above.

‡ The Judges who signed the petition were "John B. Robinson," "J. Jones," "Arch. McLean," and "Chr. A. Hagerman."

§ 45 to 34. The uncertain condition of feeling in the Assembly is shown by the fact that Mr. Baldwin voted with the minority.

Governor Cathcart's Action.—Before the close of 1845 Lord Metcalfe retired from the Governorship, and Lord Cathcart* succeeded him. Desirous of ascertaining for himself the views of all parties who might be supposed to have a special interest in the constitution of the Provincial University, the new Chancellor asked the opinions of the governing bodies of King's College, Queen's College, Victoria College, and Regiopolis College, respectively, on "the present state of the charter of the University of King's College, as amended by the statute of Upper Canada, 7th William IV., chapter 16th." This request was accompanied by a reference to the abortive legislation of 1843 and 1845, and by a hint of coming legislation, in the form of a reminder that "in the opinions of many, changes are still necessary to make the institution harmonize with the wants and wishes of the greater portion of the people of Upper Canada, for whose benefit it was created and endowed." The responses to the Governor's letter were very prompt. Before the end of March, 1846, official replies were received from all four corporations, and these valuable documents, with equally valuable enclosures, were laid before Parliament† early in May.

The reply from the Council of King's College called the Governor's attention to the report of that body in

---

* The Earl of Cathcart was sent to Canada in 1845 as "Commander of the Forces," and he acted for a short time as Administrator pending the appointment of a successor to Lord Metcalfe. Early in 1846, however, he was himself appointed Governor-General, and he thus became University Chancellor *ex officio*. In the latter capacity he took the important action referred to in the text.

† They are printed, along with other papers relating to King's College, as Appendix D. D. to the Assembly Journals for 1846.

1832 on the Colonial Secretary's request* for a surrender of the University charter, and enclosed a copy of it. It referred him also to the inaugural address† delivered by the President at the opening of King's College in 1843, for, " an authentic account of the great difficulties which attended the procuring of the charter on account of its open and conciliatory principles, which were at that time (1827) without precedent in such institutions either at home or abroad." Certain changes in the University's constitution, supplementary to those made by the Act of 1837 were suggested, namely: (1) That the Chancellor should be elected by Convocation ; (2) that the President should be *ex officio* Vice-Chancellor ; (3) that the appointment of the President, the Vice-President, the professors (except the professor of Divinity, " who is to be appointed by the Archbishop of the Province or the Bishop of the diocese "), and the Principal of Upper Canada College should be vested in a " Council of appointment," consisting of the President, Vice-President, and Senior Professor of King's College, and one representative from each of the following bodies: The Provincial Medical Board, the Provincial Law Society, and the Toronto City Council; (4) that the legislative and administrative functions of the College Council, both financial and academical, should be transferred to a " Caput," composed of the President, Vice-President, four professors selected by the faculties,‡ and the Principal of Upper Canada College ; and (5) that the Chief Justice of the Province and the Vice-Chancellor of the Court of Chancery should be *ex officio* Visitors.

---

* See p. 26, above.   † See above, p. 35, and also Appendix C.
‡ Arts, Law, Medicine, and Divinity are probably meant.

Reference was made to the establishment of Queen's, Victoria, and Regiopolis Colleges, and a suggestion offered, that these "and such other denominations as to government may seem meet" should be endowed out of the portion of the Clergy Reserves left* at the disposal of the Canadian Government, the endowment of King's College being left to it unimpaired. The reply closed with a recommendation that the whole question should, in anticipation of future attempts at legislation, be submitted to a Commission of experts, in accordance with the advice which had shortly before been given to the New Brunswick Legislature by Lord Stanley,† respecting the constitution of the chartered "King's College" of that Province.

The Attitude of Queen's College.—The reply from the Board of Trustees of Queen's College called attention to the fact that though the charter of King's College had been granted in 1827 the college itself had not been opened to students till 1843; that in spite of "widespread dissatisfaction on account of the exclusiveness" of the charter, no amendments had been made in it till 1837; that "the members of the Church of Scotland had refrained from taking any steps to originate an institution for the purpose of educating candidates for the ministry until 1836, when initiatory measures were adopted with the view of establishing merely a theological seminary," and that it was not until

---

* By the Imperial Statute, 3 and 4 Vict. cap. 78.

† Lord Stanley's despatch to Lieutenant Governor Colebrooke of New Brunswick on this subject is printed in Appendix D.D. to the Journals of the Legislative Assembly of Canada for 1846. It is dated Nov. 12, 1845.

1840 that they felt constrained to use efforts to provide for supplying, "not merely a theological but also a university education, which the Church of Scotland holds to be indispensable, before students are admitted to the study of theology." The result of these efforts had been the establishment of a university incorporated by royal charter in 1841, and opened for the reception of students early in 1842.* Later in the same year, when the authorities of King's College were preparing to organize it for academical purposes, the trustees of Queen's College had passed a resolution reiterating their abiding conviction that "it was most expedient that King's College, with its ample public endowment, should be in the proper sense the university for the whole population without respect to the religious creeds of the students;" declaring that "they have no wish to appear to stand in an attitude of rivalry to that institution, but rather to help it forward as far as they can;" announcing that they "are ready to concur in any legislative enactment that shall empower them to limit Queen's College to the department of theological instruction, and shall authorize the removal of said college to Toronto," provided that a "fair and virtual influence" shall be conceded to the "Board and Professors" of Queen's College in the administration of the Provincial University; but announcing also that they "do not in the meantime forgo any of the claims which they have on King's College," and that they "will exert themselves to the utmost to obtain the endowment of a theological professorship" from its funds, in accordance with pledges from the Government of the Province. Lord Cathcart

---

* See Chapter V.

was further informed that the trustees of Queen's College had in 1843 asked Dr. Strachan to lay before the Council of King's College a memorandum containing their views on the university question, that he had declined to do so, and that they had afterward " earnestly petitioned the Legislature to pass the bills introduced by Mr. Draper in the session of 1845, which they preferred to Mr. Baldwin's bill of 1843, because they retained the religious test for the professors of the Provincial University. The advantages which would result from the passing of Mr. Draper's measure the trustees believed to be incalculable. "The bringing together for several years at the most important periods of life of all those youth of the Province who might be expected afterwards to occupy the most influential stations in the community would be secured. The stimulus to exertion caused by a considerable number in a class, would be added to the other motives to successful literary effort,—an advantage needed in a country like Canada, where for many years to come, university students must be few." In their opinion, "unduly acquired ecclesiastical superiority" would, under the charter as amended in 1837, be "only in some measure concealed, not prevented; inasmuch as the parties who obtained the original charter, though now constrained in some measure to act on the amended one, must be expected, according to the well-known principles of human nature, to endeavour to secure the operation of the principles of the charter which they sought, and which even yet they do not scruple to maintain they have neither repudiated nor abandoned." The trustees set forth at length the grounds on which a share of the endowment of King's College was claimed for the maintenance of theological teaching in Queen's, and concluded with an expression of their conviction, "that the only effectual way of making King's College as extensively useful as it was meant to be, and at the same time of safely guarding the interests alike of literature, science, and religion, is to present inducements to the various ecclesiastical bodies in the Province, who may choose to avail themselves of such inducements, to establish merely theological colleges, with a certain amount of representation to each in the Council of King's College; and, *upon this principle*, so to deal with the question of grants of money from the funds of the University to the theological colleges which may be established as constituent parts of the University, as justice and equity may demand."

The Attitude of Victoria College.—The Principal* of Victoria replied for that institution, as it was not possible to call the "Board" together at that season, the members being scattered in various parts of the Province. He called the Governor's attention to the fact that the Board had in 1843, by formal resolutions, approved of "the general objects and provisions" of Mr. Baldwin's bill of that year, while suggesting some changes in its details, and pointing out that owing to their having erected a college building at Cobourg, the Wesleyan Methodists, as a body, would not be able to avail themselves of the "important rights and privileges" they might otherwise have enjoyed under such a university constitution. He also quoted a resolution adopted by the Board while Mr. Draper's measures were under consideration by the Legislature: "That while

---

* Then the Rev. Egerton Ryerson.

the Board of Victoria College has no desire to embarrass the government in the university measure, yet this Board deems it expedient that the operations of Victoria College be continued at Cobourg, and, should it be impracticable to divide the university endowment for the support of separate colleges, that arrangements be made to place Victoria College on terms equally favorable with all other colleges in the University in the constitution of the Caput." Claiming to "speak from a perfect knowledge of the facts," the Principal went on to point out that the Board had not been disposed to dictate to the Government any particular view as to the settlement of the university question; that "the evils complained of in reference to the University of King's College had been regarded by the Board of Victoria College as practical rather than theoretical," and as being due not so much to the amended charter as to the manner in which it had been administered; that while the Board of Victoria College had not been disposed to press on the Government any one mode of settling this question, it had not "refused to sustain any relation to the Provincial university which might be required of it in common with other colleges;" that, owing to the objects* in view in the establishment of Victoria College, it was "imperative" that the general educational operations of the institution should be continued, and that this must be done at Cobourg unless the Board should be remunerated for abandoning its building there; that the labors of the Wesleyan Methodist Church had been "confessedly more extensive and more self-sacrificing than those of either

---

* See Chapter IV.

of the other three persuasions" which had undertaken academical work—the "Churches of England, Scotland, and Rome,"—all of which had received large appropriations from the State; that the facts of the case had been repeatedly submitted for the consideration of the Government, but so far in vain; and that the result was "dissatisfaction" which seemed likely to become "deep and universal."

The Attitude of Regiopolis College.—Vicar-General Macdonell, one of the trustees of Regiopolis, replied from Montreal on behalf of that institution. He stated that though they "individually disapproved of the manner in which public property, that should have been applied for the advantage of all the members of the community without reference to sect or denomination of Christians, had been misapplied," they would have refrained from expressing any opinion on the matter if they had not been called upon to do so. Even then, though they deemed it necessary that the College of Regiopolis should be "endowed by some permanent grant from the Provincial Legislature," they would rather see it endowed in some other way than by receiving part of the funds which had been vested in the corporation of King's College. They suggested that such an endowment as they indicated could be made " without infringing on the vested rights of any other institution, and in a manner much more congenial to their own feelings and to those of the community to which they belong, out of the unalienated Estates* for-

---

* These Estates remained unappropriated until 1888, when by an Act of the Quebec Legislature they were devoted to educational work in accordance with a scheme approved of by His Holiness, Leo XIII. (Statutes of Quebec, 51 and 52 Vict., Cap. 13.)

merly possessed by the Order of the Society of Jesus the proceeds of which can never be justly diverted from the ends which the donors had in view, the education of the Catholic youth and the spread of the Catholic faith in Lower Canada." Admitting that changes were still necessary to bring the charter of King's College into harmony with "the wants and wishes of the greater portion of the people of Upper Canada, for whose benefit the College was founded, they declined to offer any advice as to what amendments should be made by the Legislature, but expressed the opinion "that it would be much more beneficial for the community at large, if the charter of the University of King's College were repealed, and the four colleges already chartered—that is, King's College at Toronto, Victoria College at Cobourg, Queen's College at Kingston (or wherever else the trustees choose to erect it), and the College of Regiopolis* at Kingston—and a College of Law and Medicine to be erected somewhere in the Province, were endowed out of the proceeds of the property now vested in the trustees of the University of King's College."

Parliamentary Action of 1846.—Almost coincident with the submission of these documents to the Legislative Assembly, was the introduction of university bills similar to those introduced by Mr. Draper in 1845, the object being to create a non-sectarian "University of Upper Canada," and to transfer to it the endowment of King's College. After the latter had again been heard by counsel, the House resolved to postpone the second reading of

---

* See Chapter IX.

the bills to a future session. The majority on the division was 40 to 20, Mr. Baldwin voting for the postponement.

Bishop Strachan, by way of supplement to the action taken by the Council of King's College, and to the official memorial of the Visitors, protested personally against the attempts made to mo.lify the constitution of the University during the years 1843-46. He addressed a letter to Governor Metcalfe in 1843, and sent the same year a still more elaborate memorial to the Legislative Assembly. In 1844 he wrote again to Governor Metcalfe, protesting in advance against the threatened legislation of 1845. In 1846 he discussed the whole question very fully in a letter to Governor Cathcart. What he thought of Mr. Draper's university bills of 1845 and 1846 may be gathered from his "Brief History of King's College," published in 1850. After characterizing in vigorous language the Baldwin bill of 1843, he says*:

"The party favorable to this measure lost the management of public affairs, and their opponents, who professed to be Conservatives, became the administrators of the Government. It was now hoped that King's College would be left in peace, and be allowed to win its way, as it was rapidly doing, in the affections of the people. But, instead of permitting it to proceed in its onward course, the new Ministry, as they were called, yielded to the clamour of a most insignificant faction, and introduced a measure in 1845, respecting the institution, little better than that of their opponents. The Conservatives made another attempt in 1847,† which, though in some respects better, because there are degrees of evil, was nevertheless liable to the most serious objections."

---

* This quotation is made from a copy in the possession of Dr. Hodgins, Librarian to the Education Department of Ontario.

† This should be 1846.

CHAPTER III.

THE UNIVERSITY OF TORONTO.

The long and acrimonious struggle over the sectarian charter of King's College came, for all practical purposes, to an end with the passage of the University Act* of 1849, which completely secularized the institution and changed its name to "The University of Toronto." Lord Elgin succeeded† Lord Cathcart as Governor-General of Canada and *ex officio* Chancellor of the University of King's College. Like his predecessor he made an effort to obtain, in the latter capacity, independent and trustworthy information respecting a question that had been so frequently discussed in Parliament, and that must sooner or later come up again for settlement. In July, 1848, a statute was passed by the Council of King's College, and assented to by the Governor, appointing a "Commission to examine into all accounts and other fiscal affairs" of the University and of Upper Canada College, "and into all matters in any way connected with such affairs," and to report as soon as possible "in order to enable the Legislature the sooner to come to a final determination thereon." The Commissioners appointed under this statute were John Wetenhall, Joseph

---

* 12 Vict., cap. 82.

† The Earl of Elgin and Kincardine was appointed to office late in 1846 and arrived in Canada early in 1847.

Workman, and Robert Easton Burns.* Though the Report† of the Commission was not completed till 1851, and was not printed till 1852, enough of light was by its early investigations thrown on the state of the University to prove beyond controversy the necessity for legislation. Accordingly in the session of 1849 a University bill was introduced into the Legislative Assembly by Mr. Baldwin. The motion‡ for its second reading was, after several amendments had been voted down, carried by a majority of 42 to 2.§ The motion for the third reading was carried by a majority of 43 to 14, after another unsuccessful attempt‖ to secure an amendment of the measure. The bill was passed by the Legislative Council without amendment. King's

---

* Mr. Wetenhall was a member of the Legislative Assembly of Canada for the County of Halton. Joseph Workman was the late Dr. Workman, for many years Superintendent of the Toronto Lunatic Asylum. Mr. Burns, who had been a law partner of Mr. (now Sir) Oliver Mowat, was at this time Judge of the Home District. In 1850 he was appointed a Judge of the Queen's Bench. Owing to the death of Mr. Wetenhall soon after the Commission began its labors, and to the frequent absences of Judge Burns on circuit, the chief part of the labor fell to Dr. Workman, who was, by his colleagues, appointed "visiting Commissioner."

† For a summary of this valuable document see Appendix D.

‡ This motion was seconded by Mr. Wetenhall, one of the King's College Commissioners.

§ The two were Mr. W. H. Boulton of Toronto, and Mr. W. B. Robinson of the County of Simcoe.

‖Made by Mr. (afterward Sir) John A. Macdonald. His amendment proposed to repeal the University Act of 1837, and to invest the endowment of King's College (increased by an appropriation of public lands) in a "General Board," for the purpose of (1) endowing the four colleges already in existence and any thereafter established by any Christian denomination in Upper Canada, (2) establishing Grammar Schools, and (3) establishing an Agricultural School in each District.

College Council was not on this occasion represented at the bar of the Assembly, but an energetic protest sent to Parliament by Bishop Strachan was treated with the utmost consideration, one thousand copies having been printed and circulated by order of the Assembly. The bill received the Royal Assent on the 30th of May, and was not disallowed by the Imperial Government though memorials* were addressed to the Queen praying that it should not be permitted to go into operation. In the following session a supplementary statute† was passed, mainly to clear up misapprehensions as to the effect of the Act of 1849, and in any attempt to comprehend the new constitution then given to the Provincial University these two statutes must be read together.

Preamble to the University Act of 1849.—The general character of the changes effected by the statutes of 1849-50, as well as the objects in view in enacting them, are indicated in the Preamble to the Act of 1849, the text of which is as follows:

Whereas a universi y for the advancement of learning in that division of the Province called Upper Canada, established upon principles calculated to conciliate the confidence and insure the support of all classes and denominations of Her Majesty's subjects, would, under the blessing of Divine Providence, encourage the pursuit of literature, science and art, and thereby greatly tend to promote the best interests, religious, moral, and intellectual, of the people at large; and Whereas, with a view to supply the want of such an institution, His late Majesty King George the Fourth, by Royal Charter bearing date at Westminster, the 15th day of March, in the eighth year of his reign, was pleased to establish at Toronto, then called

*See Dr. Strachan's "Brief History of King's College," 1850.
†13 and 14 Vict., cap. 49.

York, in that division of the Province, a Collegiate institution with the style and privileges of a university, and was afterwards pleased to endow the said institution with certain of the waste lands of the Crown in that part of the Province; and Whereas the people of this Province consist of various denominations of Christians, to the members of each of which denominations it is desirable to extend all the benefits of a university education, and it is therefore necessary that such institution, to enable it to accomplish its high purpose should be entirely free in its government and discipline from all denominational bias, so that the just rights and privileges of all may be fully maintained without offence to the religious opinions of any ; and Whereas, the Legislature of the late Province of Upper Canada, having been invited by His late Majesty King William the Fourth "to consider in what manner the said University could be best constituted for the general advantage of the whole Society," as appears by the despatch of His Majesty's Secretary of State for the Colonies, bearing date the eighth day of November, in the year of our Lord one thousand eight hundred and thirty-two*, the Parliament of that Province afterwards, by an Act passed in the seventh year of the reign of His said late Majesty King William the Fourth, chaptered sixteen and intituled "An Act to amend the Charter of King's College," did alter and amend the said Charter in certain particulars in order, as the preamble to the said Act recites, "to meet the desire and circumstances of the Colony ;" and Whereas such alteration and amendment have been found insufficient for these purposes, and therefore, as well for the more complete accomplishment of this important object, in compliance with His said late Majesty's most gracious invitation, as for the purpose of preventing the evil consequences which frequent appeals to Parliament on the subject of the constitution and government of the said University are calculated to produce, it has become expedient and necessary to repeal the said Act, and to substitute other legislative provisions in lieu thereof : Therefore, etc.

---

*Lord Goderich was then Secretary of State for the Colonies. He had sent a previous despatch on the subject of King's College, dated Nov. 2, 1831. See above, page 26.

The New Constitution.—Under the Royal Charter the administration of King's College, both academic and financial, had been vested in a "Council." The University Act* of 1837 did nothing to mar the extreme simplicity of this arrangement. The Act of 1849 repealed not merely the Act of 1837 but the Royal Charter† itself, so far as its provisions were "contradictory to, or inconsistent with" or rendered unnecessary by, the provisions of the new constitution. The latter was a very complicated mechanism, involving a distribution of administrative functions among several different bodies. The University remained, as it had been, a corporation, but its title was changed from "The Chancellor, President and Scholars of King's College at York in the Province of Upper Canada" to "The Chancellor, Masters, and Scholars of the University of Toronto." The Governor-General of the Province was made "Visitor" instead of "Chancellor" and the latter was made elective triennially by Convocation.‡ The right to appoint the "President" continued to be vested in the Crown. The Vice-Chancellor was made elective annually by the "Senate," and the "Pro-Vice-Chancellor" annually by Convocation. The management of the institution was divided up among

---

*7 William IV., Cap. 16.

†No authoritative declaration has ever been given as to the precise extent to which the Royal Charter of King's College remains in force. A Special Committee of the University Senate was appointed in 1895 to investigate the matter, but it never reported.

‡The qualifications for membership in this body remained much the same as they had been under the Royal Charter. It included the "Chancellor, Vice-Chancellor, President and professors, and all persons admitted in the University to any degree in law or medicine or to that of Master in any of the other Arts or Faculties," on payment of twenty shillings a year toward the support of the University.

these officers and several bodies, which varied greatly as to membership and functions.

Each of the three Faculties of Law, Medicine, and Arts was created an organization, composed of such of the professors as the Senate by statute directed, presided over by an elective Dean, and authorized to enact by-laws for its own government, subject to their confirmation by the Senate.

The "ordinary general discipline and government" of the University, "in subordination to the Senate," was vested in and exercised by "the Caput," which had in turn under its direction and control the Vice-Chancellor and President, except in matters in which these officers were intrusted with independent powers by the University Act, by the original Charter, or by some statute of the Senate. The Caput was composed of five members: The President of the University, the three Deans of Faculties, and a representative elected by Convocation.

An Endowment Board was created for the purpose of undertaking "the general charge, superintendence, and management of the whole property and effects, real and personal, of the University," under the direction of statutes passed by the Senate, to which it was required to report annually on the state of the "whole fiscal or financial affairs" of the University. It was composed of five members: namely, one appointed by the Governor, one elected by the Senate, one chosen by the Caput, and two representing respectively the "Council" and the "Masters" of Upper Canada College.*

---

* For the changes made from time to time in the constitution of Upper Canada College, and in its relation to the University of Toronto, see Appendix B.

The "Senate," created by this statute, was a body composed of the Chancellor, the Vice-Chancellor, the President, all the professors, and twelve or more additional members of whom one-half were appointed by the Crown and the other half by Colleges* holding to the University that kind of relationship which is now called "affiliation." The powers conferred on the Senate were very comprehensive. It was the only body within the University authorized to pass "Statutes" for the regulation of the affairs of the institution, and these when enacted by the Senate were not subject to review by any other authority except the Crown, which might disallow any statute within two years after its enactment. It was authorized to legislate as it might think "necessary or expedient" concerning "the good government of the University;" "the professors and all others holding office in the Senate;" the studies, lectures, examinations, exercises, degrees and all that related to them; the meetings of the Caput, the Senate, and Convocation; the duties of the Chancellor, and the residence and duties of the Vice-Chancellor and President; the number, examinations, residence, duties, and order of precedence and seniority of the professors; fellowships, scholarships, exhibitions, and other prizes; the number, residence, appointment, and duties of all employees of the University; the management of the property and revenues; the "salaries, stipends, provisions, fees, and emoluments of and for the Vice-Chancellor,† President, professors, fellows, scholars,

---

*This privilege was restricted "to such Colleges as now or hereafter shall be incorporated with the power of conferring degrees in Divinity, and not in the other Arts or Faculties."

†Who was to be a professor or ex-professor.

officers, and servants;" and generally "any other matter or thing for the well being and advancement of the University." It was authorized to suspend from office any "professor for any just and reasonable cause," and this suspension, if not appealed against within three months, or if confirmed by the Visitor, became a dismissal *ipso facto*. If it preferred to report to the Governor a recommendation that a professor ought to be "removed," then the Governor was *ipso facto* empowered to "remove" him. It played an equally important part in the appointment of "professors." While the actual appointment was vested in the Crown, the latter was limited in its choice to three candidates nominated by the Senate after all the applications had been reported on by the Caput, and it had a statutory right to subject candidates to a "personal, public, oral examination," or to any other non-religious test it chose to prescribe.

Secularization of the University.—The complete secularization of the Provincial University, which was the outcome of the uncompromising and unremitting polemics of more than twenty years, was effected by means of several different provisions of the Act of 1849. The spirit and purpose of the statute are clearly shown by the following enactment* :—

"No religious test or qualification whatsover shall be required of or appointed for any person admitted or matriculated as a member of such University, whether as a scholar, student, fellow, or otherwise ; or of or for any person admitted to any degree in any Art or Faculty in the said University ; or of or for any person appointed to any office, professorship, lectureship, mastership, tutorship, or

---

Section 29.

other place or employment whatsoever in the same; nor shall religious observances, according to the forms of any particular religious denomination, be imposed upon the members or officers of the said University, or any of them."

It was further provided that the Chancellor elected by Convocation should not be "a minister, ecclesiastic, or teacher, under or according to any form or profession of religious faith or worship whatsoever," and a similar restriction was placed on the Crown in its appointment of members of Senate. The Faculty of Divinity, and with it the professorship of the same subject, was abolished, and the right to confer degrees in Divinity was expressly abrogated.*

Financial Policy and Management.—The endowment of the University had prior to the passing of the Act of 1849 been seriously impaired by lavish expenditure on capital account, and also by culpable mismanagement.† In order to guard against a continuation of reckless outlay on the one hand, and a recurrence of financial malfeasance on the other, positive regulations were laid down in the Act for the guidance of the "Endowment Board" and the limitation of its powers. It was required to discharge its functions "under the direction" of statutes passed by the Senate. It was forbidden to dispose of or apply "the real property" or other capital of the University "otherwise than by authority of a

---

* Section 28. The Act of 1850 provides that while religious instruction may be given to students, no part of the funds of the University shall be spent for such a purpose. Upper Canada College also was secularized by the University Act of 1849.

† See Appendix D, for a summary of the Report of the King's College commissioners (1848-51). See also Ontario Sessional Paper No. 74, of 1895.

statute." It was directed to form an "Investment Fund" and an "Income Fund;" to pay into the former all moneys received on capital account; and to pay into the latter all revenue from fees, rents, interest, and dividends, and all annual donations not given by the donors for specific purposes. It was ordered to invest the capital of the endowment in "Government or landed securities approved of by the Senate," and to apply the annual income to the payment of the following claims, in the order given : (1) cost of management of the funds; (2) cost of management of the real property; (3) salaries of the officers, servants, and teachers not of professorial standing; (4) incidental expenses; (5) salaries of the Vice-Chancellor, President, and professors; and (6) special appropriations ordered by statutes of the Senate. All annual surpluses of income over expenditure were ordered to be transferred from the income fund to the investment fund of the University. Provision was made for an annual audit of the accounts by two auditors, one appointed by the Chancellor or Vice-Chancellor, and the other by the Senate, to which, as well as to the Visitor, they were required to report.

The Act of 1849 in operation.—The new constitution of the Provincial University went into operation on the first of January, 1850. It was amended in some points of detail by an Act* passed in the session of that year, and an ineffectual attempt was made in the Legislative Assembly to restore to the University more or less of its former sectarian character. But the system did not fulfil the expectations to which its establishment gave rise.

---

* 13 and 14 Vict. Chapter 49.

One object in view in the legislation of 1849 was to secure the abandonment by the denominational colleges of their University powers,* and to obtain their co-operation with the Provincial University in the promotion of secular culture. This purpose completely failed, partly because the change in the constitution of the University came too late, and partly because it was not in itself well calculated to produce the desired effect. None of the existing denominational colleges would consent to abandon their degree conferring powers unless they were permitted as teaching institutions to share in the proceeds of the University endowment, and from this they were expressly debarred by the provision of the Act† of 1849, which required the Endowment Board, after paying the working expenses of the University, to add all surplus income to capital. Queen's, Victoria, and Regiopolis retained their academical independence, and, through the active exertions‡ of Bishop Strachan and his associates, Trinity College was soon established in Toronto as a University of the Church of England. There was no rapid increase of students in attendance at the Provincial University, and strenuous efforts were made, not without effect, to discredit it with the people as a "godless" institution. The want of enthusiasm for the secular University, and the rising tide of denominationalism against it, alike pointed to the necessity for some further change, and this was effected after the brief interval of four years.

---

* Except the right to confer degrees in Divinity of which the Provincial University had been deprived.
† Section 42.
‡ See Chapter VI.

The University Act of 1853.—As the denominational Colleges had by this time become firmly rooted in the localities where they had been established, it was evidently useless to expect them to transplant themselves to Toronto except on terms financially profitable to them This made it necessary for the Legislature either to appropriate public money for the purpose, or to leave them where they were, for the capital of the University endowment was not in a position to stand so heavy a drain. No proposal to increase that endowment would have had the slightest chance of adoption by Parliament, which was then distracted by the agitation for the settlement of the "Clergy Reserve" question.* The alternative course was, therefore, adopted, but the privilege of affiliation to the University of Toronto was not made conditional on the surrender of degree-conferring powers by affiliated Colleges, as had been the case under the Act of 1849. To make the contemplated scheme still more workable it was deemed expedient to divest the University of Toronto of its teaching functions, and to vest these in a new corporation to be called "University College.". Lastly, an attempt to conciliate the denominational institutions was made by providing that annual surpluses should "constitute a fund to be from time to time appropriated by Parliament for academical educa-

---

* In 1853 the Imperial Parliament passed an Act (16 and 17 Vict., cap. 21,) to authorize the Legislature of the Province of Canada to make provision concerning "the Clergy Reserves in that Province, and the proceeds thereof." In 1854 the Canadian Parliament passed an Act (18 Vict., cap 2,) secularizing the clergy reserves, and devoting the proceeds to educational and other purposes.

tion in Upper Canada." The general scope of the Act* of
1853 is fairly indicated by its title,† but still more clearly
by its preamble, the importance of which is enhanced by
the fact that the statute to which it is prefixed has been
to a large extent the basis of all subsequent legislation in
relation to the Provincial University. The text of the
preamble is as follows :—

Whereas the enactments‡ hereinafter repealed have failed to
effect the end proposed by the Legislature in passing them, inasmuch as no college or educational institution hath under them
become affiliated to the University to which they relate, and many
parents and others are deterred by the expense and other causes
from sending the youth under their charge to be educated in a
large city distant,§ in many cases, from their homes ; And Whereas, from these and other causes, many do and will prosecute and
complete their studies in other institutions in various parts of this
Province, to whom it is just and right to afford facilities for obtaining those scholastic honors and rewards which their diligence and
proficiency may deserve, and thereby to encourage them and others
to persevere in the pursuit of knowledge and sound learning ; And
Whereas experience hath proved the principles embodied in Her
Majesty's Royal Charter to the University of London‖ in England

---

* 16 Vict cap 89.

† It is entitled "An Act to amend the laws relating to the University of Toronto, by separating its functions as a University from
those assigned to it as a College, and by making better provision
for the management of the property thereof and that of Upper
Canada College."

‡ The University Act of 1849 (12 Vict. Chapter 82), and that of
1850 (13 and 14 Vict. Chapter 49).

§ The construction of railways on any extensive scale in Canada
was then only beginning.

‖ The proposal to organize a purely secular University in London
was so strenuously resisted in Parliament that application was made
for a royal Charter, which was obtained in 1836. The original intention of the promoters was the establishment of a teaching University entirely free from sectarian control, but some of them se-

to be well adapted for the attainment of the objects aforesaid, and for removing the difficulties and objections hereinbefore referred to:" Therefore, etc.

The University of Toronto.—Besides repealing the University Acts of 1849 and 1850, the Act of 1853 repealed " so much of the Charter as may be inconsistent with this Act," but provided that "so much of the said Charter* as shall not be inconsistent with this Act shall remain in force." It continued the "University of Toronto" as a corporation, but prohibited the establishment in it of any "professorship or other teachership," and limited its functions to the " examining of candidates" for degrees and standing, and the granting of these after examination. The University corporation was defined as consisting of "One Chancellor, one Vice-Chancellor, and such number of other members of the Senate as the Governor of this Province shall from time to time appoint." The right to appoint the Chancellor was vested in the Crown, and the right to elect the Vice-Chancellor in the Senate, of which he was in the Chancellor's absence the presiding officer. The Governor was continued as Visitor, with powers of visitation and veto similar to those conferred upon him by the Act of 1849. The office of President was of course discontinued, and with the sole exception of the Bursar, a new official to be appointed by the Crown, all the other "officers and servants of the

---

ceded from the movement and established King's College under Church of England auspices. This led to the separation of the University from the t aching functions of the original institution, and to the issue of two charters of the same date, one incorporating the University of London, the other incorporating University College, which, with King's College and many others, is affiliated to the University.

* See note on p. 53 above.

University" together with the "examiners," were to be appointed by statutes of the Senate. "Convocation" was abolished by the repeal of the Act of 1849, and the failure to perpetuate its existence by the Act of 1853. Its chief function under the former statute had been to elect the Chancellor and one member of the Caput. The three faculties of Law, Medicine, and Arts, were retained, but, as there was no teaching, the faculty organization was discontinued, and with it the office of " Dean."

The Senate—composed of the Chancellor, the Vice-Chancellor, and at least* ten members appointed by the Crown—was made the chief governing body in the University. Subject to the provisions relating to " income and property," it was entrusted with " the management of and superintendence over the affairs and business thereof," and it was clothed with authority " to make such statutes and to act in such manner as shall appear best calculated to promote the purposes of the University," in all cases unprovided for by the Provincial statute. It was in a special manner authorized to make regulations respecting the examinations for degrees and standing, the granting of these after examination, the fees to be paid, and the use to be made of the revenue thus secured. It was required to hold an " open and public" examination at least once a year, and was authorized to confer degrees in " Arts and Faculties," and certificates of honor

---

*Section 4, 5, and 8, construed together, give the Governor-in-Council authority to appoint as many members of Senate as might seem expedient, but if the number fell below ten, and the Governor-in-Council did not think proper to make appointments, the Senate was authorized to elect enough of new members to bring the number up to the minimum. The only limitation in the choice was that they must be British subjects.

in special subjects. It was empowered to grant "scholarships, prizes, and rewards," payable out of the University income fund, and these were to be open to competition in any of the affiliated Colleges in Upper Canada. Finally, it was required to report annually to the Governor on "the general state, progress, and prospect of the University," and also to report specifically on any particular subject which he might refer to it for that purpose.

As the Act of 1853 had for one of its chief objects the recognition of educational work done by teaching colleges generally, provision was made for their "affiliation" to the University of Toronto. This privilege was by the Act conferred at once on "all Colleges* in Upper or Lower Canada, incorporated by Royal Charter or by Act of Parliament" for the promotion of literature, science and art, a description which applied to Queen's College, Victoria College, Regiopolis College, and Trinity College in Upper Canada. It was conferred also on all such arts colleges, "corporate or unincorporated," then or afterward established, as the Governor of the Province should from time to time prescribe to the Senate. Lastly, it was conferred on all such teaching colleges of law and of medicine as the Senate might from time to time approve of.

University College.—The teaching function of the former "University of Toronto" was by the Act of 1853 vested in a new "collegiate institution," called "University College." This was placed under the "direction, management, and administration" of a body

---

*It was not necessary under the Act of 1853, as it had been under that of 1849, that affiliated Colleges with degree conferring powers should cease to exercise them.

corporate, called the "Council," which was composed of the President, Vice-President, and professors[*] of the College. These, together with all the other teachers and officers, were appointed by the Crown, the Governor of the Province being *ex officio* Visitor. The Council was authorized to make statutes for "the good government, discipline, conduct, and regulation" of the College, and of its professors, teachers, students, officers, and servants; for the regulation of the fees to be paid by persons receiving instruction in it; and generally for the "management of its property and business." The Council was further entrusted with power to determine by statute the composition of the teaching staff of the College, and also the courses of instruction, subject to the proviso that the latter should be consistent with statutes passed by the University Senate respecting "the prescribed subjects of examination." The prohibition of the teaching of divinity was continued,[†] and the teaching of law and medicine was abolished,[‡] "except in so far as the same may form part of a general system of liberal education." The non-sectarian character of the institution was safeguarded by the following enactment:[§]

"No religious test or profession of religious faith shall be required of any professor, lecturer, teacher, student, officer, or servant of the said College, nor shall any religious observances, according to the forms of any particular religious denominations be imposed on them or any of them; but it shall be lawful for the Council to make such regulations as they may think expedient, touching the moral conduct of the students and their attendance on public

---

[*] The Dean of Residence was added by the University Act of 1873.
[†] See above, p. 57.   [‡] Section 32.
[§] Section 34.

worship in their respective churches or other places of religious worship, and their receiving religious instruction from their respective Ministers, and according to their respective forms of religious faith, and every facility shall be afforded for their so doing."

Financial Management. — The financial policy embodied in the University Act of 1849 was to entrust the management to an " Endowment Board," in the membership of which the Crown had only one representative, and to limit the powers of this Board, (1) by general provisions in the Provincial statute itself, and (2) by making its management of the property of the University subject to the statutory direction of the Senate.* The policy adopted in 1853 was to transfer to and vest in the Crown, for the purposes of the University Act, "all the property and effects, real and personal," which had under the Act of 1849 belonged to, or been vested in, " the Corporation of the Chancellor, Masters, and Scholars of the University of Toronto." Thenceforth it was to be managed and administered, under the orders of the Governor-in-Council, by an officer to be appointed by Commission under the Great Seal of the Province, to hold his office during pleasure, and to be called the " Bursar of the University and Colleges† at Toronto," his powers being subject to definition from time to time by the Governor-in-Council.‡

---

*See above, pp. 54 and 57-58.

†University College and Upper Canada College. For the relation of the latter to the University under the Act of 1853, see Appendix B.

‡The most important Orders-in-Council dealing with the general subject of financial management are two passed in May 1878, and May, 1884, respectively, by the Lieutenant-Governor-in-Council of the Province of Ontario. Except in so far as the second of these orders amends the first they are both still in force, and when read

With a view to guarding more effectually against such malfeasance* as the University endowment had already suffered from, he was, as to accounting for the funds under his management, placed by the Act on the same footing as " an officer employed in the collection of the Provincial revenue," and was required to report annually to the Governor, for the information of Parliament, on (1) the state of the land endowment, (2) the amount of capital invested and the amount expended during the year, and (3) the amount required to be paid out for current expenses, with a description of the various services on which it was spent. He was required to keep a "Permanent Fund," out of which no payments should be made on capital account except on the order of the Governor-in-Council, and that only for "such permanent improvements or additions to the buildings as may be necessary for the purposes" of the University and College respectively. He was similarly required to consolidate into one "Income Fund" all fees received in the University and the College, together with the rents of leased property, interest on the purchase money of property sold, interest on invested capital, "and all other casual and periodical incomings, including any donations or subscriptions touching which it shall not be otherwise ordered by the donors." Out of this income fund, after paying the expenses of the Bursar's office, the Governor-in-Council was authorized to appropriate yearly the amount " required to defray the

---

together they constitute a "Board of trustees," which controls expenditures under appropriations made by Order-in-Council, takes charge of buildings and grounds, and advises as to investments.

*See Appendix D.

current expenses" of the University of Toronto* and of University College, including in both cases the care, maintenance, and ordinary† repairs" of the property assigned to the two institutions respectively; and the appropriation for each year might, at the option of the Governor-in-Council, either be made for "particular purposes," or be placed at the disposal of the University Senate and the College Council, respectively, "to be applied under the provisions of statutes" passed by these bodies and approved by the Governor-in-Council.‡ There was added the following provision,§ which played an important part in the University controversies of the next ten years:—

"Any surplus of the said University income fund remaining at the end of any year after defraying the expenses payable out of the same, shall constitute a fund to be from time to time appropriated by Parliament for academical Education in Upper Canada."

New Site and Building.—The work of the University had for some years been carried on in the building erected‖ as part of a larger edifice to be constructed n accordance with future requirements. During the

---

*"Scholarships, Rewards, and Prizes" established by the Senate, are in this connection specifically mentioned as part of the "current expenditure" of the University.

†It was left to the Governor-in-Council "to decide what shall be deemed ordinary repairs as distinguished from permanent improvements."

‡The method of authorising the annual expenditure has usually been to make by Order-in-Council detailed appropriations for specific services, but these have been made on the basis of estimates sent in beforehand by the University Senate and the College Council, respectively.

§Section 54.

‖See above, p. 35, and note.

session of 1853 an Act* was passed authorizing the Government to take possession of the site for new Provincial buildings, and to value the land† and pay interest on the valuation into the University income fund. Both the site and the building were accordingly appropriated by the Government, and were long retained by it for Provincial uses, though the scheme for the erection of new Provincial buildings fell through. This made necessary the selection of another site and the erection of a new University building. The latter was begun in 1856 and completed in 1858. The total cost was $355,907,‡ the original appropriation by the Governor-in-Council having been $300,000. The withdrawal of so large an amount from the permanent fund caused serious embarrassment to the management of the University, the receipts from fees being at that time quite insignificant§. The following

---

*16 Vict., Cap. 161.

†No provision was made for the inclusion of the College building in the valuation, though it had cost $55,000. For a full discussion of the matter see Ont. Sess. Paper No. 74 of 1895. See also the report of the University Commission of 1861 pp. 7 and 61-62. For a summary of this valuable report, see Appendix E.

‡The building was partially destroyed by fire in 1890, and was restored, without loss to the capital of the University, by means of a special appropriation of $160,000 made by the Ontario Legislature for the purpose. The total amount taken out of the Endowment for building purposes is $652,652, made up as follows:—

King's College, East wing (1842)	$ 55,000
University of Toronto (1856)	355,907
Biological Building (1890)	129,745
Gymnasium 1894	30,000
Chemical Building 1895	82,000
Total	$652,652

§"Matriculated" Students in Arts were, prior to 1861, exempted from payment of fees for tuition, and the fees paid by

table will show the effect of the impairment of the capital of the endowment on the revenue of the institution :—

Year.	Income	Expenditure.	Surplus.	Deficit.
1853	$67,077	$54,929	$12,148	
1854	52,923	49,453	13,476	
1855	57,477	56,780	697	
1856	66,577	65,206	1,371	
1857	60,132	60,917		$ 785
1858	55,734	55,386	348	
1859	51,586	70,155*		18,569
1860	54,375	63,153		8,778
1861	50,355	61,829		11,474

Proposed Division of the Endowment.—As far back as 1846, in reply to communications† from Governor Cathcart, the authorities of Queen's College, Victoria College, and Regiopolis College had intimated very plainly that they had strong claims on the Province for aid in carrying on the work of higher education, and on behalf of Queen's it was alleged that an endowment had been promised for a chair of theology, to come out of the

---

"occasional" students were assigned as "perquisites" to the several professors and tutors in addition to their stated salaries. See Report of University Commission of 1861, pp. 8 and 127.

*Including $5,125 for "Furniture for College Residence"; $6,256 for improvement of the grounds; and $4,340 for a residence in connection with the Observatory. See Report of Commission of 1861, p. 9.

†See above, pp. 41-46.

King's College endowment. The University Act of 1849 had closed the door to any such advantage by declaring that annual surpluses should be added to the capital of the endowment, but the way to a continuation of the agitation was opened up by the provision in the Act of 1853, which placed* such surpluses at the disposal of the Legislature for the promotion of "academical education." The buoyant condition of the University revenue during the years 1853-56 naturally attracted the attention of those who felt the burden of carrying on at their own expense colleges doing work similar in character and equal in extent to that done by University College.

The pressure for a division of the funds of the University, which had been for some time growing stronger outside of Parliament, at length found expression in petitions to the Legislature. More than once the Wesleyan Methodist Conference authorized its President and Secretary to send in formal memorials on its behalf, and one of these† was in the Session of 1860 referred, with others of similar tenor, to a special committee,‡ which took a large amount of very valuable evidence§ respecting the history, organization, and work of the Provincial University. The petition of Conference in 1856 had prayed " that enlarged

---

*See above, p. 68.

† Prepared by the Rev. Dr. Ryerson. The full text is given in his "Story of my Life," pp. 520-523..

‡Composed of Hon. Malcolm Cameron, Attorney-General (John A.) Macdonald, Hon. George Brown, Hon. William Cayley, Hon. Michael Foley, and Messrs. Wilson, Roblin, Simpson, and McCann.

§No report of the proceedings of this committee was published by Parliament, the understanding being that each side should take the responsibility and assume the cost of printing its own case. See Appendix E.

assistance may be granted to Victoria College, and that part of the funds now expended on Toronto University and University College may be annually appropriated to the several chartered colleges." The occurrence of a large deficit in 1859 is a sufficient explanation of the changed form of the petition of 1860, which prayed for "an inquiry into the manner in which the University Act of 1853 has been administered, and the funds of the University expended, and that all colleges in Upper Canada (denominational or otherwise*) may be placed on the same footing in regard to the University." As the Legislature met at that time in Quebec it was obviously inconvenient for a Parliamentary committee to investigate thoroughly the state of an educational institution situated in Toronto. Partly for this reason and partly because petitions both for and against a division of its funds, presented to the Legislature in the session of 1861, made it appear that the agitation was likley to be continued, Governor-General Monck, as Visitor of the University of Toronto and University College, appointed a Commission† to conduct on his behalf a visitation of these institutions and report to him. The Commissioners held a number of meetings in the University for the taking of evidence and consulting of records, and a number of additional meetings elsewhere for the preparation of their report, which was sent‡ to the Government at Quebec. Their criticism of

---

*The only non-denominational one was University College, which was established on the University endowment.

†Made up of Hon. James Patton of Toronto (Chairman), John Beatty M.D., of Cobourg, and John Paton Esq. of Kingston. The date of the appointment of the Commission was October 28, 1861.

‡On the 29th of May 1862. For a summary of the report see Appendix E.

the management of the University was moderate in tone, and was directed against a defective system rather than against those who had to administer it. On the subject of aid to affiliated Colleges they recommended (1) that the Crown Lands Department should assume the administration of the remainder of the land endowment of the University; (2) that interest-bearing debentures, to the amount of $971,000 should, in return for the land and in lieu of annual grants by the Legislature to denominational Colleges, be added to the capital of the endowment; (3) that out of a total revenue of $84,000 a year from investments the sum of $28,000 should be appropriated to University College,* and the sum of $10,000 to each of the other four—Queen's, Victoria, Regiopolis, and Trinity; (4) that no degrees in Arts should be conferred by these institutions on their own students, the University of Toronto† prescribing the Arts curriculum, conducting the examinations in each institution, and granting the degrees; and (5) that after an appropriation of $3,500 for scholarships in the University and the colleges, the remainder should be devoted to paying the expenses incurred by the Senate in the management of the affairs of the University.

No action was ever taken by either the Government or the Legislature on this report. The controversy was kept up in the country for a time with a persistence and an acrimony that recalled the disputes over the sectarian charter of King's College. But the disputation was comparatively short-lived. Petitions both for and against the proposal to divide up the endowment were presented

---

*Under the old name of " King's College."
†Under the name of " The University of Upper Canada."

to Parliament in the first session of 1863; petitions against, but not for it, were presented in the second session of that year. The matter was then by common consent dropped, its disappearance from the Parliamentary arena being due to the insufficiency of the endowment for what was required of it already; to the reluctance of the Legislature to either add to it, or assume any further liability in connection with higher education; and to the very unsettled state of Canadian politics that resulted in 1864, in the Quebec Conference resolutions, and three years later in the passing of the British North America Act, which consigned higher as well as lower education to the jurisdiction of the Provincial Legislatures. The Ontario Parliament, in spite of the strenuous opposition of the supporters of denominational colleges, discontinued in 1869 the small annual grants that had been made to them for many years by the Parliament of Canada.

The University Act of 1873.—Apart from minor changes effected by orders of the Lieutenant-Governor-in-Council in connection with the management of the finances, no modification was made in the constitution of the Provincial University until the Session of 1873, when an Act* was passed, which left the principal functions† of the two institutions practically unaltered, while it made several important changes of a minor kind. The University corporation was changed by the addition of " Convocation " to the Chancellor, Vice-Chancellor, and Senate as

---

*36 Vict., Cap. 29 of the Statutes of Ontario.

† That of examining for degrees and standing on the one hand, and that of teaching on the other.

provided by the Act of 1853, and Convocation was defined* as including "all Doctors and Bachelors of Law, all Doctors and Bachelors of Medicine, all Masters of Arts, all Bachelors of Arts of three years' standing, all Doctors of Science, and all Bachelors of Science of three years' standing." While the Vice-Chancellor was left elective by the Senate, the Chancellor was made elective triennially by Convocation. The composition of the Senate was changed by the limitation of Government appointees to nine, by the introduction of certain *ex officio* members,† and by the addition of fifteen members elected by Convocation. The affiliation of all institutions‡ that had not been affiliated as the result of "special applications made in that behalf" was cancelled, and the right to grant the privilege of affiliation was conferred on the Chancellor, Vice-Chancellor, and Senate, subject to the approval of the Lieutenant-Governor-in-Council and to the decision of Convocation. Authority to establish, on the recommendation of the Senate, additional "professorships or chairs" in University College was given to the Lieutenant-Governor-in-

---

*By 44 Vict., Cap. 31 all graduates were afterwards declared to be members of Convocation.

†The President of University College, the Chief Superintendent (later the Minister) of Education for the Province, a representative of the Law Society, the Principal of Upper Canada College, a representative from each affiliated institution, a representative of the High School Masters, all former Chancellors and Vice-Chancellors, and two members of the Council of University College.

‡This included Queen's College, Victoria College, Regiopolis College, and Trinity College, which had been affiliated by the University Act of 1853 without having applied for the status conferred by it.

Council, and the Senate was invested with a still more important prerogative by the following provision*:—

The Senate of the University, upon representations made to it in that behalf, may enquire into the conduct or efficiency of any professor in University College, and report to the Lieutenant-Governor the result of such enquiry, and may make such recommendations as the Senate may think the circumstances of the case require."

The University Act of 1887.—The attendance of students at University College increased slowly from 1853 to 1873. Shortly after the latter date began the assimilation of the matriculation examination of the University to the examinations held by the Education Department for the qualification of Public School teachers, and the consequent simplification of the work of the High Schools in preparing candidates for both tests. The increase in the number of University Students became more rapid, until both the available accommodation and the capacity of the teaching staff were seriously taxed. This gave rise to a demand on the part of the supporters and alumni of the Provincial University for additional financial aid from the Legislature, and a spirited opposition to this demand from the friends of Victoria, Queen's, and Trinity Universites.† The outcome of the controversy was a conference‡ of representatives of these institutions with representatives of the University of Toronto and its affiliated denominational colleges. This was held in

---

*Section 49. This enactment is still part of the organic law of the University. See Section 45 of the University Act of 1897 (50 Vict., Cap. 43.

†Regiopolis College had ceased to do academic work in 1871. See Chapter IX.

‡For a brief account of the work of this conference, including the resolutions adopted, see Appendix F.

1885 at the instance of the Hon. G. W. Ross, Minister of Education for the Province of Ontario, and its deliberations resulted in the adoption of a series of resolutions embodying the general principles on which the institutions above referred to might join in a co-operative federation for the promotion of higher education. This basis of union was submitted to and adopted by the Senate of the University of Toronto, and also by Convocation. It was rejected by the authorities of Queen's and Trinity Universities. The right to deal with it on behalf of Victoria University was vested in the General Conference of the Methodist Church of Canada, and by that body it was at first rejected.* The Legislature nevertheless, embodied in an Act† passed in the session of 1887 the essential features of the scheme, which were in that statute consolidated with the provisions of the existing University constitution.

One important change effected by the University Act of 1887 was the division of the work of tuition, and the restoration of a large part of it to the University of Toronto, from which it had been taken away by the Act‡ of 1853. The object in view was to make tuition in the subjects assigned to the University, as distinguished from University College, free to the students of other universities, by way of inducement to the latter to leave their degree conferring powers (except in the faculty of Divinity) in abeyance, and join in a federal union with

---

*This action was reversed by the General Conference in 1890 and Victoria College was removed to Toronto, from Cobourg, in 1892. See Chapter IV.

†50 Vict., Cap. 43.

‡See above pp. 60 and 62.

the Provincial University. Speaking generally, the line of cleavage between the teaching functions of the University and the College respectively was the line between Science and Philosophy on the one hand, and the languages with Ethics on the other.* An equally important change was the making of provision for the re-establishment of the teaching faculties of Law and Medicine, which had been abolished by the Act† of 1853. The expediency of such re-establishment was left by the Act to be determined by the University Senate, which almost immediately moved in the matter by appointing special committees to report as to the advisability of taking such a step in the case of either faculty. The result was the creation within the year of a teaching faculty of Medicine, which has been made self-suporting so far as the endowment of the University is concerned. No teaching faculty of Law has yet been created‡ under the authority granted by the Act of 1887.

The Organization of the University.—The Act of 1887 continues the " University of Toronto " as a corporation, with power to hold real property, and " such other powers and privileges as are conferred upon it by those portions

---

*The University subjects, as enumerated in the Act are: Pure Mathematics, Physics, Astronomy, Geology, Mineralogy, Chemistry, (pure and applied), Zoology, Botany, Physiology, History, Ethnology, Comparative Philology, History of Philosophy, Logic and Metaphysics, Education, Political Economy, Jurisprudence, Constitutional Law, Engineering, Italian and Spanish. The University College subjects are: Greek, Latin, French, German, English, Oriental languages, Moral Philosophy, and Ancient History taught in connection with Greek and Latin.

†Sections 3 and 32. See above, p. 65.

‡Probably because a Law School has been established under the auspices of the Law Society of Upper Canada.

of the Charter remaining in force,* or by any former Act." The Corporation consists of the " Chancellor, Vice-Chancellor, Professors, and members of the Senate and of Convocation for the time being." The Lieutenant-Governor of the Province is continued as " Visitor " *ex officio.* The Chancellor is elected triennially by the graduates of the University, all of whom in all its faculties are members of Convocation. The Vice-Chancellor is elected triennially by the Senate, of which, in the absence of the Chancellor, he is the presiding officer. The President of the University, who is *ex officio* President of University College, is appointed by the Crown, as are also all the members† of the teaching staff. The administration of the affairs of the institution, except so much of them as belong to the Bursar's office, has been committed to (1) the Senate and (2) the University Council.

The Senate is composed of (1) members *ex officio*, namely, the Minister of Education, the Chancellor, the Vice-Chancellor, the President of University College, and the President or other head of each federating‡ University or College ; (2) appointed members, namely nine appointed by the Crown, three by the University Council, and one by the governing body of each of the following : University College, the Law Society of Upper Canada each federating University or College, and each affiliated College ; (3) elected members, namely, one for every hundred graduates in Arts on the register of each federating

---

*See above, p. 53.

†Members of the Medical Faculty must be nominated by the Senate.

‡The only " federating University " to date is Victoria ; the only " federating Colleges " are Knox College, Wycliffe College, and St. Michael's College.

University when the Act of 1887 took effect,* two for the graduates in Law without distinction of University, four for the graduates in Medicine, and two elected by "the head masters and assistant masters of collegiate institutes and high schools." Subject to the provisions of the Act† respecting the income and property of the institution the Senate is entrusted with "the management of and superintendency over the affairs and business of the University." It is authorized to prescribe courses of study, and after examination to confer degrees or grant certificates of standing in the different departments of learning except Theology.‡ It may establish "scholarships, prizes, and rewards," but is forbidden to make them a charge on the funds of the University. It may by statute, subject to the approval of the Lieutenant-Governor-in-Council, grant the privilege of affiliation to teaching institutions, and may in the same way cancel the privilege after it has been granted. It may of its own motion "inquire into the conduct, teaching, and efficiency of any professor or teacher" in either the University or University College, and report the result of its inquiry to the Lieutenant-Governor with such recommendations as the circumstances of the case seems to require. In addition to the powers specifically conferred upon it by the Act, it is authorized to pass statutes "in general for promoting the purposes of the University, and

---

*It was brought into force by proclamation of the Lieutenant-Governor in Council on the 23rd of March, 1888. The representatives of the graduates in Arts are at present twelve for the University of Toronto, and five for Victoria University.

†See below, p. 82.

‡In the older University Statutes the term "Divinity" is used.

touching all other matters whatsoever regarding the same or the business thereof, or for any purpose for which provision may be required for carrying out this Act according to its intent and spirit," in any case not provided for by the Act. All its statutes are subject to ratification by order of the Lieutenant-Governor in Council, to whom it is required to report annually on the general condition and progress of the University.

The University Council is a body created for the first time by the Act of 1887. It consists of the President and the professors in the various teaching faculties of the University, and is entrusted with full authority (1) to exercise discipline over all students in relation to the lectures and other instruction by members of the University teaching faculties; (2) to regulate the work carried on by "the societies and associations of students" organized in connection with the University; (3) to control all "officers and servants" whose services are required in connection with the work of instruction; and (4) to prescribe fees for laboratory instruction. The University Council is not a body corporate, or even a constituent element in the University corporation.

University College.—This institution is continued as a body corporate under the name of "The Council of University College." The Lieutenant-Governor is continued as *ex officio* Visitor. The Council is composed of the President, the College professors, and the Dean of residence, and it is empowered to make regulations for "the management of the property and business" of the College, and for any purpose necessary for carrying the Act into effect according to its intent and spirit in cases for which no provision is made. All the members of the teaching staff are appointed by the Crown and hold office during its pleasure, but the President may suspend any "officer or servant," and report the case to the Visitor. The Council is authorized, subject to the approval of the Lieutenant-Governor-in-Council, to determine the fees payable for tuition in the College. The non-sectarian character of the University and University College is maintained, but the Councils of the two institutions are authorized to make regulations for the moral conduct of students and their attendance on public worship, the latter being, however, left entirely voluntary.

Financial Management.—The University Income and Property Act* of 1887 effects a complete separation between the management and endowment of Upper Canada College† and those of the University of Toronto and University College, and vests the control of all the property and effects of the latter two institutions in the Crown, under the management of the Bursar, whose office is continued unchanged as to appointment, terms, powers, and functions.‡ It is provided by this statute that the former distinction between "property" and "income" shall be maintained in the Bursar's accounts; that in making appropriations out of income for the annual expenditure the Lieutenant-Governor-in-Council may either designate the special services, or leave that to be done by the University Senate and College Council; and that any surplus remaining at the end of any year to the

---

*50 Vict., Cap. 44.
†See Appendix B.
‡See above, p. 66.

credit of the income fund " shall be treated as permanent property."

The University Acts of 1887 were in the year of their enactment consolidated with the Revised Statutes of Ontario for 1887, and in this form they are at present the organic law of the Provincial University.

CHAPTER IV.

VICTORIA UNIVERSITY.

The adherents of the Methodist Church in Upper Canada shared during the early history of the Province the general regret at the absence of all facilities for obtaining a higher education. Prominent members of the Methodist communion took part in the educational controversies of the day both in the Legislature and outside of it. When the District Grammar Schools were founded under the Act* of 1807, they, with other so-called "Dissenters," resented their exclusion from what they deemed a fair share of influence in the control and direction of public schools maintained entirely at the public expense. They objected, as members of other denominations did, to the sectarian character of the charter granted to King's College in 1827, and to the surrender of the Provincial University's land endowment to the control of a single church. Their dissatisfaction was intensified when Lieutenant-Governor Colborne, without authority from the Legislature, or the concurrence of any other body except his Executive Council, established† Upper Canada College as a substitute for the Home District Grammar School. Owing to the circumstances of the case, whether it was so intended or not, the new

---

*47 Geo. III., cap. 6.

†See above pp. 23-24, and also Appendix B.

College fell at once under the virtual control* of the Church of England, which claimed then to be the "Established Church" of Upper Canada, and there can be little doubt that this acted as a stimulus to the Methodists in their efforts to promote liberal culture by the establishment of an institution under their own control, but open to students of all other denominations.

The Work of Dr. Ryerson.†—By far the most prominent exponent of the views of the Methodist body during the stirring educational controversies which agitated the country for the forty years from 1824 to 1864, was the Rev. Egerton Ryerson. The son of a United Empire Loyalist who had served as a British officer in the Revolutionary War, he was born in 1803 in that part of Upper Canada which afterwards became, and is now, the County of Norfolk. The London District Grammar School was within easy reach, and there he obtained his primary education under Mr. James (afterwards Judge) Mitchell, who had come to Canada from Scotland with Dr. Strachan. Contrary to the expressed wish of his father he joined the Methodist Church at the age of eighteen, and after spending two years as assistant teacher in the grammer school of which he had been a pupil, he took a brief course of preparatory instruction in Hamilton and there entered the itinerant Methodist ministry. Shortly

---

*From a petition sent to the Legislative Assembly by the "United Presbytery of Upper Canada" in the session of 1830, it appears that allegations of the same kind were current respecting the Grammar Schools (See Hodgins' "Documentary History," Vol. I. pp. 298-299.)

†A very good account of Dr. Ryerson's work is given in his "Story of My Life," edited and supplemented by his intimate friend and official colleague, J. G. Hodgins, LL.D.

afterward, at the instance of his fellow ministers he published anonymously, in 1825, a spirited reply to one of Archdeacon Strachan's controversial sermons, and even at the early age of twenty-two he began to be looked upon as the coming champion, not merely of Methodism but of all the other religious denominations which were then striving to secure a reasonable degree of civil rights and of religious freedom. His appointment to the Editorship of the *Christian Guardian*, which was established in 1829 by the Methodist body as its journalistic organ, gave him increased opportunities and greater influence as a publicist. He had taken an active part in the organization of an independent "Methodist Episcopal Church in Canada," which was effected in 1828,* and in 1833 he made his first journey to England to promote the union of that year between the Canadian and British Methodist Conferences. A second journey across the Atlantic was made in 1835 to secure a charter and raise funds for the seminary which had by that time been established by the Canadian Methodists. After it became a university in 1841, he was chosen its first "Principal," and this office he held until after he was appointed in 1844 "Chief Superintendent of Education" for Upper Canada. In that capacity he was able to render educational services of the greatest value to the Province. He visited many countries in Europe, as well as different States of the Union in America, and before he resigned his office in 1876 he was permitted to witness in effective

---

*Prior to that date the Methodist Church in Canada was connected with the Methodist Episcopal Church of the United States, by which it had been established.

operation a system of popular education which is not inferior to any other in the world, and which is due in its main features to his exceptional aptitude for initiating practical reforms and his phenomenal capacity for popularizing them. In all the controversies over the clergy reserves, which were finally secularized in 1854,* and over the sectarian charter of the Provincial University, which was cleared of its sectarianism by the University Act† of 1849, he, more than other person, spoke for his own denomination, and he continued to do so during the discussion over the Provincial University endowment, which lasted till 1862. After his retirement from all active duty in church and state, but busily engaged in literary work as long as his physical and intellectual powers remained vigorous, he lived in honored retirement till his lamented death in 1882.

Upper Canada Academy Established.—In the Methodist Conference held in 1829 the subject of a seminary of higher education was taken into consideration and a committee was appointed, but nothing decisive was done ‡ In the following year the matter came up again for discussion; a committee was appointed to deal with it, and a plan for carrying on the work was reported by the committee and adopted by the Conference.§ In accordance with the resolutions then passed the proposed "seminary of learning" was to be established " under the direction of the Conference

---

*By Act of the Canadian Parliament, 18 Vict., cap. 2.
†12 Vict., cap. 82.
‡Carroll's "Case and his Contemporaries," Vol. III., p. 256.
§"Life and times of Anson Green, D.D.," p. 140.

of the Methodist Episcopal Church* of Canada." It was to be placed under the control of nine "Trustees" appointed by Conference, and in them was to be vested the management of all the property belonging to the institution. Five Visitors were to be chosen annually by the Conference, and these were to be associated with the trustees in appointing members of the teaching staff, fixing their salaries, framing regulations, prescribing the course of study, and dealing with "all other matters which relate to the proper regulation, government, discipline, and instruction of the students." The seminary was to be a purely literary institution; no system of Divinity was to be taught in it, but all students were to be "free to embrace and pursue any religious creed, and attend any place of religious worship which their parents or guardians might direct." Dr. Green who was a member of the Conference of 1830, describes the scheme as "a bold and venturesome, as well as a patriotic, undertaking," and it is difficult to see how this encomium can be withheld from it. Dr. Green adds† : " We had no funds with which to provide such an institution, and we had little collegiate knowledge and experience to guide us; but the country required it, the church demanded it, and the Conference ordered it, therefore it was accomplished."

---

* Founded by missionaries from the M. E. Church of the United States at the time of the United Empire Loyalist immigration. In 1833 this body united with the Methodist Church established in Eastern Canada by British Methodist missionaries, the name of the united body being the "Wesleyan Methodist Church in Canada."

† "Life and times of Anson Green, D.D.," p. 140.

The committee* appointed by Conference to select a location and site for, and to give a name to, the new seminary, ultimately chose Cobourg from among a number of competing places,† and the name given to the college was "The Upper Canada Academy." A vigorous canvass for funds was carried on, and able expositions of the purpose in view appeared occasionally from the pen of Dr. Ryerson. The project was apparently regarded with dislike by Sir John Colborne, who in the course of a somewhat undignified reply‡ to a courteous address of the Methodist Conference, said, evidently with Upper Canada College in his mind :—"The system of education which has produced the best and ablest men in the United Kingdom will not be abandoned here to suit the limited views of the leaders of societies who perhaps have neither experience nor judgment to appreciate the value or advantages of a liberal education; but the British Government will, I am confident, with the aid of the Provincial Legislature, establish respectable schools in every part of the Province, and encourage all societies to follow this example. A seminary, I hope, will not be styled exclusive that is open to everyone, merely because

---

*This committee was composed of : Rev. John Ryerson, Thomas Whitehead, Samuel Belton, David Wright, John Beatty, William Ryerson, Thomas Madden, William Brown, and James Richardson. The two Ryersons were brothers of the Rev. Egerton Ryerson, who was then editor of the *Christian Guardian*, the denominational journal ; the Rev. James Richardson was afterwards Bishop of the Methodist Episcopal Church till his death in 1875.

†York (now Toronto), Colborne, Belleville, Kingston, and Brockville, were the others.

‡See Hodgins' "Documentary History," Vol. II., pp. 11-12. The incident occurred in 1831.

the classical masters are brought from our own universities." Dr. Ryerson's response was as pointed as the attack: "The only opinion expressed by the Methodist Conference in regard to a system of education is, that it might be such as the local knowledge of the Provincial Legislature, in respect to the circumstances of the Province, might dictate. No objection that I am aware of has ever been made to classical masters from English universities; but when seminaries are established and placed under the sole direction of the clergy of one church, without even consulting the popular branch of the Colonial Legislature, I cannot see how they are justly entitled to the character, confidence, or patronage of free public institutions."

The Upper Canada Academy Charter.—In spite of the formidable obstacles they had to encounter the promoters of the new Academy succeeded in erecting during the years 1832-35 a building* suitable for the work. The corner stone was laid† on the 7th day of June, 1832, but a heavy debt was incurred in order to secure the completion of the structure. This proved so burdensome that, after various devices‡ had been resorted to at home the Conference resolved in 1835 to send an "Agent" to England to collect funds there, and also to procure for the

---

*This edifice continued to be, until Victoria University was transferred to Toronto in 1892, the nucleus of Victoria College, Cobourg.

†By Dr. Gilchrist of Colborne. Among the memorials placed in the stone was Number 28 of Vol. III., of the *Christian Guardian* then edited, by Mr. Ryerson.

‡Among them a resolution of Conference that its members "should apply to the erection of the Upper Canada Academy all fees which they may receive for the celebration of matrimony for the four years ensuing."

Academy a royal charter. The latter had become a necessity from the fact that the Legislature of Upper Canada showed a strong disinclination* to pass such an Act of incorporation as the promoters of the institution would be justified in accepting. The agent selected was Dr. Ryerson, and in November of the same year he set out on his twofold mission. His urgent appeal to the Colonial Secretary† for financial aid to the Academy, in the shape of a grant of money for immediate relief and a land endowment for future maintenance, was met after some time by a refusal to interfere with the revenue of the Province, or make any further appropriation out of the waste lands of the Crown. He was successful, after some delays, caused by doubts on the part of the law officers of the Crown, in obtaining a royal charter,‡ which created "The Trustees of the Upper Canada Academy" a corporation, named the first Trustees and the first Visitors, and provided for the election of their successors by the "Annual Meeting§ of the Ministers of the Wesleyan Methodist Church in Upper Canada." The functions of the trustees, of the Visitors, and of the "Board" made up of the two classes of officials taken together, were defined in accordance with the resolutions of the Conference of 1830.‖ The amount of money collected

---

*See Hodgins' "Documentary History," Vol. II., p. 174.

†Then Lord Glenelg.

‡For the text of this document see Appendix G. It will be found *in extenso* in Hodgins' "Documentary History," Vol. II., pp. 268-272.

§The law officers had some scruple about the use of the term "Conference" and also about that of the word "Church." For the latter they wished to substitute "Connexion,"

‖See above, pp. 87-88.

in England was not enough to free the supporters of the Academy from embarrassment; but in spite of the discouraging state of its finances the institution was, almost immediately after the arrival of the charter, formally opened for the reception of pupils. The charter was dated the 12th of October, 1836; the Academy was opened* on the 10th of June following.

Though Lord Glenelg had not seen his way to granting either a sum of money out of the " casual and territorial revenues of the Crown " for the immediate relief of the Academy, or a land endowment for its future maintenance, he gave Dr. Ryerson a promise† that he would "not fail to direct the Lieutenant-Governor of Upper Canada to recommend to the favorable attention of the Legislature of that Province the claims of the Upper Canada Academy to their protection and support." The matter came before the Legislative Assembly in the first‡ session of 1837, on a petition from the Principal of the Academy, which was referred to a special Committee.§ The report gave full credit to the promotors of the Academy for their enterprise and public spirit, described briefly what they had already accomplished,

---

*Under the Principalship of the Rev. Matthew Richey, and with an attendance of 120 pupils, of whom 80 were boarders.

†See Hodgins' "Documentary History," Vol. II., pp. 251-252, and 255.

‡This was the regular session. The second was a special one held to deal with the financial crisis.

§Of this Committee Mr. W. H. Draper was Chairman, and the other members were Messrs. Ruttan, Hagerman, Prince, Gowan, Cameron, and Monahan. All but the last two belonged to the Church of England; Mr. Cameron was a Presbyterian, and Mr. Monahan a Catholic.

and suggested "the propriety of affording a grant of money to meet the present necessities of the institution In spite of some opposition "An Act granting a sum* of money by way of loan to the Upper Canada Academy at Cobourg" was passed by both Houses, but it was rendered useless by the addition of a provision in the Legislative Council to the effect that the Receiver-General should not advance the amount unless he had money in his hands for which he had no other use. Dr. Ryerson, who had not left England when this procedure was reported to him, at once penned an indignant remonstrance to Lord Glenelg, urging him to apply a portion of the revenue of the Crown in Upper Canada to the relief of the Academy from embarrassments which threatened its continued existence. The Colonial Secretary promptly instructed Sir Francis Bond Head to "advance" the amount specified in the Act, and half of it was paid over under this order. Before the other half was paid, the question was raised by Sir Francis whether the "advance" ordered by Lord Glenelg was to be a "loan" or a "grant." The matter was submitted to both Houses of the Legislature in the session of 1838. The Council declined to express any opinion on the point, and the Assembly requested† the Lieutenant-Governor to pay the balance of the amount specified by the Colonial Secretary, "leaving it to be decided by His Lordship whether it was the intention of the Home Government that such advance should be a loan, or a grant, a matter upon which the

---

*The sum named was £4,150 ($16,600), and the loan was to be for ten years.

†Hodgins' "Documentary History," Vol. III., pp. 103-124

House abstains from offering an opinion." Sir Francis replied that it would afford him great pleasure " to give immediate effect to the wish expressed by the House of Assembly," and thus the unpleasant incident terminated.

Victoria College.—The educational work done in the Upper Canada Academy during the first few years of its existence was intended to be similar in grade to that done in Upper Canada College. Neither of them had university powers to exercise, and each of them was designed to be a preparatory school in relation to a Provincial University, should one be established on a basis satisfactory to the community at large. Whatever hopes may have been entertained by the Methodists as the result of the partial secularization of the charter of King's College by the Act* of 1837, it soon became apparent that the Provincial University would continue under the virtual control of the Church of England, and application was made to Parliament on behalf of the Academy for legislative authority to confer degrees in the various faculties. This was granted by an Act† passed in 1841, the object of which is made clear by the terms of its preamble. After reciting the text of the Royal Charter in full, it continues :—

" And whereas, by petition of the said Board,‡ it appears that the said Academy has been in continuous operation during the last five years, and that its success and usefulness would be greatly increased if it were incorporated with the style and privileges of a

---

*7 William IV., cap. 16. See above, p. 32.

†4 and 5 Vict., cap. 87. This was the first session of the first Parliament of the Province of Canada.

‡The " Board " of the Academy, made up of nine Trustees and five Visitors. See above, p. 88.

College; and whereas the said Board have prayed for the incorporation of the said Academy under the name and style of "Victoria College" at Cobourg, with such privileges as were intended to be conferred upon a College about to be established at Kingston, in connection with the Church of Scotland, by an Act* of the Legislature of the late Province of Upper Canada, intituled *An Act to establish a College by the name and style of the University at Kingston.*"

The statute changed the name of the institution from "The Upper Canada Academy" to "Victoria College," and invested it with "power and authority to confer the degrees of Bachelor, Master, and Doctor in the several arts and faculties." It recognized the "Conference" by that name as the annual meeting so designated† in the royal charter, and it enacted that the President of the Executive Council, the Speaker of the Legislative Council, the Speaker of the Legislative Assembly, the Attorney-General, and the Solicitor-General for Canada West should be *ex officio* Visitors of the College and, as such, members of the "Board" and "Senate." The organization of the new University under this Act was therefore made up of the following constituent bodies: (1) The "Trustees," whose number and functions remained the same as under the royal charter; (2) the "Visitors," whose functions remained unchanged, while the number was increased by the addition of the *ex officio* Visitors above mentioned; (3) the "Board," whose functions continued unchanged, while its membership was increased by the addition of the *ex officio* Visitors; and (4) the "Senate," composed of the President and professors, together with the members of the Board. The last named body was

---

*3 Vict., cap. 35. See chapter V.
†See above, p. 91.

entrusted with "full power and authority to confer the degrees of Bachelor, Master, and Doctor in the several Arts and Faculties." The Act of 1841 did not repeal the royal charter granted to the Academy, but on the contrary, expressly affirmed that it applied to "everything which appertains to the constitution, government, management, proceedings, and interest of the College, as they have heretofore applied to the Academy." The Act of 1841 was amended by a statute* passed by the Parliament of Canada in 1858. By it the number of trustees appointed by Conference was increased to twelve, the number of elected Visitors to twelve, and *ipso facto* the membership of the "Board," exclusive of *ex officio* members, to twenty-four.

Provincial Aid.—From its foundation the Upper Canada Academy had depended almost entirely on the liberality of the Methodists themselves, not merely for the revenue necessary to maintain it, but also for the capital expenditure involved in its establishment. In an able and energetic protest which Dr. Ryerson addressed to the Colonial Secretary† against the Clergy Reserve bill‡ passed by the Parliament of Upper Canada in 1839, he thus stated§ the case for his denomination from the educational standpoint :—

"A very large sum has been expended in the erection of Upper Canada College, on the grounds of King's College, and with an endowment of $8,000 or $10,000 a year. This institution is wholly under the management of Episcopal clergymen, while the Upper

---

*22 Vict., cap. 67.

†Then Lord Normanby, successor to Lord Glenelg.

‡This measure was reserved for the Queen's assent, and it never became law.

§"Story of My Life," p. 252.

Canada Academy, which was built at Cobourg by the Methodists at a cost of about $40,000, could not, without a severe struggle, get even the $16,000 which were directed to be paid over to it by Lord Glenelg. The matter had to be contested* with Sir F. B. Head on the floor of the House of Assembly before he could be induced to obey the Royal instructions."

Dr. Ryerson was at Kingston† when the Victoria College Act was assented to by Governor Sydenham. In a letter written at that time he thus speaks‡ of the University and its future :—

"The establishment of such an institution by the members of the Wesleyan Methodist Church in Canada attests their estimate of Education and Science. . . . . The Act itself will advance the paramount interests of literary education amongst Her Majesty's Canadian subjects. For the accomplishment of this purpose a grant must be added to the charter, a measure honourable to the enlightened liberality of the Government and Legislature. When they are securely laying a broad foundation for popular government, and devising comprehensive schemes for the development of the latent resources of the country and the improvement of its internal communication, and proposing a liberal system of common school education, free from the domination of every church, and aiding colleges which may have been established by any church, we may rationally and confidently anticipate the arrival of a long-looked for era of civil liberty, social harmony, and public prosperity."

Later in the same year Dr. Ryerson was apppointed the first Principal§ of the new University, and in a

---

*See above, pp. 93-94.

†Then the capital of Canada. See above, p. 35.

‡"Story of My Life," p. 301.

§The appointment was made in October, 1841, but he was not formally installed till June, 1842. He occupied the position till he was appointed Chief Superintendent of Education in 1844. He continued at the head of the institution as "Honorary Principal," and afterward as "President," till the late Rev. Dr. Nelles became President in 1852. Dr. Nelles at his death in 1887, was succeeded by the Rev. Dr. Burwash.

G

public address in that capacity, after describing the Academy as "the first institution of the kind established by royal charter, unconnected with the Church of England, throughout the British Colonies," he went on to say : *

"It is a cause of renewed satisfaction and congratulation, that, after five year's operation as an Academy, it has been incorporated as a College, and financially assisted by the unanimous vote of both branches of the Provincial Legislature, sanctioned by more than official cordiality, in Her Majesty's name, by the late lamented Lord Sydenham, one of whose last messages to the Legislative Assembly was a recommendation to grant £500 as an aid to the Victoria College. A foundation for a common school system in this Province has been laid by the Legislature, and I have reason to believe that the attention of Government is earnestly directed to make permanent provision for the support of Colleges also, that they may be rendered efficient in their operation, and accessible to as large a number of the enterprising youth of our country as possible."

University Legislation, 1843 53.—The attitude taken in 1841 by Dr. Ryerson was steadily maintained by him and by the Methodist Church through the University controversy which lasted till 1862. The death of Lord Sydenham cut short the educational plans he was devising in concert with Dr. Ryerson, whom he apparently intended† to appoint to the superintendency of Common Schools. No University legislation of any kind was attempted during the brief *regime* of Sir Charles Bagot. While Mr. Baldwin's University bill of 1843 was before

---

* " Story of My Life," p. 301.

† " Story of My Life," p. 342.

Parliament the Victoria College Board passed* a series of resolutions, commending the University Act of 1837, condemning the manner in which its objects had been "entirely defeated and abrogated," and the sectarian character of the charter " virtually restored ;" approving of the bill of 1843 as likely "to provide effectually against the abuses practised under the general and indefinite provisions of the amended charter; cordially concurring in the general objects and provisions of the bill," though its passage could not confer any advantage on the Wesleyan Methodist Church ; calling attention to the obligation resting on that Church to continue Victoria College at Cobourg as "a literary institution ;" and appealing "to the just and enlightened consideration of the Government to grant such assistance " as the peculiar circumstances suggested. A few days afterward† Dr. Ryerson wrote for publication in the *Christian Guardian* a letter in which he characterized Mr. Baldwin's bill as " a measure worthy of the most enlightened government," and went on to explain how Victoria College would be affected by it :—

In the discussion‡ the authorities of Victoria College have taken no part. We have remained perfectly silent and neutral, not because we had no opinion as to the policy which has been recently pursued in converting a Provincial Ministry into a Church of England one. We, as a body, had more to lose than to gain by any proposed plan to remedy the abuse and evil complained of. As a

---

*At a special meeting held on the 25th of October, of that year. The full text of these resolutions is given in Appendix D.D., to the Journals of the Legislative Assembly of Canada for 1846. See above pp. 44-46.

†October 28, 1843.

‡Of the University bill.

body we gain nothing by the University bill, should it become a law; it only provides for the continuance of a small annual aid which Parliament has already granted; whilst, of course, it takes away the University powers and privileges of Victoria College—making it a College of the University of Toronto. Our omission, therefore, from the bill would be preferable, as far as we, as a party, are concerned, were it consistent with the general and important objects of the measure. But such an omission would destroy the very character and object of the bill. As a Provincial measure, it cannot fail to confer unspeakable benefits upon the country. Viewing the measure in this light, the Board of Victoria College have consented to resign certain of their rights and privileges for the accomplishment of general objects so comprehensive and important.

The resignation of Mr. Baldwin and his colleagues, and the consequent prorogation* of Parliament, prevented the passing of the University bill, and Sir Charles Metcalfe soon afterward entered into communication with Dr. Ryerson as to the provisions which should be embodied in a new one. Though he was appointed Chief Superintendent of Education in 1844 he was still Principal of Victoria College while Mr. Draper's University bills† were before Parliament in 1845. With respect to them the Board of Victoria College assumed‡ a friendly attitude, but at the same time resolved to ask the Methodist Conference to petition the Legislature to " grant a sufficient and permanent endowment for Victoria College where it is now located," and asserted the right of the College to fair representation on the governing bodies of the Provincial University. The personal reply §of Dr.

---

*On the 9th of December, 1843. See above, p. 37.

†See above, p. 38.

‡See Appendix D.D., to the Journals of the Legislative Assembly for 1846.

§See above, pp. 44-46.

Ryerson to Governor Cathcart's request for the opinion of the authorities of Victoria College on the amended charter of King's College was in the main a fuller exposition of the same general attitude.

As the University Act* of 1849 was similar in scope and purpose to the Baldwin bill of 1843, no opposition to its passage was offered by the authorities of Victoria College, though it cut off all hope of any portion of the income being diverted to the advantage of the denominational Universities.† By the University Act‡ of 1853, provision was made for the devotion of the surplus revenues from the Provincial University endowment to the formation of a "fund to be from time to time appropriated by Parliament for academical education in Upper Canada." Victoria College was by this Act affiliated to the University of Toronto, and Dr. Ryerson was appointed by the Crown a member of its Senate. Before long the supporters of the denominational colleges began to petition the Parliament of Canada for a share of the proceeds of the University endowment. The most important of these memorials was one§ prepared by Dr. Ryerson in 1859, adopted by the Methodist Conference of that year, and submitted on its behalf to Parliament in the session of 1860. The subsequent action taken by Parliament and the Governor-in-Council has been sufficiently noticed‖ in connection with the University of Toronto.

---

*12 Vict., cap. 82.

†See above, p. 59.   ‡16 Vict., cap. 89.

§For the text of this document see "Story of My Life," pp. 520-523.

‖See above, pp. 71-74.

Changes in the Constitution.—The union of the Wesleyan Methodists with the New Connexion Methodists made necessary some modifications of the constitution of Victoria College, and these were effected by an Act* passed by the Ontario Legislature in 1874. This statute "repealed" absolutely and expressly, not merely the Acts of 1841 and 1858, but also the royal charter of 1836, and continued the corporate existence of the institution under the name of "Victoria College at Cobourg."† It provided that " the various branches of science and literature " should be taught on "Christian principles," but that no religious test or qualification for admission should be required. The former "Board" having been abolished by the repeal of the Act under which it was constituted, a new "Board" was created with the usual corporate powers, and was clothed with authority to appoint and remove the President, professors, tutors, masters, and all other officials of the College ; to make regulations respecting its own meetings ; to control the " performing of Divine service ;" to prescribe courses of study ; and to fix salaries and other emoluments. It was to be composed of twelve laymen and twelve clergymen, and to be responsible to the General Conference of the Methodist Church of Canada, by which its members were to be appointed quadrennially, and to which it was required to report. The Senate, as before, was to be made up of the members of the "Board," together with the "President and pro-

---

*38 Vict., cap. 79.

†An Act passed by the Parliament of Canada in 1850 (13 and 14 Vict., cap. 142), had authorized the removal of Victoria College from Cobourg to Toronto.

fessors of the various faculties," and invested with authority to confer degrees in Arts, Science, Law-Divinity, and Medicine.

This constitution was modified in 1879 by an Act* of the Ontario Legislature, which made provision for the appointment by the General Conference, on the nomination of the College Board, of a "Dean of the Faculty of Theology," his duties being left to be defined and his salary to be fixed by the Board. It also enacted that the membership of the Senate should be increased by the addition of four representatives elected by the graduates in Arts, and one elected by the graduates in the faculties of Law, Medicine, and Theology, respectively, and to this enlarged body it gave authority to "determine the courses of study and qualifications for degrees, the appointment of examiners, and all matters strictly pertaining to the work of education."

In 1883 the constitution was further amended by an Act† of the Ontario Legislature, which granted representation on the Senate to affiliated institutions, and authorized the graduates of the University to elect six representatives to the "Board," of which the President was made a member *ex officio*. A proviso was added, that "no member of any faculty of the University should be eligible for election on the Board" as a representative of the graduates.

The Union of the "Methodist Church of Canada" with the "Methodist Episcopal Church of Canada"

---
*42 Vict., cap. 89.
*46 Vict., cap. 67.

took place in 1883, and in connection with it the United Church adopted the policy of maintaining only one University. It was agreed that Albert College, which had been the University of the Episcopal Methodists,* should be deprived of its degree conferring powers, and should become a college in affiliation with Victoria. This and the other academic changes caused by the union of the two denominations were effected by an Act† passed by the Ontario Legislature in the Session of 1884. The name of the institution was changed from "Victoria College" to "Victoria University," and the provision of the Act‡ of 1874 which repealed the charter granted in 1836 for the incorporation of the Upper Canada Academy" was itself repealed, thus reviving the charter except in so far as its provisions were modified by subsequent legislation. All the amendments made by the Acts of 1879 and 1883 were repealed, and the charges introduced by the Act of 1884 took the form of amendments of the Act of 1874. The "Board of Regents" took the place of the former "Board," as the "body corporate" of the University, and its membership was made to include (a) the General Superintendents of the Methodist Church of Canada, (b) the Chancellor and Vice-Chancellor§ of the University, (c) twelve laymen and twelve clergymen appointed by the General Conference, and (d) seven representatives elected by the gradu-

---

*See below p. 106.
†47 Vict., cap. 93.
‡See above, p. 102.
§The President was made *ex officio* Chancellor, and as such, the presiding officer of the Senate. The Vice-Chancellor was made elective by the graduates.

ates of the University. The Senate was defined so as to include in its membership, (a) the members of the Board of Regents, (b) the professors of the various faculties, (c) representatives of affiliated institutions, and (d) " eight graduates elected by the graduates" It was invested with authority to grant degrees in the several faculties to determine the courses of study and qualifications for degrees, to regulate all matters strictly pertaining to the work of education, and to "settle (subject to ratification of the Board of Regents), the terms on which chartered colleges and schools may become affiliated to the University."

Federation with the University of Toronto.—The changes effected in the Constitution of the Provincial University by the Act* of 1887 have been already sufficiently described†. In 1890 it was decreed by the General Conference of the Methodist Church that Victoria University should be federated with the University of Toronto under the provisions of that statute, and accordingly the degree-conferring powers of the former institution were allowed‡ to fall into abeyance; its graduates, except those in Divinity, and those who in Medicine had received their training in affiliated Medical Schools outside of Ontario, became *ipso facto* graduates in the corresponding faculties of the University of Toronto; its students became entitled to free tuition in all the

---

*50 Vict., cap. 43.

†See above, pp. 77-82.

‡The official proclamation which gave effect to the resolution of the General Conference was issued in November, 1890. Victoria College was removed from Cobourg to Toronto in 1892.

subjects assigned to the University of Toronto as distinguished from University College; and it acquired the right to an influential representation* on the University Senate.

Albert College.—The "Upper Canada Academy" was established in 1830 as a seminary of the "Methodist Episcopal† Church of Canada." When the Canadian church united with the British Methodist Conference in 1833, a minority of its ministers seceded, and in 1835 organized a Methodist Episcopal Conference. In course of time they succeeded in establishing at Belleville a "seminary designed to teach a system of classical, scientific, and commercial instruction, free from sectarian tenets and religious tests, while its moral government was based on Christian principles as revealed in the Holy Scriptures." In order to enable it to accomplish its work more perfectly an Act‡ of incorporation was in 1857 obtained from the Parliament of Canada, the corporate name given to it being "The Belleville Seminary." It was by this statute placed under the control of the General Conference of the denomination. The latter

---

*Victoria is represented by (1) the President *ex officio*, (2) a representative of the governing body of the College, (3) a representative of Albert College, (4) five representatives elected by the graduates in Arts, (5) two representatives elected by the graduates in Law voting along with those of the University of Toronto, and (6) four representatives elected by the graduates in Medicine voting in the same way.

†See above, p. 88.

‡20 Vict. cap. 184.

was empowered to appoint trustees, and these with certain other officials, appointed partly by the General Conference and partly by the Annual Conferences, constituted the "Board of Management", whose duty was to make appointments to the teaching staff, fix salaries, and devise means for carrying on the work.

By an Act* passed by the Parliament of Canada in 1866 the name of the Seminary was changed to "Albert College," and it was invested with University powers "so far as relates to degrees in Arts." The Governor-General was made Visitor of the institution, and a "Senate" was created to which was committed "the management and superintendence over all the affairs and business of the College not already under the direction of the Board of Management. The Senate was composed of the Bishops of the Church, the Principal and professors, and a variable number of additional members appointed by the General Conference. It was empowered to make regulations respecting examinations, and to confer the degrees of Bachelor of Arts, and Master of Arts, but was required to keep up a standard of qualification not inferior to that adopted in the University of Toronto.

The Victoria University Act† of 1884, divested Albert College of its degree-conferring power, but continued it as an incorporated institution under a "Board" appointed by the General Conference of the united Methodist Church.

---

*29 and 30 Vict., cap. 135.
†47 Vict., cap. 93. See above, pp. 104-105.

CHAPTER V.

QUEEN'S UNIVERSITY.

The Presbyterianism of Canada was, in its early days, the direct offspring of the Presbyterianism of Scotland, which has been, ever since the days of John Knox, earnest and persistent in promoting both lower and higher education. The Church of Scotland being an establishment,* quite as much as the Church of England, the members of her communion in Upper Canada resented keenly their virtual exclusion from the management of the District Grammar Schools which were established under the Act† of 1807. The "Trustees" of these schools were appointed by the Lieutenant-Governor-in-Council, and in 1830 the Presbytery of Upper Canada, in a memorial‡ to the Legislative Assembly, complained of their appointment from "one Communion alone," and petitioned Parliament to afford to the petitioners "provision for other schools to be placed under their superintendence." Pending the consideration by the Legislature of the allegations and prayer of this memorial the Presbytery appointed a committee to report on the feasibility of establishing a

---

*See the extract from the speech of Chief Justice Robinson, above, pp. 30-31.
†47 George III., cap. 6.
‡Hodgins' "Documentary History," Vol. I., p. 298, and 307-310.

"Literary and Theological Seminary," and in the following year resolved to apply to Lieutenant-Governor Colborne, "requesting him to procure for the United Presbytery of Upper Canada the privilege of choosing a professor of Divinity in King's College, to sit in the Council, and in every respect to be on an equal footing with the other professors in the said College." This twofold action was endorsed in 1832 at a meeting of the "United Synod of Upper Canada." "Pleasant Bay, Hillier," in Prince Edward County was selected as the location of the proposed "Seminary," and an unsuccessful attempt was made to procure the necessary financial assistance* from Presbyterians in the United States as well as in Great Britain.

The University at Kingston.—The passage of the King's College Act† of 1837 gave rise to hopes that were soon disappointed, for that institution remained about as completely as before under the control of the Church of England. Efforts‡ were made, under the authority of the Synod, to secure the disallowance of that statute, but the Colonial Secretary§ declined to interfere. The representatives‖ of the Synod in England strongly urged the establishment of two theological faculties in King's College, one in connection with the Church of England and the other in connection with the Church of Scotland, "as

---

*The Synod in 1834 authorized the application of the money that was collected to the building of a "Church connected with instruction for youth."

†7 William IV. cap. 16. See above pp. 31-33.

‡Hodgins' "Documentary History," Vol. III., pp. 285-288.

§Then Lord Glenelg.

‖Rev. Dr. Machar of Kingston, Rev. Dr. Mathieson of Montreal, and Hon. William Morris.

recommended* by the Government," but nothing came of the recommendation. Meanwhile the scarcity of Ministers to fill vacancies in the pastorate of the Church made it imperative that the education of young Canadians for the work should be undertaken, and in 1838 the Synod appointed a committee to report on the best means of carrying it on. The following year this committee reported in favor of obtaining an Act of incorporation from the Legislature of Upper Canada, and a draft bill was prepared and adopted for submission to that body. Late in the same year a public meeting in support of the scheme was held at Kingston, which had been chosen as the location of the proposed College, and during the Session of 1839-40 the Synod's bill was passed by the Legislature, incorporating it " by the name and style of the University at Kingston."

Queen's College.—The Act† of incorporation provided that the institution should be under the control of the Presbyterian Church ; that both the lay and the clerical members‡ of the Board of Trustees should subscribe to the Westminster Confession of Faith ; that the first Principal and the first professor of Theology should be appointed by a Committee of the General Assembly of the Church of Scotland ; that the Principal should always be a Presby-

---

*See above, pp. 21-22, for an extract from the report of a Committee of the British House of Commons. A similar recommendation was made by the Special Committee of the Legislative Council of Upper Canada on the Bill of 1837. (Hodgins' "Documentary History," Vol. III., p. 69.)

† 3 Vict. cap 35. This is the statute referred to in the Act passed in 1841, by the first Parliament of Canada, to confer University powers on the Upper Canada Academy. See above, p 95.

‡Fifteen of the former, and twelve of the latter.

terian Minister; and that all professors should be members of the Presbyterian Church. It was provided, however, that no religious test or qualification "should be required of any scholar or graduate in any faculty except that of Divinity. The Board of Trustees was invested, as a corporation, with full power to control the property of the institution, to make appointments to the teaching staff and prescribe the duties of its members, to fix all salaries, and to regulate all courses of study. A "Senate," composed of the Principal and the professors, was invested with the right to exercise "academical superintendence and discipline over the students," and to confer the degrees of Bachelor, Master, and Doctor in the several Arts and Faculties." The Legislature added the following interesting enactment*:—

"So soon as the University of King's College, and the College hereby instituted, shall be in actual operation, it shall and may be lawful for the Governor, Lieutenant-Governor, or person administering the government of this Province, to authorize and direct the payment from the funds of the said University of King's College, in aid of the funds of the College hereby instituted, of such yearly sum as to him shall seem just for the purpose of sustaining a Theological Professorship therein, and in satisfaction of all claim on the part of the Church of Scotland for the institution of a Professorship in the University of King's College, according to the faith and discipline of the Church of Scotland."

For some reason not now clearly apparent, the supporters of the new University, preferred not to make use of this statute, which had been passed at their request. They applied to the Queen for a royal charter of incor-

---

*Section 15.

poration, and after some difficulty* suceeded in obtaining it. The chief obstacle in the way was the opinion of the Law Officers of the Crown, who held that the incorporation or establishment of a " University " was part of the prerogative of the Crown, that for this reason the Act incorporating the University at Kingston was objectionable, but that the Act had become law in virtue of the Royal assent given to it, and that the only way to meet the wishes of the applicants was to disallow the Act and " grant a new charter framed as the original incorporation and foundation of the institution." The Act was accordingly disallowed† by proclamation, and the royal charter, creating "Queen's College" at Kingston, "with the style and privileges of an university, for the education and instruction of youth and students in Arts and Faculties," was issued‡ in its stead. A comparsion of the two documents shows that there is no important difference between them except (1) that the section of the Act which provided for the endowment of a chair of theology in Queen's College, out of the funds of King's College, was omitted from the charter, and (2) that the latter makes the corporation consist of all the " Ministers " and " Members " of the " Presbyterian Church of Canada, in connection with the Church of Scotland," while under the Act, the Board of Trustees was the corporation.

---

*For an account of the circumstances connected with the substitution of the charter for the statute, see Hodgins' "Documentary History," Vol. III., pp. 291-293.

†On the 10th of February, 1840.

‡On the 16th of October, 1841. For the text of the charter, see Appendix H.

The Sectarian Controversy.—In accordance with the provisions of the charter, the Colonial Committee of the Church of Scotland appointed as its first Principal the Rev. Thomas Liddell, and under him the college was opened in 1842.* In the course of that year the Board of Trustees, taking occasion from the laying of the cornerstone of King's College in Toronto, passed a resolution declaring that they had "no wish to appear to stand in an attitude of rivalry to that institution," but rather to help it forward as far as they could, and that they were ready "to concur in any enactment that would empower them to limit Queen's College to the department of theological instruction," and authorize its removal† to Toronto, provided the professors of Queen's College were allowed a fair influence in the administration of King's College. Early in 1843 the Board appointed a deputation to lay its views before the King's College Council. These were embodied in a written statement and placed in the hands of Dr. Strachan as its President, but he declined to lay them before the Council. The Board of Queen's College warmly supported Mr. Draper's University bill‡ of 1845, and in reply to Lord Cathcart's letter§ in the following year, it argued earnestly for the passage of some measure which would create a Provincial non-sectarian Univer-

---

* On the 7th of March.

†No great amount of expense had at that time been incurred for permanent accommodation. In the session of 1840 the Parliament of Upper Canada had by statute (3 Vict. cap. 36) granted permission to the authorities of Queen's College to occupy the building of the Kingston General Hospital, but the contemplated arrangement was never carried out.

‡ See above, p. 38.

§ See Appendix D.D., to the Journals of the Legislative Assembly of Canada for 1846.

H

sity, with the various theological colleges incorporated as integral parts of it, each having its own corporate existence and internal management. In the same communication the Board pressed its claim for the endowment of a theological chair, basing it (1) on the report of the Committee of the British House of Commons in 1828; (2) on the report of the Committee of the Legislative Council of Upper Canada on the University bill of 1837; (3) on the instruction given by Lord Glenelg to Sir Francis Bond Head in the same year; (4) on section 15 of the Act* of 1840 establishing the University at Kingston; (5) on the opinion of the Law Officers of the Crown on the Queen's College charter, to the effect that the Legislature was free to pass subsequent enactments respecting the University funds; and (6) on promises made by parties representing the Government of Canada, that Queen's College should obtain from the funds of King's College, the sum of £1,000 per annum.† The University bill failed in 1846, as it had failed in 1845, and by the time when the University Act of 1849 was passed, the institution had become too deeply rooted at Kingston to be easily transplanted.

The Agitation of 1853-1863.—The representatives of Queen's University took an active part in the agitation for a share in the endowment of the Provincial Univer-

---

* See above, p. 111.

†In 1839, the Rev. John McCaul, the Rev. H. J. Grasett, and Mr. S. B. Harrison, acting under a commission of investigation issued by Sir George Arthur, in a report on the subject of King's College recommended the establishment of theological seminaries, "one for each denomination that might appear to require such an establishment for the education of their clergy." (Hodgins' "Documentary History," Vol. III., p. 247.)

sity, consequent on the provision* in the University Act
of 1853, that the surplus revenues derived from that endowment should go to form a fund which Parliament might apply to the promotion of higher education. Convinced by the Report† of the Commission of 1861, that all hope of financial advantage from this source was vain, the authorities of Queen's devoted their energies with a considerable measure of sucess to procuring funds wherewith to endow their University, and provide it with improved accommodation.

Queen's College Act of 1874.—The early development of Queen's College was greatly hampered by the separation which took place in the Presbyterian Church in Canada, consequent on the Disruption of 1844 in Scotland. The section which sympathized with the Free Church in the Mother Country, took for its name "The Presbyterian Church of Canada;" the section which sympathized with the Establishment retained as its title, "The Presbyterian Church of Canada in connection with the Church of Scotland." The former found itself under the necessity of undertaking the training of candidates for the Ministry, and after this had been done for some time without any incorporation, an Act‡ was passed in 1858 creating for this purpose a corporate body under the name of "Knox College," which associated itself closely with the University of Toronto.§ Under the same auspices, "The Presbyterian

---

*See above, p. 68.
†See Appendix, E.
‡ 22 Vict. cap. 69.
§Under the University Federation Act of 1887, Knox College became one of the "federating Colleges." See above, p. 79. It has been authorized by the Ontario Legislature to confer degrees in Divinity.

College of Montreal," was incorporated by Act* of Parliament in 1865, and it has always been carried on in close connection with McGill University. More of a competitor for the support of that section of the Presbyterian Church in Canada to which Queen's College belonged was Morrin College, founded at Quebec in 1861, and incorporated by Act† of the Canadian Parliament for the purpose of "increasing and rendering more perfect the means of obtaining for the youth generally, and especially those who may devote themselves to the Ministry" of the Presbyterian Church of Canada, in connection with the Church of Scotland, "a liberal and enlightened education." Some improvement in the position of Queen's University took place as the result of the reunion of the Presbyterian bodies in 1874, and of the more effective organization conferred on it by an Act‡ of the Ontario Legislature passed in that year. This statute enacts that the royal charter of incorporation shall continue in force except as "modified or changed" by the Act itself. It places the University in relations to "The Presbyterian Church of Canada"§ similar to those which it formerly held to "The Presbyterian Church of Canada in connection with the Church of Scotland," and continues the "Ministers and members" of the Church as "corporators" of the College. No change is made by the Act in the composition of the Board of Trustees, but it is provided that as vacancies occur they shall be filled

---

* 28 Vict. cap. 23.
† 24 Vict. cap. 100.
‡ 38 Vict. cap. 76.
§ The name of the united Church.

by the remaining members of the Board, by the exercise of co-optation. The trustees are authorized to appoint a Vice-Principal; provision is made for the election of a Chancellor by the alumni; and the Principal is declared to be the Vice-Chancellor, *ex-officio.* The Senate is authorized to pass by-laws, subject to the approval of the Board of Trustees, " touching any matter or thing pertaining to the conditions on which degrees in the several Arts and Faculties may be conferred." A new body, the " University Council," is created with certain advisory functions; it is composed of (1) the members of the Board of Trustees, (2) the members of the Senate, and (3) " as many graduates or alumni as shall be equal in number to these aforesaid members taken together," the last named being eligible by the registered graduates and alumni of the College. As under the charter, the Board of Trustees controls all property and revenues, and makes all appointments, while the Senate is responsible for the discipline of the students in attendance.

Dominion Legislation.—In consequence of the decision of the Imperial Privy Council in a case* growing out of the union of the Presbyterian churches, a doubt was cast on the competency of the Ontario Legislature to pass the Act of 1874, and in the session of 1882 the Dominion Parliament passed a statute† re-enacting it in substance for the purpose of setting the doubt at rest. The same Parliament, in 1889, passed an Act‡ providing for an

---

*Dobie *vs.* The Board for the Management of the Presbyterian Church of Canada (in connection with the Church of Scotland) *et al.* See Appeal Cases, Vol. VII. (1881-82).
†45 Vict. cap. 123.
‡52 Vict. cap. 103.

increase in the number of the trustees by the addition of five representatives chosen by the University Council, and expressly declaring that "it shall not be necessary that any trustee elected by the Council be a member of the Presbyterian Church in Canada, or that any trustee hereafter elected* make or subscribe any religious declaration or formula whatever," before entering on the discharge of his duties as such. It is further provided in the statute that "all professors, other than those in the theological faculty, shall subscribe only such formula, declaratory of their religious belief, as the Board of Trustees from time to time prescribe." As the graduates of the University form a majority of the Council, this Act practically gives them the privilege of electing five trustees, and it also enables them to choose as their representatives persons belonging to any religious denomination.

---

*Either by the other trustees or by the Council.

CHAPTER VI.

TRINITY UNIVERSITY.

The complete secularization of King's College by the University Act* of 1849, against the earnest protests of Bishop Strachan, was the signal for renewed effort on his part to secure for his Church a University, in which secular learning might be cultivated on a strictly religious foundation, not merely by candidates for holy orders but also by all the youth of the Church of England who were in a position to secure a higher education. With characteristic energy and indomitable courage, at a time of life when rest would have been welcome, and after a struggle so severe and prolonged that few men could have endured it to the end, he undertook the herculean task of not merely securing a charter for a University of the Church of England, but providing it with buildings and an endowment out of voluntary contributions. There is a vein of pathos as well as one of acrimony in the following announcement† of his intention to visit England for this two-fold purpose, and to secure, if possible, the disallowance of the University Act by the Imperial Government :—

---

*12 Vict., cap. 82. It came into force on the first of January, 1850.

†In a pastoral letter, addressed to "The Clergy and Laity of the Diocese of Toronto" on the 7th February 1850. The printed copy from which this extract is taken is in possession of J. G. Hodgins LL.D.

I shall have completed my seventy-second year before I can reach London, of which more than fifty years have been spent in Upper Canada ; and one of my chief objects during all that time was to bring King's College into active operation ; and now, after more than six years* of increasing prosperity, to see it destroyed by stolid ignorance and presumption, and the voice of prayer and praise banished from its walls, is a calamity not easy to bear. I shall not rest satisfied till I have laboured to the utmost to restore the College under a holier and more perfect form. The result is with a higher power, and I may still be doomed to disappointment ; but it is God's work, and I feel confident that it will be restored, although I may not be the happy instrument, or live to behold it. Having done all in my power, I shall acquiesce submissively to the result whatever it may be ; and I shall then and not till then, consider my mission in this behalf ended.

Trinity College.—Furnished with numerously signed petitions, both to Her Majesty-in-Council and to the two Houses of Parliament, for the disallowance of the University Act, and encouraged by the enthusiastic support of a very large† portion of the people of his Diocese, he left Toronto on the 10th of April, 1850, and arrived in London on the last day of the same month. He "lost‡ no time in addressing letters to the Archbishops, Bishops, clergy, and laity," appealing to them for sym-

---

*King's College was opened for the reception of students in 1843. See above p. 35, and Appendix C.

†The petition to the Queen was signed by W. H. Draper, the framer of the King's College Amendment Act of 1837 which partially secularized that College, and of the University Bills of 1845 and 1846, either of which, if it had become law would have completed the secularization. Robert Baldwin, the author of the bill of 1843 and of the Act of 1849, was also a member of the Church of England, but he did not sign the petition.

‡For an account of Dr. Strachan's mission see the inaugural address delivered by him at the opening of Trinity College, on the 15th of January, 1852.

pathy and financial assistance. He received both. Donations were made both by societies and by individuals, and with these, supplemented by what had been given in the form of land and money in Canada, it was deemed best to begin as soon as possible to erect a college building.* The order for the preparation of plans was given in January, 1851, and in January, 1852, the College was opened† for the reception of students of Arts and Divinity. Meanwhile a medical school, which had been organized‡ as an independent institution, became by a mutually advantgeous arrangement, the Medical Faculty of the College, and was inaugurated as such in November, 1850, immediately after the Bishop's return from his journey to England. He was thus able to announce in his inaugural address in 1852, that they were ready to give instruction in five departments—"Theology, Classical Literature, the Mathematical Sciences, the faculty of Law, and the faculty of Medicine (including Chemistry)."

While Bishop Strachan's mission to England in 1850 was successful, so far as securing funds was concerned, it failed completely as a means of preventing the University Act of 1849, from going into operation. The petition for disallowance was presented to the Queen, but the

---

*The site selected was the one on which Trinity College still stands, at the head of Strachan Avenue, and facing Queen St., Toronto. It is described in the Bishop's address as "commanding a view of the Lake and Harbor," but its outlook has been greatly changed by the erection of buildings and the construction of railways.

†It is an interesting coincidence that the address given by Bishop Strachan on this occasion was followed immediately by one from his former pupil, Chief Justice Robinson, who had spoken immeiately after him at the opening of King's College in 1843.

‡By Doctors Hodder, Rowell, Bethune, and others.

Colonial Secretary* informed him that with respect to it he was "unable to advise Her Majesty to issue any commands." The petitions to the two Houses of Parliament were never presented† at all. Dr. Strachan found unexpected obstacles in his way when he made application for a royal charter to incorporate the College and confer on it university powers. He cited as precedents the charter granted to King's College at his own instance in 1827, the charter granted to Upper Canada Academy in 1836, and the charter granted to Queen's College in 1842, the first and third of which conferred University powers, as well as incorporation. The Colonial Secretary however, in view of the fact that the application for the Trinity charter had not been fowarded through the office of the Governor-General, informed the Bishop that he would feel it his duty to "communicate with the Provincial Government on a matter of such importance before committing Her Majesty's Government to any settled course of action." This reference of the matter to the Canadian Government led to a protracted correspondence and a considerable delay. Lord Elgin was then Governor-General, and his chief adviser was Mr. Baldwin. Acting doubtless on Ministerial advice the Governor informed Lord Grey that negotiations were in progress with a view to induce the authorities of Queen's and

---

*Then Lord Grey.

†Sir Robert Peel, in an interview with Bishop Strachan, remarked on this part of the question ; " I think you have exercised a wise discretion in not presenting your petitions to the two Houses of Parliament ; and it no doubt will be duly appreciated at the Colonial Office—for acts of forbearance are seldom lost. And indeed I do not well see what Parliament could have done in the matter."

Victoria Colleges to surrender their University powers and affiliate those institutions to the Provincial University as theological colleges, and urged that it would be "premature" to issue a general University charter to another college before it could be shown that all hope of securing this consolidation "must be abandoned." The Colonial Secretary acted on this representation, and as the result of further correspondence carried on in Canada between the Governor and the Bishop the former made an offer of such aid as was in his power to bestow in procuring from Parliament a "charter of incorporation," and this offer was not declined.

During the session of the Canadian Parliament for 1851 an Act* was passed incorporating Trinity College, with the usual powers of bodies "corporate and politic," and with the right to hold property, and to adopt any procedure necessary to the efficient performance of its academic work. Under this Act the "Corporation" of Trinity consists (1) of the Bishop† of Toronto, (2) the trustees of Trinity College, and (3) the Members of the College Council. The Trustees and Members of Council were to be named at first by the Bishop, but as vacancies occurred they were to be filled "by other persons to be named in like manner, or in such other manner as may from time to time be directed by any statute of the College to be passed for that purpose." The "Corporation" is empowered to make regulations "concerning the system of Education in, and for the conduct and government of the College

---

*14 and 15 Vict., cap. 32.
†Or the "Bishops of any dioceses into which the Diocese of Toronto may be divided."

and of a preparatory School* connected with or dependent on it, and also for the management of its property; but all such regulations are subject to the approval of the Bishop or Bishops of the Church of England in Upper C nada. Under the Statutes of Trinity, since enacted, the right toappoint and remove the "Provost and professors" of the Colleges is vested in the Corporation.

Trinity University.—The purpose of the University Act of 1849, to secure the abandonment by Queen's and Victoria Universities of their degree-conferring powers, with a view to their consolidation with the University of Toronto as theological colleges, having been frustrated by the refusal of the authorities of these institutions to avail themselves of the provisions of that statute, there was no longer any good reason for withholding University powers from Trinity College, and accordingly, a royal charter was issued† to it in 1853. In it the corporate powers granted to the College by the Act of 1851 are recognized andcontinued unchanged; the work already done in the way of creating an organization, erecting a building, appointing a teaching staff, admitting students, and providing funds is described; and it is decreed that "the said College shall be deemed and taken to be a University, and shall have and enjoy all such and the like privileges" as are enjoyed by the Universities of Great Britain and Ireland. The right to confer on students the degrees of "Bachelor, Master, and Doctor in the several

---

*Such a preparatory School under Trinity College auspices has been carried on for several years in Port Hope, Ontario.

†For the text of this instrument see Appendix I. Lord Elgin cordially concurred in securing it. See Appendix U. to the Journal of the Legislative Assembly for the session of 1852-53.

arts and faculties" is expressly conferred on the College. The office of "Chancellor" is created, and is left to be filled as the College Council, subject to Episcopal approval, may determine. The Chancellor, Provost,* professors, and such graduates as qualify for that purpose are made members of "Convocation," and this body is clothed with the usual powers in relation to academic functions.

Trinity University, as such, was affiliated to the University of Toronto by the Act† of 1853, and it became entitled to any financial advantage which might accrue to it under the operation of the clause of that Act which devotes the annual surpluses of University College revenues to the promotion of higher education in general. No such advantage ever resulted, however, and the affiliation of 1853 was cancelled by the University Act of 1873. The Medical Faculty of Trinity University, which fell into abeyance in a few years after its establishment in 1850, was revived in 1871, and in 1877 it was created‡ an independent corporation. In the same year it became affiliated to both Trinity University and the University of Toronto, and it still maintains this dual academical relationship. There is no teaching faculty of law in Trinity College, the functions of which are limited to giving instruction in arts and theology.

---

*This is the official title of the head of Trinity College under the regulations adopted by the Council. The first Provost was the Rev. George Whitaker.

†16 Vict., cap. 89.

‡By Act of the Ontario Legislature (40 Vict., Cap. 65).

Early in the history of Trinity College a dispute arose between the Bishop of Toronto and the Bishop of Huron* about the character of the theological doctrine taught in the institution. The controversies on this subject and subsequent discussions in the Synods of the two Dioceses resulted in such a cleavage in the Anglican communion of the Province of Ontario, that eventually those who felt inclined to dissent from the teachings of Trinity College established, first, Huron College in London, and afterwards Wycliffe College in Toronto, as theological seminaries. The former has since become merged† in the Western University and the latter has been affiliated to the University of Toronto, with power to confer degrees in Divinity. By the University Act ‡ of 1887 it was created a "federating College" in the Provincial University system, with increased representation on the Senate of that institution, and a right to recognition for certain arts work done incidentally by its teaching faculty of theology.

---

*This Diocese was created in 1857 out of the western part of the Diocese of Toronto, with its headquarters at London, and the Rev. Benjamin Cronyn was elected first Bishop.

† See Chapter VIII.

‡50 Vict., cap. 43.

CHAPTER VII.

McMASTER UNIVERSITY.

From an early period in the history of Canada the Baptists have been noted for two peculiarities—a strong desire for an educated Ministry, and a deep aversion to state aid in clerical education. Unwilling to accept help for themselves in providing a theological training for their preachers, they were naturally opposed to giving it to other denominations. As they have never been very numerous in comparison with some of the other Protestant bodies, this attitude of voluntary independence has entailed sacrifices and cost efforts that would form an interesting and instructive chapter in any complete history of higher education in Canada. As early as 1836 a Baptist College was established at Montreal, under the Principalship of the Rev. Dr. Davis. He had been selected for the position by the English Baptists, who paid his salary, but the difficulties in the way of success were very great, and he seems to have been ill-adapted to overcome them. One of the most formidable was the doctrinal cleavage between the Baptists of Eastern Canada, who generally sympathized with the "open communion" views of their English brethren, and the Baptists of Western Canada, who were quite as strongly in sympathy with the "close communion" theory and practice of their brethren in the United States. After a precarious existence of fourteen years the Montreal College came to an end in 1850, its building and other property having been sacrificed to pay the debts which had accumulated against the institution.

Rev. Dr. Fyfe.—No sketch of what has been accomplished by the Canadian Baptists in the way of higher education would be at all complete without some account of the personality of the Rev. Robert Alexander Fyfe. He was born a few miles from Montreal on the 20th of October, 1816. His parentage was Scottish, his father and mother having emigrated to Canada in 1809. After receiving such an early training as his native place afforded, he took up mercantile life at Laprairie, where in 1835 he joined the Baptist Church, and formed the resolution to enter the Baptist Ministry. There was at that time no Baptist College in British America, and his eyes were therefore naturally turned to the United States. After a year's attendance at Madison College in Hamilton, New York, he spent some time at the then newly established seminary in Montreal. The years 1837-42 were divided between missionary work in Canada and attendance at Baptist Colleges in the United States. He was ordained at Brookline, Massachusetts, but the intense love for his native country, which was characteristic of him through life, brought him back to Canada. His first pastorate was in Perth, Ontario, where he began to take an active part in the controversies which were then raging over the proposed secularization of King's College and the clergy reserves, and in which he afterwards became prominent. For one session, in 1844, he took temporary charge of the Monreal College on the retirement of Dr. Davis to England

and pending the arrival of the Rev. Dr. Cramp*, who was designated his successor. A missionary tour through Western Canada immediately after his release from academic duties was the occasion of his settlement in Toronto as pastor of the Baptist Church on March† St., where he remained till 1848. The next seven years were divided between his old Perth congregation and pastoral charges at Warren in Rhode Island and Milwaukee in Wisconsin. The latter he resigned in 1855 to resume the pastorate of his former Toronto Church, but he had been there only two years when the course of events constrained him to give himself up entirely to educational work. Meanwhile he had thrown himself into the University controversy‡, making free use, as a vehicle for his arguments and appeals, of the Brantford *Christian Messenger*, which in 1859 he purchased and transferred to Toronto under the name of the *Canadian Baptist*.§

Woodstock College.—From 1857 till his sad and too early death in 1878 the biography of Dr. Fyfe, is largely the history of the educational institution which was due mainly to his initiation, and was sustained chiefly by his indomitable energy, exceptional aptitude, and unflagging zeal. So far back as 1849 some leading Baptists of Western Ontario, prompted partly by their want of

---

*Afterward President of Acadia College. See Chapter XII.

†Afterward Stanley, and more recently Lombard. At Mr. Fyfe's instance, while he was its pastor, the congregation removed to Bond St., and many years afterward it built the present Jarvis St. Church.

‡The clergy reserve question had been settled in 1854. The then controversy on the Provincial University was about a division of its endowment, which he strenuously opposed.

§This journal is still edited by Mr. J. E. Wells M.A., a former colleague of Dr. Fyfe's in the Baptist College at Woodstock.

I

doctrinal sympathy* with their Eastern brethren, and partly by the provisions of the University Act† of that year, had projected a theological seminary which was intended to be located in Toronto and to be affiliated with the Provincial nUiversity. The scheme never took practical shape, but it may have had some influence as a prelude to a similar one‡ that came much nearer to realization in 1852. Dr. Fyfe was absent from Canada while these two projects were under consideration, but after his return he commenced an agitation for the establishment of a denominational college of a quite different sort. At that time many of the secondary schools of Upper Canada were in an inefficient state, and Dr. Fyfe's suggestion was that a good residential seminary should be established for the secular education of young people of both sexes, a theological department being added for the special training of candidates for the Ministry. The proposal took with the denomination. Funds were freely subscribed. Among competing places§ Woodstock offered the most liberal encouragement, and at a meeting there of the subscribers, on the 18th of March 1857, an organization was effected which was in the course of the same year created a corporation by Act|| of the Canadian Parliament. The first Trustees, fourteen in number, were

---

*See above, p. 126.

†12 Vict., cap. 82.

‡Known as the "Maclay College," from the name of its chief promoter who was to have been also its Principal.

§Brantford and Fonthill were the most persistent rivals.

|| 20 Vict., cap. 217. This was amended in 1864 by another Act of the same Parliament (27 and 28 Vict., cap. 143), and in 1877 by an Act of the Ontario Legislature (40 Vict., cap. 63), but only in unimportant details.

named in the Act, and statutory provision was made for the election of their successors by subscribers to the funds of the College, the corporate name of which was "The Canadian Literary Institute." Dr Fyfe became its first Principal, and for eight years he was the sole teacher of theology. The struggle for existence was severe and protracted, but the institution has survived it, and it still continues to do useful work as a residential Academy.* In 1875 it became actively connected† with the University of Toronto, with the privilege of having its candidates examined where they had been taught. Its name was changed‡ in 1883 to "Woodstock College," but it was expressely provided that this should not indicate or imply any change of corporation.

Toronto Baptist College.—In 1881 an Act§ was passed by the Ontario Legislature, incorporating the "Toronto Baptist College," for which a foundation was provided by the liberality of the Hon. William McMaster. He had been for many years a generous contributor to the funds of Woodstock College, and by his aid it was found practicable to organize a strong Theological Faculty. The Act of incorporation named the first trustees, and invested them and their successors with the right to "appoint, dismiss, or remove" members of the Board, and to "appoint new trustees from time to time" in accordance with by-laws enacted by

---

*On the establishment of "Moulton College" in Toronto in 1888, the admission of women to Woodstock College was discontinued. See Ontario Statute, 56 Vict., cap. 114.

†This affiliation was discontinued after the establishment of McMaster University.

‡By Act of the Ontario Legislature (46 Vict., cap. 69.)

§44 Vic. cap. 87.

the Board for that purpose. The trustees were further invested with "full and exclusive power and authority as to the appointment and dismissal of all professors, tutors, and teachers, and all officers and servants of the said College, and for and in respect of every matter and thing connected with the control, maintenance, and regulation." The College was by the same statute empowered to confer the degrees of "Bachelor of Divinity" and "Doctor of Divinity." It was by a statute of the Senate of the University of Toronto affiliated to that institution in 1885. In the same year the organization of the College was modified by an Act* of the Ontario Legislature, which created a "College Senate" composed of representatives of (1) the Board of Trustees, (2) the Faculty of the College, (3) the Faculty of Acadia College, (4) the Faculty of Woodstock† College, (5) the Alumni of the Toronto Baptist College, and (6) each of the four Baptist Conventions of Canada. The Senate was granted by the statute a concurrent power in the appointment and dismissal of members of the teaching staff of the College, and was invested with the "control and management of the system and course of education" pursued in it, and of the examinations conducted in connection therewith.

McMaster University.—The further donation by Mr. McMaster of an endowment, deemed by the promoters of Baptist higher education sufficient to warrant the consolidation of the above two institutions into one University, was the occasion of an application to the Ontario

---

*48 Vict., cap. 9℃.

†The teaching of Theology was discontinued at Woodstock immediately on the establishment of the Toronto Baptist College, and it was discontinued at Acadia College soon afterwards.

Parliament for the necessary legislation. This was granted in 1887 by an Act* which created a new corporation, and conferred on it the right to grant degrees, not merely in theology, but in the "several arts, sciences, and faculties." This statute had the effect of abolishing the separate corporations of "Woodstock College" and "Toronto Baptist College," and of vesting in the new corporation of "McMaster University" all the "real and personal property, rights, franchises, and privileges" which had belonged to them. The University was placed under the "management and administration of a Board of Governors," the members of which, to the number of sixteen† were to be chosen by the Baptist Conventions of Ontario and Quebec.‡ The Governors were given "full power and authority to fix the number, residence, duties, salary, provision, and emolument of the Chancellor, Principal, professors, tutors," and all other officers of the University, including any "preparatory or academical department ;§ to remove any of the above named officers at their discretion ; and to appoint any of them on the recommendation of the Senate. To the latter body was entrusted the "control of the system and course of education pursued in the University, and of all matters pertaining to the management and discipline thereof, and of the examination of all departments thereof; also the right to confer degrees, and to determine the courses of

---

*50 Vict., cap. 95.
†Exclusive of the Chancellor, who is a member *ex officio*, and also the presiding officer.
‡See Ontario Statute, 52 Vict., cap. 91, sec. 2.
§There are two of these—Woodstock College and Moulton College.

study and qualifications for them, subject to the proviso that the standard for the matriculations and subsequent examinations should be as "thorough and comprehensive" as that maintained by the University of Toronto in the same departments of study. The Senate was authorized to make recommendations from time to time for the appointment of the Chancellor and of the members of the teaching staff, and the Governors were forbidden to make such appointments except on such recommendations. The conditions on which teaching institutions, other than theological colleges, might affiliate with the University, subject to the approval of the Lieutenant-Governor in Council, were left to be prescribed by the Senate. The composition of the Senate, as defined by the Act of incorporation, was changed by an Act* passed in 1893. For ordinary academical purposes it is now made up of (1) the members of the Board of Governors, (2) six representatives of the University Faculty to be elected by the Faculty annually, (3) five representatives elected by the graduates in theology, (4) five representatives elected by the graduates in Arts, (5) two representatives elected by the teachers of Woodstock College, and (6) two representatives elected by the teachers of Moulton College; when the Senate is dealing with the theological course, its membership is *quoad hoc* increased by the addition of (1) eight representatives elected by the Baptist Convention of the Maritime Provinces, (2) the President and two professors of Acadia University, and (3) two representatives elected by the Baptist Convention of Manitoba and the North-

---

*56 Vict., cap. 114.

west Territories. As to denominational character, while McMaster University is declared to be "a Christian school of learning," and the study of the Bible or Sacred Scriptures" is prescribed by the Act as "part of the course of study," it is also provided that every member of both the Senate and the Board of Governors must be "a member in good standing of some regular Baptist Church in Canada." Each member of the teaching Faculty of theology is required to be of the Baptist communion, but of other teachers it is required only that they shall be members in good standing of "an Evangelical Christian Church," while it is provided that "no compulsory religious qualification, or examination of a denominational character, shall be required from, or imposed upon any student whatever, other than in the faculty of theology."

CHAPTER VIII.

THE WESTERN UNIVERSITY.

For reasons on which it is unnecessary to dwell, the establishment of Trinity College did not completely satisfy the views of the Anglican Church in all parts of Upper Canada. In 1857, the western portion of the Province was erected into the diocese of Huron, with its headquarters in London and the Rev. Dr. Cronyn as its first Bishop. The progress of settlement in the northern part of his district was then very rapid, and he found it difficult to receive an adequate supply of clergy. The remedy that suggested itself was the establishment of an independent theological college, and Bishop Cronyn early cherished the project of founding and endowing one.

Huron College —In the interest of the scheme a visit to England was made in 1861 by the Rev. Dr. Hellmuth, then Archdeacon * of the Diocese, and his mission was so successful that steps were soon taken to provide a building, and begin the work of teaching. The latter was greatly facilitated by a donation † of £500 sterling for the endowment of the chair of Divinity, and by several other contributions of less value. In 1863 Huron College was incorporated by Act‡ of Canadian Parliament. Bishop Cronyn was the principal petitioner, and the cor-

---

*He afterward succeeded Dr. Cronyn as Bishop.

†From the Rev. Alfred Peach, M.A., incumbent of Downend, near Bristol. This donation is still known as "The Peach Fund."

‡26 Vict., cap. 31.

poration was made up of himself and the members of the College Council, whom he was authorized in the first instance to appoint. Vacancies, as they occur in the Council, are filled up by the practice of co-optation. Archdeacon Hellmuth was the first Principal, and the first session was held in 1864.

The Hellmuth Colleges.—In 1865, by an Act* of the Canadian Parliament, a second educational institution was incorporated in the same city, and to some extent under the same auspices, by the name of "The London Collegiate Institute." The chief promoter and sole proprietor was Archdeacon Hellmuth, but he had associated with him, among others, the present Bishop Sweatman of the Diocese of Toronto, and Mr. Adam Crooks, afterward Minister of Education for the Province of Ontario. The "Institute" was intended to be a residential school for the education of boys In 1868, by an Act† of the Ontario Legislature, its name was changed to "Hellmuth College," and the corporation was turned into a joint stock company. In the following year a similar College for young ladies was established by Dr. Hellmuth, equipped with the college building proper, a chapel, and grounds containing forty acres of land.

The Western University. The educational work done in these institutions eventually led to an application to the Ontario Legislature for permission to establish "a college with university powers in connection with the Church of England," and this was granted by an Act‡ passed

---

*28 Vict., cap. 96.
†31 Vict., cap. 58.
‡41 Vict., cap. 70.

in the session of 1878. The corporate name selected for the institution was "The Western University of London, Ontario," and the corporation was declared to consist of (1) a number of specified persons, (2) those who might be afterward appointed Chancellor or members of Senate, and (3) all future graduates of the University. The chief governing body was to be a "Senate," composed of the Bishop, the Principal of Huron College, the persons named specifically as members of the corporation or their successors, and the ten senior graduates. The Senate was invested with the "management of and superintendence over the affairs concerns, and property of the university," and with authority to make regulations respecting the "number and appointment of professors and lecturers in the different faculties or departments of learning," and also the examinations for degrees and standing. It was provided, however, that no religious tests should be imposed on any students except those in divinity, and that the standard of qualification in secular learning should be as high as that maintained in the University of Toronto. Permission was given by the statute for the affiliation of Huron College to the University as its faculty of divinity, and for the acquisition by the University of the "control and management of Hellmuth College." In 1882 the original statute of incorporation was amended by an Act[*] of the Ontario Legislature, which made the management of the University more distinctively Anglican by requiring that every member of the Senate should be a member of the Church of England. It also changed the name to "The Western University and College of London, On-

---

[*] 45 Vict., cap. 89.

tario," and enacted that "its teaching functions in the faculty of arts, or in science, or literature shall be exercised by such College as distinct from the University, but subject to the by-laws and regulations of the Senate of the University." Under this constitution work has been carried on for some time in the Arts Department, but no full course has yet been taken by students. In 1882 there was established a Medical Department which has enjoyed a continuous existence till the present time.

In 1892 an Act* was passed by the Ontario Legislature modifying the constitution of the University in various ways, but leaving it to be determined by the Senate whether these changes should be adopted. As that body has not so far resolved to give them effect the Act has not yet come into operation. Should it do so hereafter the name of the institution will be changed to "The Western University and London University College"; the corporation will consist of the "Chancellor, the Vice-Chancellor, the Professors, the Members of the Senate, and the Graduates"; and the Senate will be composed of (1) the Chancellor, (2) the Vice-Chancellor, (3) the Principals of all affiliated Colleges, (4) the Principal of the London Collegiate Institute,† (5) the persons named in the original Act or their successors, (6) the Mayor of London, and (7) ten graduates elected by the graduates.

*55 Vict., cap. 107.
†Not the original of Hellmuth College, but the public secondary school maintained by the city of London under the High School Act of the Province.

CHAPTER IX.

ROMAN CATHOLIC UNIVERSITIES OF ONTARIO.

The Roman Catholic Church in Upper Canada was from an early period earnest and persistent in promoting higher education, and this duty it still discharges with undiminished energy and a fair degree of success. Its efforts in this connection are mainly identified with the organization and work of three institutions—Regiopolis College at Kingston, Ottawa College at Ottawa, and St. Michael's College at Toronto. The first of these discontinued its academic work a quarter of a century ago, but the others are still actively performing the functions for the discharge of which they were called into existence.

Bishop Macdonell.—The name of the Honorable and Right Reverend Alexander Macdonell, first Roman Catholic Bishop of Upper Canada, is so inseparably connected with the early educational work of the Church, that a brief account of his career is indispensable to a clear understanding of her aims and undertakings. He was born on the 17th of July, 1762, at Glen Urquhart on the shore of Loch Ness, Scotland. He was educated for the Church, partly in Paris, partly at Valladolid, and at the latter place was ordained a priest in 1787. The time was one of great distress in the Highlands of Scotland, owing to the number of small farmers dispossessed of their holdings through the general consolidation of farms, and Mr. Macdonell obtained leave from the British Government to organize volunteers from among them into a regiment known as the "Glengarry Fencibles." Of this regiment he was appointed chaplain, and with it he served in Ireland during the rebellion of 1798. It was disbanded after the Peace of Amiens in 1802, and Mr. Macdonell was able to secure for each officer or soldier whom he could induce to settle in Upper Canada a grant of 200 acres of land. The locality selected for the settlement was the present County of Glengarry, where there were already a number of United Empire Loyalists of Highland extraction. Taking up his abode with them as a missionary, he made his headquarters at St. Raphael's, and when Canada was threatened with invasion in 1811 he organized a Canadian Glengarry regiment which he accompanied as chaplain during the war of 1812-15. For his patriotic services he received from the British Government a pension, which was bestowed for life and was increased from time to time till it finally reached five hundred pounds sterling per annum, at which amount it was continued to his successors in the See of Kingston. In 1819 he was created "Bishop of Rhœsina," and Administrator of Upper Canada as Vicar-General of the Bishop of Quebec, to whose diocese this extensive territory belonged. In 1826 Upper Canada was cut off from Quebec and made a separate diocese, and he was appointed its first bishop with the title* of Bishop of "Regiopolis or Kingston." He died in 1840 at Dumfries

---

*The title of Bishop is taken from his "See," or seat of ecclesiastical government.

in Scotland, whither he had gone on a visit during a trip to Great Britain, undertaken to promote emigration, from the Highlands to Canada.

THE UNIVERSITY OF REGIOPOLIS.

Bishop Macdonell's first academic institution was carried on for a time at St. Raphael's, but when his ecclesiastical headquarters was transferred to to Kingston he transferred thither his educational work also. He gave a sufficient amount of land for a site for the proposed College, and in the session of 1837 the Parliament of Upper Canada passed an Act* incorporating a Board of Trustees under the name of " The College of Regiopolis," and empowering it to hold real property " in trust for the erection, use, and support of a Roman Catholic Seminary." Of this Board the Bishop of Kingston was made an *ex officio* member. The other trustees† designated by the statute were the Rev. Angus Macdonell, Bishop Gaulin, the Rev. John Cullen of Ottawa, the Hon. John Elmsley of Toronto, and Walter McCuniffe of Kingston, provision being made for the filling up of vacancies by co-optation. The Board was empowered to make such regulations as might be necessary not merely for " the due management of the land," but also for the administration of the " Roman Catholic Seminary to be erected thereon." In the session of 1845 the Parliament of Canada passed an Act‡ to enable the heirs of

---

*7 William IV., cap. 56.

†The first named was the Bishop's nephew, who afterwards became the head of Regiopolis College. See above p. 46.

‡8 Vict., cap 79.

Bishop Macdonell to convey to the College of Regiopolis an additional portion of the real property devised by him to them, and to enable the college to hold other lands than those conveyed to it under his will or belonging to his estate. Regiopolis College, like Victoria College and Queen's College, found it difficult to carry on educational work with a slender revenue, and repeated applications were made to Parliament for assistance. Petitions were sent in during the sessions of 1843-50, and in 1846, in answer to Lord Cathcart's letter* asking for an opinion respecting King's College, Vicar-General Macdonell suggested that the Jesuit's estates in Lower Canada might be utilized as a source of relief.

The Parliament of Canada, in the session of 1866, at the request of the college authorities, passed an Act† conferring university powers on Regiopolis and making some other changes in its constitution. The corporation under that statute, consists of the Roman Catholic Bishop of Kingston, the Principal and professors of the College of Regiopolis, and the trustees, and is entitled "The University of Regiopolis." The powers of the Senate,‡ as to conducting examinations and conferring degrees, are very similar to those of the University of Toronto under the Act of 1853, and the standard prescribed is that which obtains in the University of London, England. Under this constitution the University carried on its work till the withdrawal of its annual grant by the Ontario Legislature in 1869, after which it succumbed to its financial difficulties.

---

*See above, p. 46.
†29 and 30 Vict., cap 133.
‡Composed of the Bishop, the Principal, the professors, and the trustees.

OTTAWA UNIVERSITY.

This institution has enjoyed a corporate existence since 1849, in which year an Act* was passed by the Parliament of Canada creating the Roman Catholic Bishop and Curé of Bytown,† the Superior, the Director, and the professors of Philosophy and Belles Lettres, a corporation under the name of "The College of Bytown," with power to hold real property and to enact such regulations for its adminstration and for the management of the College as might be "deemed useful or necessary for the interests" of the institution. The property and functions of the unincorporated seminary already in existence under the same name were vested in the new corporation, which was required to report to Parliament annually the state of its finances, the character of its equipment, and the number of students in attendance. The change of the name of the city in which it is located from "Bytown" to "Ottawa" necessitated a like change in the title of the institution, and this was effected by an Act ‡ passed by the Parliament of Canada in 1861. The same Act, while it expressly provides that the corporation of "The College of Ottawa" is not a new one, but a continuation of the one already in existence, declares that the Bishop and Curé of Bytown shall no longer be members of it, and that its composition shall remain otherwise unchanged.

---

*12 Vict., cap. 107.
†Now Ottawa.
‡24 Vict., cap. 108.

In 1866 University powers were granted by statute*
to the College, the examining and degree-conferring
powers being vested in a "Senate" composed of
the President and Bursar of the College, the Prefect of Studies, and the Professors of Divinity,
Philosophy, Rhetoric, and Belles-Lettres, with the Roman
Catholic Bishop of Ottawa *ex officio*. The Act provides
that the standard of attainments shall approximate as
closely as practicable to that of the University of London, and that the Senate shall, with this proviso, have
authority to confer, "after proper examination," the
degrees of Bachelor and Master of Arts, Bachelor and
Doctor of Laws, and Bachelor of Medicine. A public
character is imparted to the institution by the fact that
the Governor of the Province is created the "Visitor" of
the University, and that the Senate is required to report
to him on its "general state, progress, and prospect.
The constitution of the University was modified
in certain respects by two statutes† passed by
the Ontario Legislature in 1885 and in 1891, respectively.
Their joint effect is (1) to enlarge the membership of the
Senate by the addition of certain professors in the College;
(2) to increase the number of different degrees which the
Senate may grant after examination ; (3) to confer on the
Senate the right to grant *ad eundem* degrees; (4) to invest the Senate with authority to affiliate to the University, under certain limitations, other teaching institutions
with a view to the admission of their students to exam-

---

*29 and 30 Vict., cap. 135.
†48 Vict., cap. 92, and 54 Vict., cap 105.

J

inations for degrees, standing, or scholarships ; and (5) to substitute the Lieutenant-Governor of Ontario for the Governor of Canada as the Visitor of the College.

ST. MICHAEL S COLLEGE.

In 1852 the religious order of St. Basil, in France, established an educational institution under this name in Toronto. As the attendance of students increased additional accommodation was from time to time provided, and the course of study was extended so as to include work of a University character in Philosophy and History. In 1881 St. Michael's was affiliated to the University of Toronto by statute of the University Senate. Under a special arrangement the subjects of Philosophy and History may be taken in the College, instead of the University, through the whole undergraduate course. When the University Act* of 1887 was passed, St. Michael's was accorded the status of a " federating College," with increased representation on the University Senate, and certain privileges in the way of special options for such of its students as may choose to avail themselves of them.

---

*50 Vict., cap. 43,

CHAPTER X.

PROTESTANT UNIVERSITIES OF QUEBEC.

The Parliament of Lower Canada passed an Act* in in 1801, "for the establishment of free schools and the advancement of learning." This statute created the machinery for the administration of a system of public schools, but did not provide for their support, the King having announced his intention to make a suitable appropriation of lands for that purpose. "Foundations of a more enlarged and comprehensive nature," were contemplated, as well as "schools for the instruction of children in the first rudiments of useful learning." Each school, when established, was to be put in charge of a corporation by the name of the "Royal Institution for the Advancement of Learning," the members of which were to be appointed by the Governor† of the Province. In order to secure the advantage of the Royal appropriation the inhabitants of each local district were required to erect a school building at their own cost, the amount being collected by a public assessment.

McGILL UNIVERSITY.

Hon. James McGill, of Montreal, died in 1813, leaving

---

* 41 George III., chap. 17. See "Revised Acts and Ordinances of Lower Canada" (1777-1841), pp. 516-521.

† The appointment of teachers and the fixing of their salaries were also vested in the Governor.

by will to four trustees* a parcel of land as a site for a university or college " with a competent number of professors and teachers to render such establishment effectual and beneficial for the purposes intended." He bequeathed on the same conditions the sum of £10,000 to be expended in founding and maintaining it. Both the land and the money were to be conveyed by the trustees to the " Royal Institution for the Advancement of Learning," but if the university or college were not established within ten years, the bequests were to be reclaimed from that corporation and otherwise applied. One of the conditions of the will was that the testator's name should be given to the college, if only one were established, or to one of the colleges, if several of them were established as parts of one university. It was with great difficulty that these conditions were complied with sufficiently to prevent the land and money from reverting to the estate of Mr. McGill. To aid in securing their permanent application to the development of higher education the " Montreal Medical Institute," which had been organized in 1824 in connection with the Montreal Hospital, was in 1828 invited to become the medical faculty of the McGill University. The invitation was accepted, and the union then established has endured to the present time.

The McGill Charters.—At its inception McGill College was entirely under the control of the " Royal Institution for the Advancement of Learning," but that corporation applied for and obtained,† in 1821, a royal charter " for

---

* These were John Richardson, James Reid, and James Dunlop, of Montreal, and the Rev. John (afterwards Bishop) Strachan, who was then Rector of Cornwall.

† From George IV. This charter was issued six years before that of King's College, Toronto. For its text see Appendix J.

the more perfect erection and establishment of the said College." One of its avowed objects was the " education of youth in the principles of true* religion," another was the exercise of university functions, the most characteristic of which is that of conferring degrees in " the several arts and faculties." The members of the Royal Institution were made "Visitors " of the College, but its administration was handed over to *ex officio* " Governors," namely " the Governor of Lower Canada, the Lieutenant-Governor of Lower Canada, the Lieutenant-Governor of Upper Canada, the Bishop† of Quebec, the Chief Justice of Montreal, the Chief Justice of Upper Canada," and the Principal of the College. The Governors were empowered, subject to the approval of the Crown, to appoint the Principal and the other members of the teaching staff, to fix their salaries, and to make regulations for academical work, and " the good government of the College." The College was created, for business purposes, a corporation by the name and style of " The Governors, Principal, and Fellows of McGill College," with power to acquire and hold real property and administer it for academic purposes.

For over thirty years the McGill College and University were carried on under the organization conferred by

---

* There is some reason to believe that the original intention was to make McGill College a Church of England University, but this idea was long ago abandoned. The present statutes of the institution require that the Governors shall be "laymen of some Protestant denomination," but require also that they shall be "selected with a view to the representation of the several Protestant denominations in Lower Canada."

† Of the Church of England.

this charter, but in 1852 application was made to the Crown, with the assent of the Rôyal Institution which still held the original property in trust, for certain modifications of it which were embodied in a new charter* granted in that year by Her Majesty Queen Victoria. By it the members of the " Royal Institution for the Advancement of Learning," were made " Governors" of the College, the *ex officio* " Governors" were dropped, and the Governor-General of Canada was created " Visitor." The name and powers of the corporation were continued unchanged, but it was provided that university statutes should be operative unless disallowed by the Visitor, instead of being left inoperative, as formerly, until the Crown assented to them.

Present Organization of McGill.—" The Royal Institution for the Advancement of Learning," which was created a corporation by the Parliament of Lower Canada in 1801, and which received the property bequeathed by Mr. McGill and administered it in trust for the College founded by his bequest and called by his name, was the subject of several statutory enactments of the Parliament of Canada. Owing to legal difficulties connected with both the land and the money devised by him to the Royal Institution, legislation was obtained by the latter, not merely to invest it with fuller powers in dealing with the property, but to make changes in its own organization. For these purposes Acts† were passed

---

* See Appendix J.

† 8 Vict. cap. 78 ; 16 Vict. cap. 58 ; 20 Vict. cap. 53 ; and 22 Vict. cap. 53. These were all consolidated in 1860 with the original Act (41 George III. cap. 17), and published as chapter xvii. of the " Consolidated Statutes of Lower Canada."

in 1845, in 1852, in 1857, and in 1859, respectively. The most important legislative enactment in its bearing on the constitution of McGill is the Act* passed in 1863, the preamble of which states that the "Royal Institution for the Advancement of Learning" had not for many years had any functions to perform "other than those incident to their capacity" as Governors† of McGill College, and "no property or funds to administer, other than those appertaining to the College and University, or to departments or institutions of learning belonging or affiliated thereto." Accordingly the two corporations—that of McGill College under its charter, and that of the Royal Institution under its statutory powers—were practically consolidated by giving the members of the Royal Institution, acting as Governors of McGill College, authority to increase their number; to regulate by their own statutes the mode in which they should be appointed; to fix their own terms of office; to prescribe the mode of appointment, duties, title, and term of service of the "President or Principal of the Royal Institution;" and to provide generally for conducting the affairs of the University.

Under statutes passed by the Governors, as thus authorized, the President of the "Royal Institution for the Advancement of Learning," elected by the Governors from among themselves, is *ex officio* the Chancellor of the University. The Principal is appointed by the Governors, and is *ex officio* Vice-Chancellor. The Fellows‡ of

---

* 26 Vict. cap. 6.

† See above, p. 149, and the charter of 1852.

‡ They are an element in the College Corporation. See above, p. 148.

the University are (1) the Deans of the respective faculties; (2) any Acting or Vice-Dean whom the Governors may appoint for any faculty, not more than one at a time; (3) four members elected by the faculty of Arts, and one member elected by each of the other faculties; (4) the Principal of the McGill Normal School; (5) the representatives of affiliated colleges; (6) eight members of Convocation, elected by their fellow-graduates, two for each of the faculties of Arts, Law, Medicine, and Applied Science; (7) "such other members of Convocation, not more than seven in number, as the Governors may appoint;" and (8) the Chairman of the Protestant School Commissioners of Montreal, if appointed a Fellow by the Governors.

To the "Corporation," which is composed of the Governors, Principal, and Fellows, is assigned the task of framing regulations dealing with the general course of study and teaching in the several faculties and in the affiliated colleges; with "all examinations and other matters appertaining either to matriculation or to graduation in the university;" and with "academic dress, or other matters of general academic interest."

"Convocation" consists of (1) the Chancellor and other Governors; (2) the Vice-Chancellor; (3) the professors and other instructing officers, members of the several faculties; (4) the instructing officers of affiliated colleges being graduates of any university; (5) the Registrar, being a graduate of any university; and (6) the graduates of the University. Members of convocation who are graduates of McGill University, and who pay the prescribed fee, elect the Fellows who represent the graduates in the Corporation.

The organization of the various faculties is an interesting feature of the constitution. It is left to the Governors to decide how the members of the teaching staff shall be classified into the several faculties of "Law, Medicine, Arts, and Applied Science," and to organize other faculties whenever they see fit. The Dean of each faculty must be a Professor, and he is appointed by the Governors, and is responsible for the keeping of its records and for a general superintendence over its affairs under the Principal. The Dean of the Arts Faculty is *ex officio* Vice-Principal of the College, and in the absence of the Principal he discharges the latter's duties. Each faculty regulates "the details of the course of study and teaching in its own department; the number, times, and modes of all examinations belonging to it; the admission of students to it; the amount and mode of payment of all fees in it; and its discipline and internal government; but all faculty regulations must be approved by the Corporation before they become operative and are subject to alteration or repeal by the Corporation afterward. It is expressly provided that "no student shall be expelled without the consent of the Corporation, and that the Corporation if it sees fit, may entertain appeal from any decision of a faculty, whereby any punishment more severe than a reprimand may have been imposed on any student."

Financial Position.—The accounts of the "Royal Institution for the Advancement of Learning" for the year ending on the 30th of June, 1894, showed that the donations to McGill College and University from its foundation amounted then to $2,184,961, of which $447,424 was represented by grounds and buildings, and $120,423 by other property, while $1,501,291 was invested as a revenue producing endowment. During the year 1893-94 the fees amounted to $25,614; the income from investments to $72,498, and donations and subscriptions to $12,197. With these and some less important sources of revenue, the income for the year fell short of the expenditure by $13,000.

MORRIN COLLEGE.

The foundation of this College was a " deed of gift " by Joseph Morrin, bearing date the 26th day of September, 1860. He had been for more than fifty years a citizen of Quebec, in which the College is located, and had been twice Mayor of the city. He was himself a man of culture as well as of public spirit, having been a physician and surgeon with a large practice, and his object in establishing the college which now bears his name was partly a desire to leave "some permanent memorial of his regard for the city of Quebec," and partly a wish to mark " his attachment to the church in which he was reared, and to which he had always belonged "—the Presbyterian Church of Canada in connection with the Church of Scotland. Dr. Morrin placed his gift, which consisted of "certain immovable properties and sums of money," in the hands of three trustees,* who applied for and obtained an Act† of Parliament creating " Morrin College " a corporation, and vesting its management in a board of " Governors." As the avowed object of the establishment

---

* Rev. John Cook, D.D., William Stewart Smith, LL.D., and James Dean, all of the city of Quebec.

†24 Victoria, chapter 109.

was the instruction of "young men intended for the ministry of the Church of Scotland in Canada," it was natural that the Governors should be selected from that denomination.* Provision was made in the statute that as vacancies occurred they should be filled by co-optation in cases where no other method of appointment was prescribed, and the total membership of the board was limited to fourteen. The property donated by the founder was vested by the Act in the Governors, who were authorized to receive and hold, for the use of the College, any other lands or other property that might be sold, donated, or bequeathed to it. It was stipulated on behalf of the trustees that accommodation should be furnished free of charge in the College building for the High School of Quebec, provided the corporation of that school were willing to have it made "subject to the government of the corporation of the College, and ancillary to it." The Governors were authorized to make regulations for "the superintendence and management of all the property belonging to the corporation," and also for the control of the educational work done in the College, or in "any other school or institution connected with or dependent upon it." It was also provided by the statute that Morrin College might become affiliated to one of the three Universities—Queen's, Toronto, or McGill. It has for some years past been one of the affiliated colleges of the last named institution.

---

* Rev. Dr. Cook was named in the statute as the first Principal and as the Chairman of the Board of Governors.

BISHOP'S COLLEGE AND UNIVERSITY.

Stimulated, no doubt, by the energy and persistence shown by the "United Church of England and Ireland," in promoting higher education for its own advantage in Upper Canada, the members of the same communion in Lower Canada began early to exercise similar foresight. The founder of McGill University belonged to the Anglican Church, and his desire to make his bequest helpful to that denomination was apparently indicated by his naming Dr. Strachan, then of Cornwall, one of the trustees of his gift. A few years afterward a movement was begun to establish a University more directly under the auspices of the Church of England. The place selected was Lennoxville, in the "District of St. Francis, and within the Diocese[*] of Quebec," and the name given to the institution was Bishop's College. It was incorporated under that title in 1843, by an Act[†] of the Parliament of Canada, the preamble of which stated that it was to be a college "in connection with the United Church[‡] of England and Ireland." The corporation was defined as consisting of (1) the Lord Bishop of Quebec, or other Superior Ecclesiastical Functionary of the church in that diocese ; (2) the trustees of the College, not less than three in number ; and (3) the members of the College Council, not less than three in number. Both the trustees and the members of the Council were to be ap-

---

[*] At that time it included the whole of Lower Canada.

[†] 7 Vict., cap. 49. This statute was passed in the year of the opening of King's College, Toronto.

[‡] Members of other churches were from the first admitted to both matriculation and graduation without being subjected to religious tests.

pointed by the Bishop, and their successors were to be appointed in the same way as vacancies should occur. To the corporation thus created was given full authority to make regulations alike for the conduct and government of the institution, and "concerning the system of education" in it, but all such regulations were to be inoperative until sanctioned and confirmed by the Bishop.

The Anglican Diocese of Montreal was not established till 1850, but the records of Parliament show that the then Bishop of Quebec and Montreal petitioned the Legislative Assembly in 1848, on behalf of the "Corporation of Bishop's College," that it might "receive the privilege of conferring degrees in Divinity, and the Arts and Faculties professed in the learned Universities." Whatever the reason may have been, the University powers then asked for were not granted by Parliament. In 1852 by an Act* amending the original statute, it was declared that the new Bishop of Montreal, as well as any other Bishop or Bishops who might be appointed for any diocese of the Church in Lower Canada, should be a member of the college corporation, co ordinate with the Bishop of Quebec in all respects, except that in the event of their being equally divided in the exercise of their powers, "the opinion of the Bishop who is senior by priority of appointment shall prevail, and his decision shall be final." In 1853, University powers were conferred by Royal Charter† on the corporation as thus enlarged, and by the same instrument the offices of Chancellor, and Vice-Chancellor were created. Under the charter all gradu-

---

*16 Vict., cap. 60.
†See Appendix J.

ates in Divinity, Law, and Medicine, and all Masters of Arts become members of Convocation on payment of twenty shillings a year. In 1870 the corporation of the College was further enlarged,* at its own instance, by granting to the synods of the various dioceses a nominating voice in the selection of trustees and members of Council, and increasing the members of each class of appointees. In 1879, an Act† was passed by the Quebec Legislature to provide for the more effective admistration of the "Bishop's College School" by incorporating an "Association" for the purpose of carrying it on in harmony with the corporation of the College.

*By Act of the Quebec Legislature (34 Vict. cap. 68).
†42 and 43 Vict., cap. 74.

CHAPTER XI.

ROMAN CATHOLIC COLLEGES IN QUEBEC.

The first permanent settlement in Canada was effected when Champlain, in 1608, planted a small colony on the site of the present City of Quebec. He possessed personal qualities which fitted him to become a pioneer of discovery and settlement, but he was characterized also by a religious disposition which prompted him to make provision for the conversion of the Indians to Christianity. One of his mottoes is said to have been that "the salvation of a single soul is worth more than the conquest of an empire," and in furtherance of this view he brought[*] to Canada in 1615 four priests of the religious order of Franciscans, known as "Recollets." The most noted of these was Joseph Le Caron, who founded the famous Huron Mission in the district lying between lake Simcoe and the Georgian Bay. In 1625 the vigorous and powerful Order of Jesuits, when solicited to take part in the task of spreading Christianity among the Indian tribes, sent out five members of their Society. The most prominent of these were Charles Lallemant, who became the intimate friend and spiritual adviser of Champlain, and Jean de Brebœuf, whose martyrdom at the hands of the invading Iroquois, took place in 1649,

---

[*] Authority for the continuance of this mission was obtained in 1618 from Pope Paul V. and from Louis XIII, king of France. The texts of the Papal brief and the Royal patent are given in Le Clercq's "First establishment of the Faith in New France." (Shea's translation Vol. 1, pp. 74-80)

while he was in charge of the Huron mission established by Le Caron. The headquarters of the Recollets and Jesuits were at first near the river St. Charles, but after the capture of Quebec by the British in 1629 and its restoration to France in 1632, the Jesuits alone were allowed to resume mission work in Canada, and they established themselves near the fort on the summit of the promontory occupied by the upper part of the city. Members of the Order of Sulpicians took up their abode at Montreal, and founded there a "Seminary" which still exists as an educational institution. The first proprietors transferred to them the ownership of the island, and this was long afterwards confirmed to them by legislative enactments.*

Bishop Laval.—Want of concord among the religious orders thus engaged in missionary and educational work in Canada showed the necessity of appointing some one with the necessary ecclesiastical authority to harmonize the various conflicting interests, and the choice of the Pope fell on Francois Xavier de Laval-Montmorency Abbé de Montigny, who was already an Archdeacon and had been, as far back as 1651, nominated as Bishop for Cochin China. He was a member of one of the highest families in Europe, but early in life he discarded all worldly aspirations and gave himself up to a life of religious devotion. He was born at Laval, in Maine† in 1623, and was the son of Hugh de Laval, Sieur de Montigny. He was educated at Caen, in the "Hermitage" there, and at

---

*2 Vict. cap. 50 (Ordinances of the Special Council in "Statutes of Lower Canada") and 3 and 4 Vict., cap. 30 (Revised Acts and Ordinances of Lower Canada.)

†In France.

the age of thirty-five was appointed by the Pope his Vicar Apostolic in Canada with the title of Bishop of Petræa. His consecration and departure were delayed by dissensions which it is needless to dwell on, and he did not arrive at Quebec till the spring of 1759. For some time the extent of his authority remained doubtful, but it was in 1661 made coterminous with the colony. Bishop Laval brought with him some secular clergymen, and as others came to New France from time to time they were assigned to parishes which had till then been ministered to by Jesuits, the latter devoting themselves thereafter more and more to missions among the Indians. The parochial work of those days was of an extremely laborious kind,* and the Bishop, in 1663, decreed the establishment of a "Seminary" at Quebec, for the twofold purposes of affording to worn-out priests a retreat in which to recruit their exhausted powers, and of providing a college for the training of young Canadians for the priesthood. His decree appropriated to the support, of the Seminary tithes collected from the people, and it was formally approved† of by Louis XIV in the following year. Vicar-Apostolic Laval was created Bishop of Quebec in 1674. In 1688 he retired from the position, and spent the remainder of his life in the Seminary of his establishment. His death took place in 1708.

The Seminary of Quebec.—The Seminary established by Bishop Laval in 1663 as a training school and home

---

*For a graphic description of it see Parkman's "Old Regime in Canada," chap. XIX.

†For the texts of the Bishop's decree and the King's "Approbation," see the collection of "Edits, Ordinances, etc." published in 1803, Vol. 1, pp. 25-29.

K

for the secular priests was, and is still, called *Le Grand Seminaire de Quebec*;* in 1668 he founded a minor Seminary, which has always borne the name of *Le Petit Seminaire de Quebec.*† A third educational institution, established about the same time, was an industrial school, in which the children of the lower classes were taught agriculture and various mechanical arts, and which was attached to the Seminary. These institutions were liberally endowed by their founder out of his own estate, or with donations obtained for them by his potent influence. Mention has already been made of the tithe imposed by the decree which established the Seminary. Louis XIV. endowed the Quebec bishopric with the revenues of three French abbeys. The Bishop received at various times grants of land from the French Crown, and in 1680 he conveyed to the Seminary, by way of endowment, three seigniories, of which the most important was Beaupré, a district stretching sixteen leagues along the shore of the St. Lawrence, and six back from the river. As these lands were free from the feudal burdens attaching to ordinary seigniories, the property rapidly became valuable, all the more because the stream of immigration was directed toward it by the Government.‡ During the century that elapsed between the establishment of the Seminary of

---

*It is one of several major Seminaries which give a theological training, all affiliated to Laval University. One of these is *Le Grand Seminaire de St. Sulpice de Montreal*.

†There are a number of these minor Seminaries affiliated to the University, for which they serve as preparatory colleges.

‡In 1667, Beaupré and Orleans, both at that time belonging to Bishop Laval, contained 1,185 out of the 4,312 settlers in the whole colony.

Quebec and the treaty of Paris, which in 1763 terminated the French *regime*, the work thus inaugurated was carried on without interruption. The institution continued its career of usefulness with no material change* for well nigh another century, until in 1852 the educational edifice was crowned by the addition of a university, which was fittingly made a means of perpetuating the name of the illustrious founder of the original Seminary of instruction.

Laval University.—The Seminary of Quebec has, from an early period in its history, enjoyed corporate powers, in virtue of which it has always been enabled to control its own property and manage its own affairs, and has existed as an organized society, with the right to exercise its functions through its own duly appointed officials. Prompted, no doubt, by the general academic activity consequent on the union of Upper and Lower Canada in 1840, the society made application to Her Majesty Queen Victoria, for authority to confer degrees and exercise other university powers. This was granted by Royal Charter,† dated the 8th of December, 1852. By it the corporate character of the Seminary was recognized and continued, the members of the corporation being the Superior and the Directors of the "Seminaire de Québec," which in the performance of all acts done under the Charter was thenceforth to be called the

---

*In the Session of 1843 the Parliament of Canada passed an Act (7 Vict. cap. 54), which gave authority to increase the amount of property held by the "Superior and Directors of the Seminary of Quebec, all laws of mortmain to the contrary notwithstanding."

†For the text of this interesting document see Appendix K. It is published in an official pamphlet entitled "Constitutions et Reglements de l'Université Laval."

"Université Laval." As such, it was clothed with the usual powers and privileges "for the education and instruction of youth and students in Arts and Faculties." The Roman Catholic Archbishop of Quebec was made its "Visitor" *ex officio*, and the Superior of the Seminary its "Rector." The University was created a corporation by the name and style of "The Rector and Members of l'Université Laval, at Quebec, in the Province of Canada," the term "members" including "professors" and "all persons duly matriculated" into the institution. The entire management of the University was vested in a "Council" composed of the Rector and Directors of the Seminary and the three senior professors of the University, subject to the right of the Visitor to disallow any enactment of the Council. The latter waa authorized to "nominate and appoint" the professors of Law, Medicine, and Arts, and to nominate candidates for the professorships of Divinity, the right of appointment in the latter case being vested in the Visitor The Council was further authorized to confer the degrees of Bachelor, Master, and Doctor, in the several Arts and Faculties, in accordance with its own regulations, not merely on students of Laval, but on those of all Colleges or Seminaries affiliated to it within Lower Canada. Provision was made that no religious test or qualification should be required or appointed for any person matriculated as a student, but declarations or subscriptions might be required of candidates for degrees in all the Faculties.

Laval à Montreal.—For nearly a quarter of a century Laval University continued to educate students, examine candidates, and confer degrees at Quebec under the Royal

Charter of 1852. Meanwhile the demand was increasing in Montreal for a Roman Catholic University in that city, which had become a great commercial and industrial centre. In order to strengthen the claim of Laval to be regarded as the University for the whole Province it was deemed expedient to obtain special Papal sanction for the exercise of its powers, and this was granted by a "Bull* of canonical establishment" which was issued at Rome on the 15th of May, 1876. This decree confirmed a decision of the Sacred Congregation of the Propangada, to the effect that while Laval remained the sole Catholic University of the Province of Quebec, it should be required to establish in Montreal a branch†, the maintenance of which should be a charge on the Diocese of Montreal, while its professors should be members of the various faculties created in the University under the Royal Charter. It was further decided that the courses of instruction in the two cities should be co-extensive and coterminous, that the professors in the two places should be on a perfect equality in all respects, and that the fees charged for instruction should be the same in the same courses. The work at Montreal was to be placed under the supervision of a Vice-Rector nominated by the University Council, subject to the approval of the Bishop of Montreal, and his functions in relation to the branch were to be similar to those of the Rector in the University itself. In short, " Laval à Montreal," so far from being a separate institution or a mere affiliated college, is·not even an

---

* For the original Latin text, and an authentic French translation of this document, see the official pamphlet entitled "Constitutions et Reglements de l'Universite Laval."

† Officially called a "Succursale."

annex to Laval, but an integral part of the University which confers degrees on the students of Quebec and Montreal on exactly the same conditions and in virtue of precisely the same authority. The separation between the branch and the stem is simply a geographical one. Though the "Succursale de l'Université Laval" was organized under the authority conferred by the Papal Bull, doubts were soon raised as to the legal right of the University to carry on its work under the Royal Charter elsewhere than in the city of Quebec. Applicaation was then made on its behalf (1) to Her Majesty the Queen for a supplementary charter, and (2) to the Quebec Legislature for a statute, which would place this right beyond all doubt. The British Secretary of State for the Colonies hesitated to recommend the granting of additional powers, pending the settlement of certain litigation then in progress. The application to the Legislature was more successful, as an Act* was passed in the session of 1881 empowering Laval University to increase the number of its chairs of Arts and other faculties within the limits of the Province of Quebec.

Laval Financial Syndicates.—The Quebec Legislature, in the session of 1887, passed two Acts,† one incorporating the " Financial Syndicate of Laval University at Quebec," the other incorporating the " Financial Syndicate of Laval University at Montreal." The object in each

---

*44 and 45 Vic. cap. 46. The preamble to this Statute expressly states that it was passed to remove doubts " with reference to the right of Laval University to give a university course elsewhere than at Quebec.

† 50 Vic. cap. 32, and cap. 33.

case is to improve the financial position of the institution, by providing a means of raising and managing funds for its use. Each corporation exercises its functions through a bureau of "Governors," and the Archbishop of Quebec is *ex officio* President of the one while the Bishop of Montreal is similarly President of the other. Some members of each syndicate hold their positions *ex officio* while others are elective, and of these latter a certain number are chosen by alumni of the University.

ST. MARY'S COLLEGE.

Reference has already been made* to the missionary work of the Jesuits in Canada. The " Society of Jesus " was organized in 1540 by Ignatius de Loyola, a Spanish nobleman, who had spent his early life as a soldier. Within a century of its foundation it had spread its ramifications over a large part of Europe, and had sent missionaries into many other lands. The mission to the Acadians was established in 1611, and in 1625 the work was begun in Canada. For some years the Jesuits divided their time between ministering to the spiritual wants of the French settlers and preaching the Gospel to the Indians; but in 1635, true to the enlightened policy of their Order, they undertook the two-fold task of training their own missionaries, and of giving to such French youth as desired it a general education. Their College at Quebec was enlarged and improved from time to time as the attendance increased until, after nearly a century and a half, their work was discontinued as the result of the Papal brief by which Clement XIV., in 1773, decreed the suppression

---

*See above, p. 159.

of the Order. The building was occupied by members of
the Society until the death of the last survivor* in 1800,
and it was used by the British Government as a military
barrack until 1879, when it was condemned as unsafe and
allowed to go to ruin. The Jesuits had before 1773 acquired much valuable property in Montreal, but had
never engaged there in the work of education. The last
survivor† in that city died in 1791, after which the
property was regarded as escheated to the Crown. By a
brief of Pius VII., the Order was revived in 1814. Work
in Canada was not resumed for some years, but in 1842,
at the instance of the late Bishop Bourget, several Jesuit
fathers took up their abode in Montreal, and in 1848 they
commenced giving instruction in temporary quarters pending the erection of a college building.

St. Mary's College.—The present Jesuit College building
was begun in 1847, but was not ready for occupation till
1851. Owing to the fact that provision was made for teaching English the attendance rapidly increased. A very thorough course of instruction, one section " classical " and
one " commercial," has been provided, while another
division is made between preparatory and advanced work.
The institution was incorporated in 1852 by an Act‡ of
the Canadian Parliament, but, unlike the Quebec Seminary,
the Jesuits did not thereby acquire university powers.
The Bishop of Montreal was one of the petitioners for the
Act, and he is *ex officio* a member of the corporation,
which includes the Rector, the bursar, and other officers.

---

*Father Cazot.
†Father Well.
‡16 Vict., cap. 57.

The corporation is authorized to make regulations for the management of the affairs of the College, subject to the provision that the revenue must be applied (1) to the maintenance of the institution, (2) to the construction and repair of buildings for its use, and (3) to the "advancement of education by the instruction of youth." The Act requires the authorities to report annually to Parliament. In 1889, St. Mary's College received, by a brief of His Holiness Pope Leo XIII., the privilege of "conferring the degrees of Laval University." The question of the disposition of the estates owned by the Jesuit Order before its suppression in 1773 was finally settled by an Act* of the Quebec Legislature in 1888. The estates† themselves were by this settlement left in the possession of the Province, which agreed to pay for a "full, complete, and perpetual cession" of them the sum of four hundred thousand dollars.

---

*51 and 52 Vict., cap. 13.

†Except the land known as "Laprairie Common," which is held by the "Society of Jesus" under corporate powers conferred by Act of the Quebec Legislature passed in 1887 (50 Vict. eap. 28).

CHAPTER XII.

NOVA SCOTIA UNIVERSITIES.

The history of the university system of Nova Scotia is a narrative of struggles more arduous and sacrifices more costly than have generally fallen to the lot of young communities in their efforts to provide the means of obtaining a higher education. This Province has the honor of being the first part of the Dominion of Canada to enjoy the privilege of parliamentary government,* and its people have been marked all through their history by a robust progressiveness which could not fail to find expression in the desire for and the promotion of popular culture. The whole of the territory now comprised in the Provinces of Nova Scotia and New Brunswick, with the exception of the Island of Cape Breton, was ceded by France to Great Britain under the treaty of Utrecht in 1713. For many years afterward a straggling border warfare was kept up between the British settlers on the one hand and the French and Indians on the other. The French Government fortified Louisburg, and the use made of it as a basis of local military operations against the British colonies prompted the expedition sent against it by the Province of Massachusetts in 1745. Louisburg was captured by the colonial forces, but was restored to France by the treaty of Aix-la-Chapelle in 1748. In the

---

* The first " Assembly " was held in 1758. It consisted of 22 members, of whom 12 were elected for the Province at large, four for Halifax, two for Lunenburg, and one each for Dartmouth, Lawrence, Annapolis, and Cumberland.

following year steps were taken by the British Government to establish a new settlement on Chebucto Bay, and its was named after the Earl of Halifax, then First Lord of the "Commissioners of Trade and Plantations." One object in view was to create an effective military counterpoise to the French settlement at Louisburg; another was to furnish with grants of land the officers and soldiers dismissed from the army on account of the restoration of peace. Many of these were from the New England States, where both parliamentary and collegiate institutions had been long* in operation, and others came from the same settlements as ordinary immigrants.† To these were added many who came direct from England and Scotland, and, after the close of the Revolutionary War, a large influx of United Empire Loyalists.

THE UNIVERSITY OF KING'S COLLEGE.

As far back as 1787 the House of Assembly appropriated £400 for the purpose of establishing at Windsor a classical school under the auspices and control of the Church of England in Nova Scotia. This action was due mainly to the exertions of the Right Reverend Charles Inglis, D.D., the first Bishop of the Province. An academy was inaugurated in 1788 on the above foundation, and in the following year the Legislature made a special grant of £500, and an appropriation of £400 a year, to

---

* The foundation of Harvard College was laid by the Legislature of Massachusetts in 1636, and that of Yale College by the Legislature of Connecticut in 1701.

† The first Chief Justice of Nova Scotia was Jonathan Belcher, son of Governor Belcher, of Massachusetts. This colony supplied a large part of the force which deported the Acadians in 1755 from the shore of the Basin of Minas.

found a "College" in connection with the school. In 1790 the Imperial Parliament supplemented these amounts with a grant of £4,000.

King's College Charter.—A Royal charter, granted by George III. in 1802, incorporated the seminary under the title of "The Governors, President, and Fellows of King's College" and conferred on it the style and privileges of a university, including the right to confer degrees. In the same year the Imperial Parliament voted a yearly subsidy of £1,000 sterling for the support of the institution. Its already exclusive character was in 1803 intensified by the adoption of a rule that all candidates for matriculation should be required to subscribe to the "Thirty-nine Articles" of the Church of England. This was a serious barrier to its usefulness, but in spite of its want of popularity it early acquired a high reputation for sound scholarship. The appropriation of public funds to a purely sectarian college did not pass without protest, and the constituency of the University was too narrow to afford it either financial support or a large attendance of students. The matriculation test was afterward withdrawn, but not till other colleges had been established in the interest of those denominations that had been debarred by it from sharing in the advantages of King's College, and too late to enable King's to become, as perhaps it might otherwise have been, the sole university of Nova Scotia. When Lord Dalhousie was Governor * of the Province he endeavoured to found a college at Halifax. His scheme failed for a time, and an effort was then made to unite

---

* In 1817. See below, p. 176.

his projected institution with King's College. A basis of union was agreed to in 1823 by the two boards of Governors, but the consummation of the union was prevented by the veto of the Archbishop of Canterbury *, who was then, as " Patron " of King's College, in a position to control the action of its authorities. Another unsuccessful attempt was made in 1829, and, at the instance of the promoters of the scheme for one Provincial University, a despatch was in 1835 sent from the Colonial Office calling on the Governors of King's College to surrender their charter and assist in establishing one well-equipped college. This they refused to do, and the Imperial grant of £1,000 a year was then withdrawn.

Legislative Incorporation.—In 1853 an Act † was passed by the Nova Scotia Legislature " To incorporate the Governors of King's College," and to repeal the Act of 1789, which was for the purpose of " founding, establishing, and maintaining " it. Under this statute the Lord Bishop of Nova Scotia became *ex officio*, a Governor the President of the Board of Governors, and the Visitor. There were twelve other members of the Board, eight of whom were made elective by the alumni, while the other four were named in the statute as life members, but their places were to be taken at death by elective members. The usual corporate powers were conferred on the Board, which was also authorized to enact regulations for the " instruction, care, and government " of the students, the management of the property, and the appointment of the President, professors, fellows, and scholars. The only

---

* Then Dr. Charles Manners Sutton.

† 16 Vict. cap. 66.

limitation was the requirement that the President should be a member of the Church of England. Though it was expressly provided that the Royal charter should not be affected by the Act, except so far as might be necessary to give effect to the latter, it was provided by the statute that the College should be "taken to be an university, with all usual privileges of such an institution, whether relating to the conferring of degrees and honors, or otherwise." This constitution was modified in 1883 by an Act [*] of the Legislature which increased the number of Governors to fifteen, the two additional ones being chosen by the Diocesan Synod of Nova Scotia. It also made provision for the election of two more members by the Diocesan Synod of Fredericton, and the addition of the Bishop of Fredericton as an *ex officio* member, whenever, and so long as, the Synod of Fredericton should accept King's College as the training school for its Divinity students. The latest amendment to the constitution of King's College was made by an Act [†] of the Legislature in 1895. By it the membership of the Board of Governors was increased to thirty-seven, one of the additional Governors being elected by each of the deaneries in Nova Scotia and New Brunswick, and three of them by the arch-deanery of Prince Edward Island.

The Collegiate School.—King's College grew out of a school, or was superadded to it, and the policy of providing for secondary education is still maintained. The "Collegiate School for boys," under the control of the governors of King's College, is now in the one hundred

---

[*] 46 Vict. cap. 63.
[†] 58 Vict. cap. 147.

and seventh year of its existence. It serves as a preparatory school for the University, and prepares candidates for other examinations similar in standard to those for university matriculation. A "Church School for girls" is also maintained under the same auspices.

The Alumni of King's College.—With a desire to promote the interests and improve the condition of their *alma mater* the alumni of King's College many years ago formed themselves into an association and undertook to raise money in aid of both the College, and the Collegiate School, With a view to enable them to accomplish their purpose more effectually they sought and obtained in 1847 an Act* of incorporation, which conferred on them the usual powers as to acquiring, holding, and disposing of property of all kinds to the aggregate value of £10,000. The annual membership fee was fixed by the statute at twenty shillings, and the fee for life membership at twenty pounds. Later legislation permitted the association to reduce these sums, and they were fixed in 1882 at two dolllars and twenty-five dollars, respectively.

DALHOUSIE COLLEGE AND UNIVERSITY.

During the war of 1812-15 between Great Britain and the United States the port of Castine, in the State of Maine, was occupied for some time by Sir John Sherbrooke, then Lieutenant-Governor of Nova Scotia. The customs revenues collected during that occupation were subsequently appropriated by the British government to

---

*10 Vict. cap. 130.

provincial purposes. Governor Dalhousie* was authorized to expend the fund "in defraying the expenses of any improvement which it might seem expedient to undertake in the Province," and his proposal was to "found a college or academy on the same plan and principle of that at Edinburgh," in the belief that "a seminary for the higher branches of education was much needed in Halifax, the seat of the Legislature, of the courts of Justice, and of the military and mercantile society." The actual foundation of a College was laid in 1821; the design of the institution was announced to be "the education of youth in the higher branches of science and literature;" the name given to it was that of its founder. It was intended to be "open to all occupations and sects of religion," and, though restricted at first in its scope, to have the "power to expand with the growth and improvement of society." The only collegiate institution at that time in the Province was King's College, at Windsor, and that was strictly sectarian.

Dalhousie College.—The original Board of Governors, appointed by the Crown, consisted of the Governor-General of British North America, the Lieutenant-Governor of Nova Scotia, the English Church Bishop, the Chief Justice and President of the Council, the Provincial Treasurer, and the Speaker of the House of Assembly. The amount appropriated out of the "Castine Fund" was £9,750. A college building was soon erected, but no educational work was done for nearly twenty years.

---

*The Right Honourable George Ramsay, ninth Earl of Dalhousie. He succeeded Sir John Sherbrooke in the Governship of Nova Scotia in 1819, and held the office till his appointment as Governor of Lower Canada in 1820.

Lord Dalhousie's intention had been to create a single non-sectarian University for the whole Province. With a view to carry out such a scheme, an effort was made by the Board of Governors to effect a union with King's College but it proved unsuccessful,* owing to the opposition of the Archbishop of Canterbury, its Patron. The negotiations between the authorities of the two institutions, after having been protracted till 1835, were finally closed and all hope of union was abandoned. Steps were taken to organize Dalhousie College for academical work, and in 1838 it went into operation under the Presidency of the Rev. Dr. McCulloch, who had in 1816 established the Pictou Academy. Though Dalhousie College was avowedly Provincial and non-sectarian, the first professors were all Presbyterians,† and this appearance of denominationalism seems to have hampered the work of the institution by virtually limiting it to one denomination without enabling it to secure even that. In 1841 University powers were conferred on the College by Act of the Nova Scotia Parliament, and by the same statute the constitution of the Board of Governors was changed, the right to appoint its members being vested in the Lieutenant-Governor in Council of the Province. In 1843 President McCulloch died and two years afterward the institution was closed, the Governors deeming it advisable to allow its funds to accumulate. In 1848

---

*See above, p. 173.

†The Rev. E. A. Crawley, an alumnus of King's College but then pastor of a Baptist Church in Halifax, was an unsuccessful applicant for the chair of Classics, and the belief that he was rejected on account of his creed had much to do with the establishment of Acadia College. See below, p. 182.

L

an Act was passed authorizing the Lieutenant-Governor in Council to appoint a new Board of Governors and "to take such steps for rendering the institution useful and efficient as to His Excellency may seem fit," and from 1849 to 1859 the funds of the University were used to support a high school. An attempt to galvanize the College into life was made in 1856-57 by uniting with it the Arts Department of Gorham College, Liverpool, Nova Scotia, but it was unsuccessful.

Dalhousie College and University.—A successful effort was made in 1863 to re-establish Dalhousie College as a teaching institution with University powers. An Act* was passed by the Legislature of Nova Scotia "to extend the basis on which the said College is established, and to alter the constitution thereof, so as the benefits that may be fairly expected from its invested capital and its central position may, if possible, be realized, and the design of its original founders, as nearly as may be, carried out." The statute repealed all previous Acts relating to Dalhousie College, except one passed in 1824 to authorize the loan of a sum of money to the then Board of Governors. It created a new corporation under the name of "The Governors of Dalhousie College at Halifax;" gave it the "title, control, and disposition" of the building, property, and funds of the institution; and provided for filling up vacancies in the Board of Governors by appointment of the Governor-in-Council, on the nomination of the remaining members of the Board.* To the Governors

---

*26 Vict. cap. 24.

*The Governors named in the Act were: Hon. William Young, Hon. Joseph Howe, Charles Tupper, S. Leonard Shannon, John W. Ritchie, and James F. Avery.

was given "power to appoint and to determine the duties and salaries of the President, professors, lecturers, tutors and other officers of the College, and from time to time to make statutes and by-laws for the regulation and management thereof," while the "internal regulations" of the institution were entrusted to the "Senatus Academicus formed by the respective chairs and professorships thereof." It was enacted that "no religious tests or subscriptions" should be required of "professors, scholars, graduates, students, or officers of the College," but provision was made that "any body of Christians of any religious persuasion whatsoever" might, with the approval of the Board, endow and support one or more chairs or professorships, thus securing the right to nominate a member of the Board for each such chair, and to nominate also its incumbent, subject in both cases to the Board's approval. The same privilege was by another provision of the Act conferred on "any individual or number of individuals," who chose to endow chairs or professorships. The Act also invested the College with the character of a University, "with all the usual and necessary privileges of such institutions," including authority to confer the degrees of bachelor, master and doctor in the several arts and faculties at the appointed times." In 1875, by an amending Act,* the membership of the Board of Governors was increased to fifteen, and power was given to affiliate to the University any other college or school in arts, theology, law, or medicine.

---

*38 Vict. cap. 27.

Under the operation of this constitution, Dalhousie College has from time to time greatly expanded its academical work. The two Presbyterian Synods* soon endowed three chairs between them, and the college was opened under the presidency of the Rev. James Ross, D.D., and with a staff of six professors. In 1868 a Faculty of medicine was organized, and in 1875 this became the "Halifax Medical College." In 1883 there was added a Faculty of Law, and in 1891 one of Pure and Applied Science. In addition to other donations and endowments, it is worthy of note that eight professorships have been endowed by two men, five† by Mr. George Munro, of New York, and three‡ by Mr. Alexander McLeod, of Halifax. The Senatus Academicus now consists of eleven professors, inclusive of the President.

ACADIA UNIVERSITY.

The Baptists of Nova Scotia were, during the first quarter of this century, few in number, far from wealthy, widely scattered over the Province, and not specially interested in either secular or religious education. Among their preachers were a few uneducated men of great natural force of character and of apostolic zeal, and the mass of the people seemed to rest contented in the belief that such men would always appear to supply the demand for them. A new element was infused into the denomination by the advent of a number of educated

---

*That of the "Presbyterian Church of the Lower Provinces," and that of the "Presbyterian Church of the Maritime Provinces in connection with the Church of Scotland."

†Those of Physics (1879), History and Political Economy (1881), English Language and Literature (1882), Constitutional and International Law (1883), and Philosophy (1884).

‡Those of Classics, Modern Languages, and Chemistry.

young men in Halifax, some of whom had been educated at King's College. Three of them were lawyers practising at the Halifax bar, and of these, Mr. J. W. Johnston afterward became eminent as a statesman and jurist, while Mr. E. A. Crawley entered the Baptist ministry, and took a leading part in the educational movement which resulted in the establishment of the denominational university.

Horton Academy.—Though the Baptist educational movement emanated chiefly from Halifax, it first took practical shape in Horton township.* In 1828, at an association of Baptist churches held there, a resolution was unanimously adopted to establish a seminary for the higher education of Baptist youth. An organization, which was afterward incorporated under the name of "The Nova Scotia Baptist Education Society," was started, and its membership included the great majority of the prominent Baptists of the Province. "That part of Horton now called Wolfville" was selected as the site of the proposed seminary. Sixty-five acres of land were procured, a building was soon fitted up, and in 1829 Horton Academy went into operation. Under the general educational system then in operation, the school became entitled to provincial aid, and received it. Along with Pictou Academy, and others of a similar class, it still forms part of the secondary school system of Nova Scotia, but it has for some years past declined all grants from the Provincial Treasury.

Acadia College.—It was from the beginning intended that the Horton Academy should be developed into a

---

* In King's County.

collegiate institution, capable of doing higher educational work, and the managing committee of the Education Society appealed more than once to the Baptists to carry the scheme to completion.* In 1836 they urged the establishment of a seminary "which shall become so fully possessed of the highest literary merit as to deserve every immunity that the law can grant to chartered institutions." In 1837 they gave a gloomy account of the state of higher education. Windsor Academy was only beginning to revive after a long period of depression. King's College at Windsor was "too sectarian to allow dissenters, with any confidence, to seek its advantages for their sons," and still suffered from "that depression which its contracted system inevitably involved." All efforts to open Dalhousie had failed. Pictou Academy was said "to be hastening to decay" as the result of dissensions among its supporters. "There is therefore," the committee urged, "at once a loud call and an open field for all who feel the importance of a liberal education, to engage in the important work of forming and animating an enlarged system of instruction such as the country urgently needs, and is sought in vain within its borders." To many Baptists the only feasible way to provide the means of collegiate instruction seemed to be the opening of Dalhousie College, which had a building and a partial endowment out of public funds. It was opened to students in 1838, but when the Rev. E. A. Crawley, then pastor of a Baptist church in Halifax, applied for the professorship

---

*See the "Vaughan Prize Essay" in "Memorials of Acadia College and Horton Academy for 1828-1878."

of Classics, he was unsuccessful, and as his failure was attributed to an intention on the part of the Board of Governors to make Dalhousie virtually a Presbyterian institution, an agitation was at once set on foot to organize at Wolfville a college for which Horton Academy would be a preparatory school. The name selected for the new institution was "Queen's College," and in the following year it was formally opened with twenty matriculated students in attendance, and three professors* on its staff. It was deemed essential that the College should have a charter of incorporation, and its promoters applied to the Legislature of Nova Scotia for one. At that time, however, there was in that body a strong desire to have one thoroughly efficient University in the Province, and the hope of accomplishing their wish caused the defeat of the Baptist application. A second one was more successful. The Legislature in 1840 passed an Act incorporating the institution under the name of "The Trustees, Governors, and Fellows of the Queen's College." It conferred on the College corporation the ordinary university powers, and while the institution was placed under denominational control it was left perfectly free from religious tests as to both teachers and students. In the following session, at the suggestion of the Colonial Secretary,† the Legislature amended the charter so as to change the name of the institution to "Acadia College." In 1851, by another Act of the Legislature, the power of appointing the Governors was transferred from the "Education Society" to the

---

*Rev. J. Prior was appointed to teach Classics; Rev. E. A. Crawley to teach moral Philosophy, Logic, and Rhetoric; and Mr. Isaac Chipman to teach Mathematics and Natural Philosophy.

*Then Lord John Russell.

Baptist Convention of the Maritime Provinces. Minor amendments were made in the constitution from time to time, as experience showed the necessity for them, and in 1891 the Legislature passed an Act* which was a revision and consolidation of all previous enactments, with such new provisions as were then considered expedient.

Acadia University.—The Act of 1891 created a new corporation under the name of the "Governors of Acadia University," to which all the property, rights, privileges, and immunities of the former corporation were transferred, and provision was made by it for the continuation of all the functions of the institution, and of the terms of office of all who held positions in it, until the new Board should otherwise decide. The latter was invested with complete control over not merely Acadia College but the Horton Academy and the Acadia Seminary,† and was authorized to receive and hold "gifts, devises, and bequests" on behalf of these institutions, jointly or severally, It was authorized also to "establish and manage professional, and technical, and other schools," and support them out of the funds of the University. It was empowered to "grant degrees in theology, and the degrees of bachelor master and doctor in the several arts, sciences, and faculties," and to "determine the course of study, and the qualification for degrees." It was invested with "full power and authority to fix the number, residence, duties, salary, provision, and emolument of the President, professors, principals, teachers, tutors, instructors, officers,

---

*Entitled "An Act respecting Acadia University." It is 54 Vict., cap. 134.
†A higher school for girls, as the Academy is for boys. Students of both sexes are admitted to Acadia University.

agents, and servants," of the University, the Academy, and the Seminary, and to remove any or all of them. The Board is under the Act required to appoint a "Senate," consisting of the President and others who are not Governors, to advise the Board on purely academical matters such as the courses of study, conduct of examinations, and the "literary welfare" of the various institutions. The "right to nominate" one-third of the members of the Senate is granted by the statute to the "Associated Alumni" of the University, and this body* nominates also one-fourth of the members of the Board of Governors.

Dr. Crawley and Dr. Cramp.—No sketch of Acadia University would be complete without some reference to the work done in its earlier history by these two men. They were both born in England, Dr. Cramp in 1796 at St. Peter's in the Isle of Thanet, and Dr. Crawley in 1794, at Ipswich in Suffolk. By courses of life and activity widely apart they were brought together in Acadia College, and each of them died under its shadow while still a member of its academic staff. Dr. Cramp's death took place in 1881, three years after the jubilee of the Horton Collegiate Academy; Dr. Crawley's in 1888, a few weeks after the jubilee of Acadia College. Though Dr. Cramp was senior in age, Dr. Crawley preceded him in his connection with Baptist educational work in Nova Scotia, Dr. Cramp having been brought from Montreal in 1851, to take the Presidency of the College. Dr. Crawley, while still within the communion of the Church of England, was educated at King's College, Windsor.

*Incorporated in 1860.

He subsequently studied law and practised with success in Halifax, but abandoned a lucrative profession to become pastor of a small Baptist Church there. He was largely instrumental in moving the Baptist Association to establish the Horton Collegiate Academy in 1828, and he was still more peculiarly identified with the foundation of Acadia College, ten years later. In 1847 he resigned his place on its staff to resume his pastoral work in Halifax   In 1852 he was induced to return to Acadia, as the President of its Arts faculty, Dr. Cramp remaining President of the faculty of Theology, and this cooperation was continued for three years. After another prolonged absence, spent largely in the United States, Dr. Crawley was appointed in 1865 to the chair of Belles Lettres. He accepted the position and remained a professor, active or emeritus, until his death. Dr. Cramp's early life was spent in his native place, where he joined the Baptist Church, and soon after became a preacher under Baptist auspices. He received his collegiate training in Stepney College, but his education was mainly the result of his own persistant and lifelong habits of study. After many years of ministerial work in England, his reputation as a preacher and author secured for him a call from the Baptists of Canada to take charge of their College in Montreal. The unfortunate career of that institution has already been referred* to. Dr. Cramp after its close took up journalistic† work in Montreal, but he accepted the call to Acadia from a sense of duty, and with his eyes fully open to the arduous nature of the task imposed

---

*See above, pp. 126-128.
†He was for a time chief editorial writer on the *Pilot*, which had been started by Mr. (afterwards Sir) Francis Hincks.

upon him. For many years he was the chief mainstay of the institution, teaching, preaching, and collecting funds with unwearying assiduity. He retired from active work in 1869 but was continued on the staff of the University till his death. Largely as the result of the efforts put forth and the sacrifices made by Dr. Cramp and Dr. Crawley, the educational work of Acadia has been made effective, and the institution has been put on a greatly improved financial basis.

The Theological Faculty.—From an early period in Dr. Cramp's incumbency, he was for many years the sole teacher of theology in Acadia College. In 1874, five years after his retirement, the work of theological instruction was revived, and was maintained until 1883, when the head of the department retired to take a chair in the Toronto Baptist College.*

THE UNIVERSITY OF HALIFAX.

The idea of having one Provincial University for Nova Scotia, which should be the examining and degree-conferring body for the various teaching colleges, was not permanently lost sight of after the failure of Lord Dalhousie's efforts to secure a union between King's College and the one he proposed to establish in Halifax. After having been driven into the background by the controversies and efforts of the generation after 1838, it was revived in 1876. During the session of that year

---

*See above, p. 131.

the Nova Scotia Legislature passed an Act* creating "The University of Halifax," with power, after examination, to confer degrees in arts and science, other than degrees in medicine and surgery, on candidates sent up by any of the following teaching Colleges: King's College in Windsor, Dalhousie College in Halifax, Acadia College in Wolfville, Saint Mary's College in Halifax, the College of St. Francis Xavier in Antigonish, and Mount Allison Wesleyan College in Sackville, N. B. The corporate powers of the University were vested in "A chancellor, Vice-Chancellor, fellows, and graduates," and these for the time being were declared to constitute the "Senate," to which was entrusted "the entire management and superintendence over the affairs, concerns, and property" of the University. It was specially empowered to make regulations for the conduct of examinations and the granting of degrees and standing, with the proviso that it should not be lawful "to impose on any person any compulsory religious examination or test, or to do, or cause or suffer to be done, anything that would render it necessary or advisable, with a view to academical success or distinction, that any person should pursue the study of any materialistic or sceptical system of logic, or mental or moral philosophy." The chancellor was to be appointed by the Governor-in-Council, and the Vice-Chancellor to be chosen by the Senate. The "fellows" were to be twenty-four in number, exclusive of the Chancellor

---

*39 Vict. cap 28. See also Revised Statutes of Nova Scotia, 1884, cap. 30,

and the Vice Chancellor, and were to be appointed out of a larger list nominated by Convocation. The latter body was declared to include "all doctors of law, doctors of medicine, doctors of science and masters of arts, all bachelors of law and bachelors of medicine of two year's standing," and those holding such other degrees as Convocation might by resolution agree to. Under the authority conferred by this constitution the University of Halifax was organized, but it never succeeded in drawing to its examinations any considerable number of candidates, though the teaching institutions affiliated to it by the statute were not required to leave in abeyance their own degree-conferring powers, and those who entered into a working arrangement with it became entitled to a special Provincial grant. After examinations had been held for a very few years, and one or two degrees had been conferred, the University became dormant, though the statute creating it has not been repealed.

ROMAN CATHOLIC UNIVERSITIES.

The Roman Catholics of Nova Scotia have long been awake to the importance of higher education, but the difficulties in the way of carrying on the work successfully have been very great. For some years an effort to do so was made in Halifax, but the St. Mary's College formerly maintained in that city no longer exists. There are still two institutions in operation in the Province, each invested with university powers, and of these a brief account may be given.

St. Francis Xavier's College. — This College was founded at Antigonish in 1854, by the Right Reverend Colin F. McKinnon, D.D., Bishop of Arichat, for the higher education of students aspiring to the priesthood and to the learned professions. Under the peculiar secondary school system of Nova Scotia, the college was affiliated with the Antigonish County Academy, and in this way became instrumental in furnishing a valuable non-professional training to many of the teachers of the public schools. Its position, in fact, was analogous to that of the Windsor and Horton Academies. Like them, it was denominational in its management, but was aided in its maintenance by a Provincial subsidy. In 1866 an Act* was passed by the Nova Scotia Legislature, declaring that " St. Francis Xavier's College shall be held and taken to be a university, with all the usual privileges of such an institution," including the right to confer on its students the degrees of " Bachelor, Master, and Doctor in the several Arts and Faculties," according to the regulations prescribed by the college authorities. In 1882 the institution was incorporated by another Act† of the Legislature, under the name of " The Governors of St. Francis Xavier's College, Antigonish." The Roman Catholic Bishop, two other clergymen, and two laymen constitute the board; the Bishop is a member *ex officio,* and the other four are governors for life, unless they resign, remove permanently from the Province, or withdraw from the communion of the Roman Catholic Church. Vacancies are filled up by co-optation, subject to the approval

---

*29 Vict , cap. 93.

†45 Vict., cap. 77.

of the Bishop, and with the same proviso the governors are authorized to make regulations for the business administration and academical management of the institution. By them all members of the teaching staff are appointed, their duties defined, and their remuneration fixed. The Act of 1882 expressly continues the university status granted to the college by the Act of 1866.

Sainte Anne's College. —This institution was established in Digby County in 1890, at the instance of Archbishop O'Brien, who invited the co-operation of the Congregation of the Eudist Fathers for the purpose. In 1892, by an Act* of the Legislature of Nova Scotia, it was incorporated under the name of "The Directors of Sainte Anne's College, Church Point," the first directors being five members of the Eudist Congregation, who are authorized to fill vacancies by co-optation, and to increase their number in the same way. All directors hold their places only so long as they remain in the communion of the Roman Catholic Church. The directors are empowered to elect a President; and to appoint members of the teaching staff, and other officers. As a corporation they have full control of the college property, and as a university they are authorized to confer degrees and prescribe the conditions on which they may be obtained in the "several Arts and Faculties." Sainte Anne's College, for purposes of secondary educational work, is affiliated with the Clare County Academy, but it has not yet begun to confer degrees.

---

*55 Vict., cap. 135.

CHAPTER XIII.

NEW BRUNSWICK UNIVERSITIES.

Many of the United Empire Loyalists settled on the north shore of the Bay of Fundy, at the mouth and along the banks of the St. John River. The natural resources of the locality attracted other immigrants, and very soon the settlers found themselves in a position to ask for an independent Provincial organization. The Colonial Office deemed it expedient to divide Acadia, and in 1774 a commission was issued to Thomas Carleton as Governor of New Brunswick, the boundaries of the Province being defined as they have ever since remained. The progress of settlement was rapid and continuous, and with its development grew the desire for improved means of education.

THE UNIVERSITY OF NEW BRUNSWICK.

As far back as 1800 a charter was issued* under the Great Seal of the province for the establishment and incorporation of a seminary of learning, named "The College of New Brunswick," which was located at Fredericton, and was endowed in the course of the same year with certain Crown lands in that vicinity. By an Act* of the New Brunswick Parliament passed in 1805, a grant of £100 a year was made to it out of the Provin-

---

*On the 12th of February.
*45 George III., cap. 15.

cial treasury, and this was in 1816 supplemented, under similar authority*, by a further grant of £150 per annum. Acts† were passed in 1820 and 1822 to confirm agreements between the College authorities and their tenants, and in 1823 authority was given by another Provincial statute‡ to the "Governor and trustees" of the College to surrender their charter to the King on condition that he would issue another in its place, making him the founder of the college. The same Act appropriated an additional grant of £600 a year to the institution out of the treasury of the Province.

King's College.—The desired Royal Charter was issued§ in 1828. It reincorporated the institution under the name of "King's College," and conferred on it university powers, but made it at the same time a Church of England college. By an educational Act* passed in the following year, the various annual subsidies payable out of the Provincial treasury were consolidated, and their amount was increased to £1,000 currency per annum, which was supplemented by a yearly grant from the the Crown of £1,000 sterling out of its "casual and territorial revenues." The period between 1828 and 1845 was marked, as it was in Upper Canada, by controversy over the sectarian character of an institution that had

---

*56 George III., cap. 20.

†Though these did not receive the Royal Assent till 1824, they are known as 60 George III., cap. 36, and 3 George IV., cap. 36.

‡4 George IV., cap. 33.

§One year later than the issue of the Royal Charter to King's College at Toronto. The date was the 15th of December. It is recited in the preamble to 8 Vict., cap. 3, of the Statutes of New Brunswick referred to below.

*9 and 10 George IV., cap. 29.

been thus liberally endowed out of the public funds of the Province, and in 1845 the agitation for its secularization resulted in the passing of an Act* which abolished all religious tests, except in the case of the Professor of Theology, and made other changes in the constitution of the College, without, however, impairing its revenues or altering the relations existing between it and the Crown. This measure was reserved for the assent of the Queen, and an opportunity was afforded for the consideration of the objections urged against allowing it to go into operation. One of these was the contention that it was beyond the competence of a Provincial Parliament to amend a Royal Charter, and in the course of the correspondence which ensued between the Provincial and Imperial Governments, the Colonial Secretary† conceded that there was no valid constitutional objection to the measure. The Act was ultimately assented to near the close of 1846, and for the next thirteen years the constitution of King's College was left undisturbed by legislation.

The University of New Brunswick.—In 1854 the New Brunswick Legislature authorized the Lieutenant-Governor of the Province to appoint a Commission to enquire into the state of King's College, with a view to its improvement. Action was taken on this initiative,‡

---

*8 Vict., cap. 3.

†Then Lord Stanley. One of his letters to Lieut.-Governor Colebrooke was enclosed in the reply of the Council of King's College, Toronto, to Lord Cathcart's letter in 1846. It is printed *in extenso* in Appendix D.D. to the Journals of the Legislative Assembly of Canada for that year. See above, pp. 33 and 41.

‡The Lieut.-Governor was the Hon. J. H. T. Manners-Sutton. The Commission was composed of J. H. Gray (Chairman), Egerton Ryerson, J. W. Dawson, John S. Saunders, and James Brown.

and before the close of the year the Commission sent in a report, in which special prominence was given to the advantage of a high standard of university education, the necessity for including religious training in the scheme of university work, the futility of expecting the best results from underpaid teachers, and the advantage of careful supervision of students by the college authorities, whether in private boarding houses or in a college residence. One of the commissioners,* in a letter to the chairman, added a statement of his own opinion on the question of residence:—

In connection with this subject, I attach much importance to the opinion expressed in the report, that the residence of pupils within the college building is not of such utility as has hitherto been supposed. From my own observation of its effects, I cannot doubt that college residence is, even under the most favorable circumstances, more dangerous to the health, manners, and morals of the students than to reside in respectable houses. The Scottish and German universities are old illustrations of the successful working of colleges without any provision for residence, and the best authorities in the United States now decidedly lean to the opinion that this method is most suitable for America. The saving of building accommodation and annual outlay, and of time, labor, and anxiety to the professors are important advantages.

The recommendations embodied in the report of the Commission, supplemented by the proposals of the Council of King's College in 1857, became the basis of an Act† passed by the New Brunswick Legislature in 1859. The name of the institution was changed to the University of New Brunswick. A new governing body, called

---

*Mr. Dawson (afterward Principal of McGill University).

†This statute was reserved for the Queen's Assent, which was given in 1860.

the "Senate" was created, of which the President was a member *ex officio*, and the others were appointed by the Governor-in-Council. The Senate was invested with authority to manage the financial business of the university, and to appoint all the members of the teaching staff and all the officers except the President. The secularization of the University was completed by the abolition of the professorship of theology, and provision was made for the affiliation of other institutions with it.

The present constitution of the University is embodied in an Act* passed by the New Brunswick Legislature in 1891. The corporation, as defined in it, consists of (1) nine† members appointed by the Governor-in-Council, (2) two members, being graduates, chosen by "The Associated Alumni of the University of New Brunswick," and (3) one member elected by "The Provincial Educational Institute." The Act makes the Senate coincident in membership with the corporation, and its presiding officer is the President, who is also *ex officio* "Chief Superintendent of Education" for the Province. The Chancellor, like the President, is appointed by the Governor-in-Council, but he must be selected "from among the professors and Faculty of the University." It is his duty to personally superintend the academic work, to see to the enforcement of discipline, to preside at the conferring of degrees, and to take charge of the buildings and grounds. "The Faculty of the University" consists of the Chancellor and Professors, and it is empowered to adjudge penalties for violations of rules, to determine

---

*54 Vict., cap. 12.

†Two of these are the President and Chancellor *ex officio*.

the relative standing of students, and to regulate the times and places for classes and lectures.

THE UNIVERSITY OF MOUNT ALLISON COLLEGE.

The Methodist Church in the Maritime Provinces has felt itself bound, like other religious denominations, to undertake and carry on the work of higher secular education. A beginning was made with the founding of an "Academy" at Sackville, in New Brunswick, in 1842. The occasion of this educational enterprise was a liberal offer made in 1841 to the "Wesleyan Conference of Eastern British America" by Mr. C. F. Allison, a Sackville merchant, who donated a site for the institution, contributed a sum of money to establish it, and agreed to make an annual payment for some years toward its support. Like the corresponding schools at Horton, Pictou, and Windsor, the "Mount Allison Wesleyan Academy" was at first only a secondary school, but its efficiency soon won for it such recognition that its alumni were readily admitted to third year standing in the Arts course of the Methodist University at Middletown, Connecticut, to which many Canadians went in those days for a culture training. With the other academies, it received a certain amount of Provincial* aid, but in the main it has been forced to look for support to the Methodist denomination. The school is still continued under the name of "The Mount Allison Academy and Commercial College," and a corresponding school has been

---

*Though situated in New Brunswick it has been allowed a share of the Nova Scotia grant for secondary Education.

established under the name of "The Mount Allison Ladies' College and Conservatory of Music." Since they were instituted they have educated many students from New Brunswick, Nova Scotia, Prince Edward Island, Newfoundland, and the Bermudas.

Mount Allison Wesleyan College.—The New Brunswick Legislature, by an Act* passed in 1858 empowered the corporation then charged with the management of the Academy to " found, establish, maintain, and manage a collegiate institution at Sackville, to be designated and known as the Mount Allison Wesleyan College." By this statute it was provided that whenever the College should have a Faculty consisting of a President and two or more professors, with a minimum attendance of ten regularly matriculated students, it should have "full power and authority to confer the degree of Bachelor, Master, and Doctor in the general arts and faculties in the manner and on the conditions ordered by the College Board" The collegiate and university functions thus authorized came into operation in 1862, and " The Mount Allison Wesleyan College " was organized as a teaching and degree-conferring university. From the outset it has been conducted under denominational control but on strictly non-sectarian principles, and it is claimed on its behalf that it was the first chartered university to admit women to all the privileges of regular collegiate courses and degrees. The partial union of the Methodist sects in 1874 became the occasion of an Act † passed the

---

*21 Vict. cap. 57. Previous Acts passed by the same body, relating to the Academy, are 12 Vict. cap. 65, and 19 Vict. cap. 65.
†38 Vict. cap. 74.

following year, by which some modifications were made in the constitution of the University, and the name of the corporation was changed to "the Board of Governors of the Mount Allison Wesleyan College and Academies." The first governors, eighteen in number, were named in the statute, and provision was made for the periodical election of their successors, sixteen by the General Conference of the Methodist Church, and two by the Alumni Society.*

University of Mount Allison College.—The complete union of the various Methodist denominations in 1883 gave occasion in a similar way for the passage in 1886 of an Act † which changed the name of the corporation to "The University of Mount Allison College," enlarged the number of "Governors or Regents" to twenty-six, of whom twenty-four were to be elected by the General Conference, and declared all graduates of the institution under its previous title to be graduates *ipso facto* of the University under its new name. In 1895 another statutory change‡ in the constitution increased the total membership of the Board of Governors to thirty-two, of whom the alumni of the College and the Academy were to elect six, and the alumni of the Ladies' College, two. The Board of Governors thus constituted is invested with complete control over the property and management of the college and the two preparatory schools. It appoints, and may remove, the President, professors, tutors, and other instructors,

---

*This association had been incorporated by Act of Parliament in 1874 (37 Vict. cap. 78.)

†49 Vict. cap. 41.

‡ Made by 58 Vict. cap. 65.

prescribes their duties, and fixes their remuneration. Conjointly with the "Faculty," which is made up of the President and the professors, the Governors form the "College Board," which is authorized to prescribe the requirements for matriculation and the course of study for undergraduates, and to "regulate all other matters relating directly to the department of education."

The jubilee of the establishment of the educational institution which has been developed under the different titles specified above, was celebrated on the 19th of January, 1893, the fiftieth anniversary of the opening of the Mount Allison Wesleyan Academy for the reception of students. The last report of the Board of Governors to the General Conference of the Methodist Church of Canada, shows that the aggregate attendance during the session of 1893-94 was 344; that the annual average attendance of students in the University proper had for the years 1890-94 been 118; that the total number of graduates from the foundation of the University was 214; and that the endowment of the University apart from the academies, was $117,518.

ST. JOSEPH'S COLLEGE.

Prior to Confederation, the Acadian French manifested but little interest in higher education, or indeed in education of any kind. Not many of them were cultured in either the academical or the professional sense. They had few French journals, French schools, or French teachers, and they were in consequence greatly behind other sections of the population, even the Canadian French, in political influence. A great change for the better has in a generation come over the French people of the Maritime Provinces. They now enjoy educational opportunities of a kind entirely unknown a few years ago, and they seem disposed to take full advantage of them. Besides schools doing primary and secondary work, they have several of a more advanced character, one of which is part of the educational system of New Brunswick.

The College of St. Joseph.—This institution was founded at Memramcook in 1864 by the late Very Rev. Camille Lefebvre, a priest of the Congregation of the Holy Cross. This is a Roman Catholic religious society devoted to educational and missionary work, and the College is still conducted by the Fathers of the Congregation. Four years after its establishment it was incorporated by Act* of the New Brunswick Legislature under the title of "The College of St. Joseph." The members of the corporation and of the "Board of Governors" specified in the statute were the Roman Catholic Bishop of the diocese, certain Roman Catholic missionaries, and a few laymen. The governors were invested with authority to appoint and remove the President, professors, tutors, and other officers, to prescribe their various duties, and to fix their remuneration. The President and professors composed the "Faculty," and the Faculty and Governors were united to form the "College Board," whose duty it was to prescribe "requisites for matriculation and courses of study for under-

*31 Vict., cap. 63.

graduates, and to regulate all other matters relating directly to the department of education." It was provided in the statute of incorporation that whenever the collegiate staff should include a President and two professors, and the attendance of regularly matriculated students should reach ten, the college should become a university with power to "confer upon properly qualified persons the degree of Bachelor, Master, or Doctor in the several arts and faculties in the manner and on the conditions which may be ordered by the College Board."

St. Joseph's College.—In 1894 a new Act* of incorporation was obtained from the New Brunswick Legislature. The only members of the corporation under this constitution are seven members of the religious order under whose auspices the institution has been carried on since its foundation—"The Fathers of the Holy Cross"—and these seven corporators are also the only members of the Board of Governors. The name of the institution is changed to "St. Joseph's College, and its university powers are continued, under the control of the College Board, as before. The Board of Governors is empowered to elect from among its own members the President and the other officers of the college, and also to change its own *personnel* by the exercise of co-optation, the choice of new members being limited to those who belong to the order of the "Holy Cross." All the acts done and degrees conferred by the authorities of the "College of St. Joseph" are by this statute placed on a par, as to legality, with acts done and degrees conferred by the

---
*57 Vict., cap. 87.

authorities of "St. Joseph's College," and all the property, claims, and franchises of the former are transferred absolutely to the latter.

The motive of St. Joseph College, as an educational institution is sufficiently explained in its announcement. Special attention is given to moral and religious training, but a varied arts course is prescribed for those who desire to take any one of the three degrees, Bachelor of Science, Bachelor of Literature, or Bachelor of Arts. The manner of testing candidates for degrees is sufficiently peculiar to merit special attention. The subjects of the course are divided into two groups as follows: (1) Latin, Greek, English, History and Geography; and (2) Philosophy, Mathamatics, and the Sciences. The degree of Bachelor of Literature is conferred on a candidate who passes a "successful" examination in the first group and a "partially successful" one in the second. The degree of Bachelor of Science is conferred on a candidate who is successful in the second group and partially successful in the first. The degree of Bachelor of Arts is conferred on a candidate who is successful in each group. To be "successful" the candidate must secure two-thirds of the maximum for a group of subjects and one-third of the maximum for each subject; to be "partially successful" he must secure one-half of the maximum for a group and one-fourth for each subject.

CHAPTER XIV.

THE UNIVERSITY OF MANITOBA.

The Province of Manitoba was created* in 1870 out of the region annexed† to the Dominion of Canada under the name of "Rupert's Land and the North-Western Territory." The constitution given to the new Province authorized its Legislature to "make laws in relation to education," subject to certain provisions relating to "denominational schools." Under this authority an Act‡ was passed in 1877 to "establish one University for the whole of Manitoba on the model of the University of London, for the purpose of raising the standard of higher education in the Province, and of enabling all denominations and classes to obtain academical degrees." The corporate name given to the new institution was "The University of Manitoba," and the corporation was declared to consist of "A Chancellor, a Vice-Chancellor, and a Council," which was composed of (1) seven representatives to be selected by each incorporated College affiliated to the University, (2) three representatives to be selected by Convocation, and (3) one member for each of the two sec-

---

*By Act of the Dominion Parliament (32 and 33 Vict., cap. 3), subsequently validated by Act of the Imperial Parliament (34 and 35 Vict., cap 28).

†By Imperial Order-in-Council, dated June 23, 1870.

‡40 Vict., cap. 11.

tions of the Board of Education. The first Convocation included "all bachelors and masters of arts, all bachelors of law, licentiates of law, doctors of law, bachelors and doctors of science, and all bachelors, licentiates, and doctors of medicine" of any university in Her Majesty's Dominion, who had resided in Manitoba for two months previous to the passing of the Act. The University was limited in its functions to "the examining of candidates for degrees in the several faculties, or for certificates of honor in different branches of knowledge, and to the granting of such degrees and certificates after examination." The Chancellor was appointed by the Lieutenant-Governor in Council, the Vice-Chancellor was made elective by the University Council. The Lieutenant-Governor was created "Visitor." In the Council, of which the Chancellor and Vice-Chancellor were *ex officio* members, was vested "the entire management of and superintendence over the affairs, concerns, and property" of the University, and, in general, the right to act "in all cases unprovided for," in such manner as might seem best calculated to promote the purpose for which the University was established. There were affiliated to the University by the Act, (1) the College of St. Boniface, (2) the College of St. John, and (3) the Manitoba College,* with a view to the admission of their students to the examinations for degrees and standing, and provision was made for the affiliation by the Lieutenant-Governor in Council of other

---

*These three institutions belonged to the Roman Catholic, Anglican, and Presbyterian denominations respectively.

incorporated Colleges which could show that they were possessed of adequate appliances and a sufficient staff. Theological Colleges affiliated to the University were empowered to grant degrees* in divinity, and the holders of such degrees became entitled to the same rights and privileges as if they had graduated in the University. Provision was also made for the affiliation of one or more Provincial Normal Schools, should they be established. By an Act† passed in 1887 the number of representatives of Convocation was increased to seven, and in 1893 it was provided by another statute‡ (1) that seven additional members of Council should be appointed by the Crown, and (2) that the seven medical representatives, who had been elective by the Provincial College of Physicians and Surgeons, should be distributed so as to leave four to be chosen by that body and three by the Manitoba Medical College, an affiliated teaching institution. The Act of 1893 further provided that the Lieutenant-Governor in Council might appoint professors and assistant professors in modern languages, mathematics, and natural sciences, whose salaries should be paid by the Provincial Government, and whose lectures should be free to the students of affiliated colleges.

---

*An amending Act passed in 1880 (43 Vict., cap. 31) made it obligatory on candidates for such degrees to be examined by the University in Greek, Latin, and Mathematics.

†50 Vict., cap. 43.

‡56 Vict., cap. 35.

Present Constitution of the University.—As the result of its evolution under these various statutory enactments the University of Manitoba has now affiliated with it and represented in its Council the following teaching institutions :

ST. BONIFACE COLLEGE.

This College is conducted under the auspices of the Roman Catholic Church and the presidency of the "Archbishop and Metropolitan of St. Boniface." It was in existence before the creation of the University of Manitoba, and was affiliated to it by the original Act of incorporation of the latter institution. It has, besides, assistant teachers, a staff of ten "professors," who collectively have charge of the following university subjects: Mental philosophy, physics, chemistry, mathematics, English, French, rhetoric and humanities, Latin and Greek. It has contributed twenty-two graduates to the University list.

ST. JOHN'S COLLEGE.

This was one of the three Colleges affiliated to the University by the Act of 1877. It is an Anglican institution, its "Chancellor and Warden" being the Archbishop of Rupert's Land. Besides the tuition given in theological subjects it provides instruction in Hebrew, mental and moral philosophy, Greek, Latin, mathematics, natural science, history, English, French, and German. It has added ninety graduates to the University register.

MANITOBA COLLEGE.

This institution was founded in 1871 by the Presbyterian Church of Canada, and was affiliated to the University of Manitoba by the original Act of University incorporation. It is still conducted under the direction of the Presbyterian General Assembly of Canada, which makes provision for instruction in arts as well as in theology. The arts staff is composed of eight teachers, who give instruction in science, English, Greek, Latin, French, German, Hebrew, mathematics, mental and moral philosophy, logic, and political economy. Manitoba College has given one hundred and sixty graduates to the University.

WESLEY COLLEGE.

In 1888 this College, established and conducted under the control of the Methodist General Conference, of Canada was affiliated to the University by order of the Lieutenant-Governor in Council. In its curriculum provision is made for teaching mental and moral philosophy, pure and applied mathematics, geology, physics, Greek, Latin, English, and history. It has added forty to the list of University graduates.

MANITOBA MEDICAL COLLEGE.

This training school of medicine was established in 1883, and was affiliated in the following year to the Provincial University, from which its students obtain their degrees. Formerly the right to examine candidates for license to practise medicine was vested in the Provincial College of Physicians and Surgeons, but under the authority of the Medical Act of 1886 all the examining powers which previously belonged to that body were transferred to the University of Manitoba, to the Council of which the College of Physicians and Surgeons is authorized to elect four representatives. The Medical College has three representatives in the same body. During its twelve years of operation the " Manitoba Medical College " has given over one hundred graduates to the University.

COLLEGIATE CO-OPERATION.

As adequate tuition in the subjects assigned to it has not yet been provided by the University of Manitoba, efforts have been made from time to time to secure among the affiliated colleges such working arrangements as will lessen to each the cost of efficient instruction. St. John's, Manitoba, and Wesley Colleges have for four years co-operated in scientific instruction, and the result has been highly advantageous, the increased efficiency of the work having entailed comparatively little extra cost on each of the institutions benefited. A further measure of co-operation has been carried into practice by Manitoba and Wesley Colleges, the former instructing the students of both in honor mental and moral science and classics, and the latter instructing them in higher honor mathematics.

N

PART II.

UNIVERSITIES OF GREAT BRITAIN.

CHAPTER XV.

THE UNIVERSITY OF OXFORD.

The University of Oxford is a corporate body, known for ages by the historic title of the "Chancellor, Masters, and Scholars of the University of Oxford," a title confirmed by Parliament in the time of Queen Elizabeth. With the exception of rare interventions on the part of the Crown, the University has always been governed by statutes of its own making.

Organization of the University.—By the Oxford University Act, 1854, the constitution of the University is framed as follows :—

1. THE HEBDOMADAL COUNCIL (so called from its meeting every week), consists of certain official and of certain elected members. The official members are the Chancellor, Vice-Chancellor, ex-Vice-Chancellor, (for one year after leaving office, or till the next triennial election), and the two Proctors ; the elected members are six heads of Colleges, or Halls, six University professors, and six members of Convocation (of not less than five years' standing). These are elected by the Congregation of the University of Oxford for six years, in such a way that one-half of each class vacate their seats every three years, being, however, re-eligible. This Council meets every Monday in

term-time and whenever convoked by the Vice-Chancellor; it has the initiative in all the legislation of the University, and from it all petitions, decrees and statutes are referred for approval to Congregation and Convocation.

2. THE HOUSE OF CONGREGATION, consists of Regents either *necessario* or *ad placitum*. All Doctors of every Faculty and all Masters of Arts are *necessario regentes* for two years after taking their respective degrees; and all the following if members of Convocation, are *regentes ad placitum*: Professors, Doctors of every Faculty who are resident, Heads of College and Halls or their deputies, Public Examiners, Moderators, and Masters of the Schools, Censors and Deans of Colleges. To make a House, the presence of the Chancellor, or Vice-Chancellor, or his deputy, and of the two Proctors or their deputies, and of nine other Regents, is required. This body, described in the statutes as 'venerable,' exists chiefly for ceremonial purposes; its business is confined almost exclusively to ratifying the nomination of examiners by the Vice-Chancellor and Proctors, and the granting of degrees.

3. THE CONGREGATION OF THE UNIVERSITY of Oxford, consists of members of the Hebdomadal Council, the Heads of Colleges, Professors, and examiners, and certain University officers; also all members of Convocation who are in residence within the University limits (between 300 and 400 qualify in this way). The Chancellor, or Vice-Chancellor or one of his deputies, and the two Proctors or their deputies, preside at its meetings. Its business is almost entirely confined to legislation. When

the Hebdomadal Council has passed a new statute it must first be promulgated, after due notice, in this assembly. At the time of such promulgation any members of Congregation may propose amendments; such amendments (if seconded, and not considered by the Chancellor or his deputy to be inconsistent with or irrelevant to the principle of the statute, as set out in its preamble) must be printed and considered at a subsequent meeting; the Council may also, at such times, propose any amendments, and when these have been adopted by Convocation, there is still a power of proposing further amendments vested in the Council or any twelve members of Congregation; when all amendments have been considered, the Statute after three days' notice, is submitted to the Congregation for approval. No right of negative is allowed to the Vice-Chancellor or Proctor, but every question is decided on a majority of votes. A statute approved by Congregation must then be submitted to Convocation, after seven days' notice, for final adoption or rejection.

4. THE HOUSE OF CONVOCATION, consists of all Doctors of every Faculty and all Masters of Arts who are still members of the University (*i.e.* whose names are still on the books of a College or other recognized institution, and who have paid all statutable fees to the University), whether they are resident or not. To make a House, the presence of the Chancellor, or Vice-Chancellor or one of his deputies, and of the two Proctors or their respective deputies is required. In this House is transacted all the formal business of the University as a corporate body, except what is named as belonging to the House of Con-

gregation. No statute is binding until it has received the assent of Convocation; matters of special and individual concern, anything that demands immediate provision, payments from the University chest, are settled by decree of Convocation. This House also confers Honorary degrees, and degrees by diploma or decree; it decides whether the University seal shall be affixed to any document, whose validity depends on such seal, and it makes most elections to University offices. In the election of burgesses, members of Convocation may send in their voting-papers without attending the poll; in other elections members must vote in person. In this House and in the House of Congregation, the Chancellor, or Vice-Chancellor or his deputy, and the two Proctors together, have the right of veto in all matters except elections; otherwise questions are decided on a majority of votes.

The Chief Officers of the University.—(a) The Chancellor of the University is elected by the members of Convocation; his is an honorary office, with no stipend attached, and is held for life; in most matters and on most occasions the Chancellor is represented by the Vice-Chancellor.

(b) The Vice-Chancellor is annually nominated by the Chancellor from the heads of Colleges. The letters of nomination are read in Convocation by the Senior Proctor; the Vice-Chancellor appoints four deputies from the heads of Colleges, to exercise his power in case of illness or absence; up till 1884 the office of Vice-Chancellor was usually held for four years; but the duties are arduous, and since then the office has not been held for so long. The annual income is made up to £600 from the University chest.

(c) The Proctors, two in number, are elected annually by the several Colleges and by the Halls conjointly according to a cycle of thirty years beginning from 1889. The electors are all those members of the several societies who being members of Convocation are also, or have been, members of the Congregation of the University, and all those Fellows and Scholars of a College who are members of Convocation. Each Proctor, on election, nominates two deputies. A Proctor's salary is annually the sum of £350. It is the duty of the Proctors to see that students conform to the statutes which regulate their dress and conduct; for this purpose they patrol the streets of Oxford after dark, during term-time, and take the names and addresses of students found in prohibited places, or walking in the public streets without the University cap and gown; they summon delinquents to appear in the Chancellor's Court, and act the part of police in all cases where a member of the University is concerned. They are elected from the resident fellows or tutors of a College.

(d) The Chancellor has jurisdiction in almost all causes, civil, spiritual, or criminal, in which students or privileged persons within the University precincts are parties. A court is held every Friday of term-time, at which the Vice-Chancellor presides, and the two Proctors may sit as assessors; the Vice-Chancellor may, if he chooses, appoint a D.C.L. or B.C.L. to sit as his assessor for the better despatch of business. The so-called 'Proctorial System' for the control of students forms part of the

Chancellor's jurisdiction. This jurisdiction is quite independent of the ordinary course of justice in the land; it usually takes the form of a fine in the case of students, but often that of suspension (rustication), or expulsion; it has also the power of 'discommuning' tradesmen *i.e.*, of forbidding them to have dealings with students, if they have abetted the extravagance of students by allowing them to run up heavy accounts; it has the power of incarcerating or excluding from the city limits after daylight any persons of immoral character who have had dealings with students. This system has its counterpart at Cambridge, where the place of incarceration has been known from time immemorial by the name of "spinning-house."

(*e*) Two burgesses, are elected to represent the University in Parliament; all members of Convocation are electors.

(*f*) The Registrar is elected by Convocation, must attend all meetings of the Hebdomadal Council of both Congregations, and of Convocation, and must register all Acts of the University that require the common seal. His annual stipend is £600.

University Professorships.—The following is a list of the chief professorships in the University of Oxford:

(1) Regius professorships of Divinity, Civil Law, Medicine, Hebrew, and Greek. These five professorships were founded by King Henry VIII., and to each is still assigned the yearly stipend of £40; but this endowment has in every case been augmented. To the chairs of Divinity and Hebrew is annexed a canonry of Christ Church. The stipend of the professor of Greek is made up to £500

a year from Christ Church. The professorships of Medicine and of Civil Law have been connected with other stipendiary offices, or been further endowed.

(2) Margaret Professorship of Divinity, the oldest in the University, was founded in 1502, by Margaret, Countess of Richmond, mother of Henry VII. The Professor is elected by all Graduates in Divinity, and those members of congregation who are at least in deacon's orders.

(3) Savilian Professorships of Geometry and Astronomy. founded and endowed in the year 1619 by Sir Henry Savile, warden of Merton college. The Professors may be chosen from any part of Christendom. They are elected by the Archbishop of Canterbury, the Lord High Chancellor of Great Britain, the Chancellor of the University, the Bishop of London, the Home Secretary, the two Chief Justices, the Chief Baron of the Exchequer, the Dean of the Arches, and the Warden of New College, with the Vice-Chancellor of the University. The endowment of each chair now amounts to £675 a year.

(4) Sedleian Professorship of Natural Philosophy, founded by Sir William Sedley in 1621. The electors are the Vice-Chancellor, the Provost of Queen's College, the President of the Royal Society of London, the Astronomer Royal, and alternately the President of Magdalen and the Warden of All Souls'. The stipend is £570 a year.

(5) Whyte's Professorship of Moral Philosophy, founded by Thomas Whyte, D.D., Canon of Christ Church. The Professor is elected for life, and the electors are the Vice-Chancellor, the two Proctors, the Dean of Christ Church, the Presidents of Magdalen and St John's, the

Margaret Professor, the Vinerian Professor, and the Professors of Modern History and Logic. The stipend is augmented to £400 out of the University chest.

(6) Camden Professorship of Ancient History, founded in 1622 by William Camden, Clarencieux King at Arms. The Professor is elected by Convocation and his stipend augmented to £600 out of the University chest.

(7) Professorship of Music, founded by William Heather, Doctor in Music, 1626. The Professor is elected for life by certain heads of colleges and professors.

(8) Laudian Professorship of Arabic, founded in 1636, by William Laud, Archbishop of Canterbury and Chancellor of the University. The stipend is now fixed at £300. The professor is elected by eight specified persons—four heads of colleges and four professors; in the case of an equality, the Vice-Chancellor has a casting vote.

(9) Professorship of Botany; in connection with the Botanic Garden, founded by the Earl of Danby in 1622-33. The chair was endowed in 1728 by W. Sherard, D. C. L., with £3,000 and since 1855 by an annual payment from the University of £100; to the same foundation is attached a professorship of Rural Economy with a stipend of £200 a year.

(10) Professorship of Poetry, founded in 1708, with a yearly stipend of £100. The Professor is elected by members of Convocation for five years, on the expiration of which he may be re-elected for five years more.

(11) The Lord Almoner's Professorship of Arabic, with a yearly stipend of £50; the Professor is appointed by the Lord High Almoner.

(12) Regius Professorship of Modern History, founded by King George I., in 1724 with an annual stipend of £621.

(13) Professorship of Experimental Philosophy, founded by Lord Crew and first filled in 1749. The Professor is elected by a board consisting of the Vice-Chancellor, the Warden of Wadham and three specified Professors; the stipend is £500 annually.

(14) Vinerian Professorship of English Law. In 1755 Charles Viner left £12,000 to the University for a professorship and certain scholarships in English law.

(15) Clinical Professorship, in connection with the Radcliffe Infirmiary, founded by the Earl of Lichfield, in 1780 and endowed with £7,000; the *ex-offico* trustees of this fund are the Chancellor, the Bishop of Oxford, the President of St. Johns.' The professor is elected by Convocation.

(16) Rawlinsonian Professorship of Anglo-Saxon, founded in 1795 and open to all members of Convocation; the range of the lectures includes the language and history of the Anglo-Saxons, the old Low-German dialects, and the antiquities of northern Europe. The Professor is elected in Congregation, and the stipend is made up by the University to £300 a year.

(17) Aldrichian Professorships of Anatomy, Practice of Medicine and Chemistry, founded in 1798 by George Aldrich, and endowed with a sum of £12,950; the first is now annexed to the Linacre Professorship of Physiology, and the second to the Regius Professorship of Medicine; the third is suppressed and its stipend applied to the payment of an assissant or demonstrator.

(18) Professorships of Mineralogy and Geology endowed by the Prince Regent, afterwards George IV., with a stipend of £100 each; the University has augmented them by a further annual sum of £150 to the former, and £300 to the latter. The Professors are appointed by the Vice-Chancellor.

(19) Professorship of Political Economy, founded in 1825 by Henry Drummond; the professor is elected by Convocation. He must be a graduate of Oxford, and has a stipend made up by the University to £400 a year; he is elected for five years but is re-eligible.

(20) Boden Professorship of Sanskrit. The late Joseph Boden, Colonel in the East India Company's service, left his property to the University for promoting the study of Sanskrit; a Professorship and scholarships have been established. The Professor is elected by Convocation, and his stipend, now £900, may not exceed £1,000.

(21) Professorship of Logic. The Professor is elected by Convocation, at a salary of £400 a year.

(22) Regius Professorships of Pastoral Theology and Ecclesiastical History, established by Her Majesty, Queen Victoria, in 1842.

(23) Professorship of the Exegesis of Holy Scripture, founded by John Ireland, D.D., Dean of Westminster, who bequeathed, in 1842, £10,000 to the University for this purpose. The Professor is elected by the heads of colleges and halls.

(24) Corpus Professorship of Latin Literature, founded in 1854 by the President and Fellows of Corpus Christi College, according to the intention of their founder, Bishop Fox, and endowed with an annual stipend of

£900. The Professor is elected by the Vice-Chancellor, the two Proctors, the President and one Fellow of Corpus, three specified Professors of the University, the public orator and three examiners in classics.

(25) Chichele's Professorships of International Law and of Modern History, founded in connection with All Souls' College, in 1854. The Professors are elected by the Visitor and Warden of the College, the Lord High Chancellor, Judge of the High Court of Admiralty, and the Foreign Secretary.

(26) Waynflete Professorships of Moral and Metaphysical Philosophy, and of Chemistry, founded in 1854 in connection with Magdalen College, with a stipend of £600 a year each; the Professors are elected by the Chancellor of the University, the Visitor and President of the College, and two other persons.

(27) Linacre Professor of Physiology, founded in 1854, in connection with Merton College, and endowed with an annual stipend of £800. The Professor is elected by the Visitor and Warden of Merton, and the presidents of the College of Physicians, the College of Surgeons and the Royal Society.

(28) Hope Professorship of Zoology, founded in 1861, by the Rev. Frederick William Hope, to whose munificence the University also owes a large entomologcial collection, a library of natural history, and a vast collection of engraved portraits; to the endowment of the professorship and the care of the collections, Mr. Hope and subsequently his widow, transferred to the University sums amounting to nearly £22,000.

(29) Professorship of Comparative Philology, founded by the University in 1868 and endowed with a stipend of £600 a year. The election is vested in the Vice-Chancellor and five professors, (of ancient languages), the Vice-Chancellor having a casting vote.

(30) Corpus Professorship of Jurisprudence, founded in 1869 by the President and Fellows of Corpus Christi College, and endowed with a stipend of £600 a year. The professor is elected by two specific professors, two lawyers selected by the College, (and approved of by Convocation), and one deputed member of the College.

(31) Slade Professorship of Fine Art, founded in 1869, and endowed with a capital sum of £12,000. The Professor is elected for three years only, but can be re elected. The election is made by a board of seven persons.

(32) Readership of Ancient History, instituted by statute in 1868, and endowed with a stipend of £200 a year from the revenue of Brasenose College; the Reader is elected by a board of seven persons, two of whom are the Principal and one fellow of Brasenose.

(33) Professorship of Chinese, instituted in 1876 and endowed with a sum of £3,000 raised by promoters of the study of Chinese; to this are added the proceeds of a Corpus Fellowship, and an annual sum of £100 from the University.

(34) Professorship of Celtic, founded in 1876 by the Principal and Fellows of Jesus College, and endowed by them with £500 a year; to this the University adds an annuity of £100.

(35) Readership in Roman Law, founded in 1881, the Reader to be appointed from time to time for periods of

three years; the Reader must lecture and give private instruction; he receives an annual stipend of £400 from revenues of All Souls' College.

Teacherships of Modern European Languages. In fulfilment of the intention of Sir Robert Taylor, and in connection with the Taylor Institution, there are teachers of German, French, Italian, and Spanish, appointed (with the approval of Convocation), by the Curators of the Institutions; each receives an annuity of £200 and a fee of £1 from everyone who attends a course of lectures.

Teacherships of Hindustani and Persian, and of Telugu, and Readerships in Indian History and Indian Law; founded by the University in 1878 in view of the needs of selected candidates for the India Civil Service. Each receives an annual sum of about £300; the Teachers are appointed for three years, the Reader for seven years.

Courses of Study and Examinations.—The various bodies that regulate the work and conduct the examinations are as follows:—

1. The Boards of Faculties:—Every faculty or branch of study at the University is controlled by a Board, at whose head is a chairman, annually elected by members of the Board, but the Faculty of Arts has three separate Boards, viz., in Literae Humaniores or Classics, in Oriental Languages, and in Modern History. These Boards are made up in about equal proportions of two distinct kinds of members, viz, (a) the University Professors, who are *ex officio* members of the Board or Boards controlling those branches of study to which their professorships belong; and (b) a number of fellows or tutors from the different colleges whose membership is the re-

sult of election. Each Board of Faculties has the duty of regulating, from time to time, the amount and nature of the work to be included in the honor examinations of the Faculty controlled by that Board; each Board has also the further duties of electing representatives to sit on the various Board of Studies, and of appointing members to form a committee for the nomination of examiners.

2. The Boards of Studies:—These Boards exist for the purpose of supervising the work in the pass (as opposed to the honor) examinations, and consist of: (a) Representatives elected by the Boards of such Faculties as are concerned in the examination, and (b) members added by co-optation. The following is the constitution of the Board of Studies regulating Responsions (Matriculation):—

(a) Four members (to serve for two years); two being annually elected by the Board of Faculty of Arts (Classics) one by the Board of Arts (Orientals), and one by the Board of Faculty of Natural Science.

(b) Three members (one to retire each year), added by co-optation from the number of those who have examined in Matriculation during any of the three preceding years.

The Board of Studies for Pass Moderations and Pass Finals are similarly constituted. At present two of the Honor departments of the final schools are supervised by a Board of Studies, not by a Board of Faculties: These are the Honor Finals in Orientals and the Honor Finals in English Language and Literature; the latter department of Honors was instituted for the first time only in 1894, and the first examination held in 1896; its

Board of Studies is thus made up: The chief Professor of Greek, of Latin, of Celtic, of Anglo-Saxon, of English, of Comparative Philology, two professors of Modern History, and the Professor of Poetry, such Professors as may be added by decree, and eight elected members; the Board so constituted may further, from time to time, add three members by co-optation.

3. Examiners:— Those who actually conduct the examinations and correct the papers of the students, are nominated by special committee. These committees must have at least six members each, viz., three *ex officio* members (*i. e.*, the Vice-chancellor and the two Proctors) and three members chosen by the Board or Boards of Faculties concerned in the examination. The persons nominated by these committees must before actual appointment be approved by Congregation and Convocation. The examiners at Responsions, Moderations, and Final Schools, are known respectively as Masters of the Schools, Moderators, Public Examiners; they need not be members of the University and are re-eligible after the expiration of one year from the termination of their former service. The Masters of the Schools are six in number, nominated annually, and serving for not more than two years in succession. The Moderators are fourteen in number, five for Honors in Classics and three for Honors in Mathematics, to serve for not more than two successive years; and six for Pass Moderations to serve for three examinations.

The Public Examiners are nearly sixty in number, viz., eighteen for Pass Candidates; seven for the Preliminary Examination in Science; three for the Preliminary Examination in Jurisprudence; and in the Honor Schools (Finals)—five in Literae Humaniores, three in Mathematics, six in Natual Science, three in Jurisprudence, five in Modern History, three in Theology and three in English Language and Literature. These all hold office during three examinations. It is further provided that no two persons who are members of the same College or Hall shall be nominated to serve at the same time as examiners in the same department of the same school. This provision is due to the intimate relations subsisting between the Fellows or Dons of a College and the students or undergraduate members of such College; the admission of two examiners in the same subjects at the same time from the same College, would create suspicion (if not danger) of favoritism towards examiners of that College

University Scholarships. — (1) Craven scholarships, founded by Lord Craven in 1647, are six in number, tenable for three years with an annual stipend of £80 a year each. Two scholars are elected annually, and candidates must have passed the second public examination and not exceeded twenty-four terms from the date of their matriculation. The subjects of examination are Greek and Latin.

(2) Travelling fellowships, founded by Dr. Radcliffe in 1714, are three in number of the annual value of £200, and tenable for three years. Candidates must have passed all the examinations necessary for the B.A. degree and obtained a first-class in one of the public examinations, or a university prize or scholarship. The Fellowships are intended for medical students and the examination is in Medical Science.

(3) Vinerian scholarships are three in number, tenable for three years, each with an annual stipend of £80. One scholar is elected annually after an examination in Civil Law, International Law, General Jurisprudence, and especially English Law.

(4) The Ireland scholarships, founded by Dean Ireland in 1825 and endowed with a capital sum of £4,000, for the promotion of Classics (Greek and Latin); they are four in number and tenable for four years, one scholar being elected annually. Candidates must be undergraduates and not have exceeded the sixteenth term from their matriculation.

(5) Eldon Law scholarship, established in 1830, tenable for three years. Candidates must be members of the Church of England and of the University of Oxford, must have passed the examinations required for the B.A. degree, and have obtained at least one first-class; they must also intend to follow the profession of Law.

(6) Boden scholarships in Sanskrit, established by the Court of Chancery in 1830 and 1860. One scholar is elected each year and holds his scholarship for four years with an annual stipend of £50.

(7) Mathematical scholarships, four in number, two senior and two junior, with an annual stipend of £30 each. One scholar is elected annually to each of the two classes, senior and junior. Candidates for the Senior Scholarships must have passed all examinations required for the B.A. degree, and not have exceeded their twenty-fifth term from matriculation. Candidates for the Junior scholarships must not have exceeded their eighth term from matriculation. The scholarships are tenable for two years.

(8) Pusey and Ellerton scholarships for the promotion of Theology through Hebrew, three in number, each of the value of £50 and tenable for three years. One scholar is elected annually and may not be above twenty-five years of age.

(9) Denyer and Johnson scholarships in Theology, two in number, of the annual value of £50 each, and tenable for one year. Any B. A. who has not exceeded twenty-seven terms from his matriculation may be a candidate.

(10) Hertford scholarship for the promotion of Latin, founded in 1834, and endowed with a capital sum of £1,110, tenable for one year. Candidates must not have completed two years from their matriculation.

(11) Taylor scholarships of Modern Languages. One scholarship of £50 and one exhibition of £25, each tenable for one year, are awarded annually for proficiency in one or more of the modern languages, a year's notice is given of the language chosen for the next competition. Candidates must not have exceeded their twenty-third term from matriculation.

(12) Burdett-Coutts scholarships, two in number, and tenable for two years, one being awarded each year; these scholarships have for endowment a capital sum of £5,000; they are for the promotion of geological study; candidates must have passed all examinations necessary for the B.A. degree and not have exceeded their twenty-seventh term from matriculation.

(13) Abbott scholarships for the sons of clergymen of the Church of England, who require pecuniary assistance at the University.

(14) Derby scholarship, open to candidates who have completed their twentieth and not exceeded their twenty-fourth term; candidates must have received the following distinctions: (1) First-class honors in Classical Moderations; (2) First-class honors in Classical Finals, or second class honors, together with two of the three Chancellor's prizes—one of which must be Latin Verse; (3) Two of the three Classical University Scholarships, viz., the Hertford, Ireland, and Craven Scholarships.

(15) Davis Chinese scholarship, of the annual value of £50 and tenable for two years, is open to all candidates who have not exceeded their twenty-eighth term.

University Prizes.—The subjects for all prize compositions are announced about midsummer, and each candidate is required to send in this composition under a sealed cover and distinguished only by a motto, his name and the same motto being enclosed separately.

(1) The Chancellor's prizes for (1) Latin Verse, candidates not to have exceeded their fourth year; (2) English essay; (3) Latin essay, candidates not to have exceeded their seventh year.

(2) English verse, Sir Roger Newdigate's prize; candidates not to have exceeded their fourth year.

(3) Ellerton Theological prize; open to candidates between the sixteenth and twenty-eighth terms from their matriculation.

(4) English poem on a sacred subject; this prize is awarded every three years, and is open to all candidates who have passed the examinations required for the degree of B. A.

(5) Arnold historical essay, awarded annually, the subjects being Ancient and Modern History in alternate years; no candidate must have exceeded his eighth year from matriculation.

(6) Stanhope historical essay, of the annual value of £20, to be awarded in books, on a subject of Modern History; no candidate must have exceeded his sixteenth term.

(7) The Gaisford prizes, in Greek verse and Greek prose; no candidate must have exceeded his seventeenth term.

(8) Johnson Memorial prize essay, awarded every four years for an essay on Astronomy or Meterology; two years' notice of the subject is given.

(9) Hall and Hall-Houghton prizes, awarded annually, two in the Greek Testament, two in the Septuagint, and one in the Syriac Version of the Scriptures.

(10) Marquis of Lothian's historical prize essay, on a subject of foreign history in the period between the dethronement of Romulus Augustulus and the death of Frederick the Great; candidates must not have exceeded their twenty-seventh term.

(11) The Conington prize, awarded every three years for a dissertation in English or Latin on a subject of classical learning, open to candidates between the sixth and fifteenth years from matriculation.

(12) The Cobden prize, awarded every three years for an essay on some subject bearing on Political Economy.

University Institutions.—(1) Bodleian Library, founded by Sir Thomas Bodley and opened in 1602; it is open every week-day to graduates of the University and any other person who presents a satisfactory recommendation; an adjoining building known as the Camera serves as a reading room in connection with the Bodleian Library; it contains all the newest works and is available for the use of other books, printed or manuscript.

(2) Clarendon Press, a new building completed in 1830; in the south part the Oxford Bibles and Prayer Books are printed; in the north part, all other books.

(3) Sheldonian Theatre, opened in 1669, used for academical ceremonies.

(4) Ashmolean Museum, completed in 1683; its basement is the repository of the Arundel marbles, etc.; the first floor is a museum of antiquities, and the top floor an examination room.

(5) The Clarendon Building, erected partly from the profits of the sale of the Lord Chancellor Clarendon's History of the Rebellion, the copyright of which was given to the University. The University Press was not set up here until 1830; it is now used for meetings of the Hebdomadal Council, of University delegates, and so forth.

(6) Radcliffe Library, opened in 1749; its scientific works have now been placed in the University Museum Library, and the building, now known as the Camera, serves as a reading-room (cf. 1 supra.)

(7) Radcliffe Observatory built in 1772, daily meteorological and frequent astronomical observations are made here.

(8) Taylor Institution (cf. Modern Language Teacherships connected herewith); this building contains a library and the leading foreign periodicals; it is open to

all members of the University and other literary persons.

(9) University Galleries, forming the central and western portions of the building, of which the Taylor Institution is the eastern; it is open daily; connected with it is the Ruskin Drawing School, established by John Ruskin in 1872.

(10) University Museum, erected by the University in 1855; it contains lecture rooms, workshops and laboratories, library and reading room.

(11) University Observatory, provided with a large refracting telescope of the highest order (1873), and presented with a large reflecting telescope and other astronomical apparatus.

The Colleges.— The Colleges, over twenty in number, are distinct corporate bodies, founded at various times for the purpose of study, and nearly all of them for the purpose of education also; within the University, but independent of it; governed, as to their own concerns, by their respective statutes; each having a mansion for the residence of members of the Foundation and for the reception of academical students; and holding property of various kinds through the munificence of founders and benefactors.

The corporation of a College comprises a Head, Fellows and Scholars in various numbers, and a few other members whose offices and titles differ in different societies. All these are members of the Foundation, and receive stipends from the corporate revenues. The Head and fellows are the governing body in each College. The Colleges contain also undergraduates or students, varying in numbers, according to the size and popularity of the College, from 50 to 200; each of these students is under the control of his College and has assigned to him a Tutor, one of the College Fellows, who arranges his work, and to whom the student is responsible for his private study and attendance at lectures.

The Resident Fellows, besides acting as Tutors to undergraduate members of their College, are also appointed by their College as Lecturers in Subjects required by the University examinations; it is the College Lectures, and not those of University Professors, that undergraduates attend in view of the examinations for which they are reading; these Lectures are thrown open by a system known as 'Inter-Collegiate' to members of any College.

The following are the Colleges in the University :—

(1) University College, said to have been founded in the year 872 by Alfred the Great. It was restored by William of Durham, who died in 1249. The present foundation consists of a Master, twelve Fellows, together with one Civil Law Fellow and eighteen Scholars, with certain Exhibitioners (*i.e.*, holders of an Exhibition or Minor Scholarship.) The number of undergraduate members of this College in 1884 was 103.

(2) Balliol College, founded by John Balliol and his wife (parents of John Balliol, King of Scotland), between 1263 and 1268. There are on the foundation the Master, 14 Fellows, and 33 Scholars. The number of undergraduate members (in 1884) was 265.

(3) Merton College, first founded at Maldon in Surrey in 1264, and removed to Oxford before 1274 by Walter de Merton, Bishop of Rochester, and Lord High Chan-

cellor of England. The foundation consists of a Warden, 20 Fellows, 19 Post-Masters (*i.e.*, a, form of Scholar), 3 Exhibitioners and 2 Chaplains. The number of undergraduates (in 1884) was 134.

(4) Exeter College, founded in 1314 by Walter de Stapledon, Bishop of Exeter. The foundation consists of a Rector, 12 Fellows, 28 Scholars and 15 Exhibitioners. The number of undergraduates (in 1884) was 164.

(5) Oriel College, founded by Edward II. in, 13.6. The foundation consists of a Provost, 15 Fellows, 10 Scholars and about 6 Exhibitioners. The number of undergraduates (in 1884) was 103.

(6) Queen's College, founded 1340 by Robert de Eglesfield, Chaplain to Philippa, Queen of Edward III. The College consists of a Provost, some 15 Fellows and 25 Scholars, and 2 Bible-Clerks (a sort of Exhibitioner); there are also some 27 Exhibitioners, but these are not open to the public, being confined to particular schools or Shires of England. The number of undergraduates (in 1884) was 128.

(7) New College, founded in 1386 by William of Wykeham, for a Warden, 70 Fellows and Scholars, 10 Chaplains, 3 Clerks, and 16 Choristers. Fellowships are of 3 kinds:—(*a*) Professor Fellowships; (*b*) Not more than 10 Tutorial Fellowships; (*c*) Not less than 14 Ordinary Fellowships. The Scholarships are of 2 classes:— (*a*) Winchester (about 24, 6 annually); (*b*) Open Scholarships (about 16, 4 annually). The number of undergraduates (in 1884) was 200.

(8) Lincoln College, founded by Richard Fleming, Bishop of Lincoln. in 1427. It consists of a Rector, 10 Fellows, and 14 Scholars The number of undergraduates (in 1884) was 65.

(9) All Souls College, founded in 1437 by Henry Chichele, for a Warden, 40 Fellows, 2 Chaplains, and 8 Clerks. The Statutes provide for the following Fellowships: 14 to be filled after examination in Law and History; 7 to be filled after examination in other subjects; 7 to be filled by a board of persons (5 belonging to the College), tenable on condition of undertaking some literary or scientific work; 3 tenable in connection with certain College offices by late Fellows; 2 tenable in connection with certain University offices by late Fellows; 12 tenable by persons who have been Fellows under the provisions of these Statutes; 5 tenable in connection with 5 Professorships, in International Law, Modern History, Civil Law, English Law, and Political Economy. There are also 4 Bible Clerks; the College is not intended for students, but chiefly for Fellows and Professors in Law and in History; it contains a valuable library (chiefly legal books) known as the Codrington. The number of undergraduates (in 1884) was 5.

(10) Magdalen College, founded in 1458 by William of Waynflete, for a President, 40 Fellows, 30 Scholars (called Demies), and certain other persons; 6 of the Fellowships are attached to Professorships. The number of undergraduates (in 1884) was 130.

(11) Brasenore College, founded in 1509 for a Principal and 12 Fellows; there are about 10 open scholarships, 14 close scholarships and some exhibitions. The number of undergraduates (in 1884) was 123.

(12) Corpus Christi College, founded in 1516; by the statutes now in force it is to consist of a President, 5 Professorial Fellows, 5 or 6 Official Fellows, 3 Extraordinary Fellows, 14 Ordinary Fellows, and 36 Scholars; it has also some Exhibitions. The number of undergraduates (in 1884) was 69.

(13) Christ Church, projected by Cardinal Wolsey and and established by Henry VIII. in 1546; it consists of a Dean, 6 Canons, 101 Students, 6 Chaplains and other Cathedral functionaries; the body of students is now split up into students (equivalent to Fellows), Junior students and scholars. There are also many exhibitions. The number of undergraduates (in 1884) was 242.

(14) Trinity College, founded in 1554 for a President, 12 Fellows, and 12 Scholars; there are now 10 Fellows and about 20 Scholars. The number of undergraduates (in 1884) was 121.

(15) St. John's College, founded 1555. Under the present Statutes the foundation is to consist of (*a*) Not less than 14 Fellowships; (*b*) Not less than 28 Scholarships, 6 of which are open, and 15 are appropriated to Merchant Taylors' School; (*c*) 4 Senior Scholarships (Merchant Taylors'). The number of graduates (in 1884) was 115.

16 Jesus College, founded by Queen Elizabeth in 1571. The College consists of a Principal and at least 10 Fellows; there are also about 24 scholars on the foundation; natives of Wales or Monmouth are specially privileged in this Society. The undergraduates (1884) numbered 70.

(17) Wadham College, founded about 1613 for a Warden, 15 Fellows and 15 Scholars, besides some other officers. There are now 10 Fellows and 18 Scholars. The number of undergraduates (1884) was 56.

(18) Pembroke College, founded in 1624 by King James I., at the costs and charges of two other gentlemen; the present constitution consists of a Master and not less than 10 Fellows and 12 Scholars. There are at present 23 Scholarships. The undergraduates (1884) number 81.

(19) Worcester College, established originally, as Gloucester Hall, as a school for Benedictine Monks in 1283, was incorporated under its present title in 1714. By the present statutes it consists of a Provost, 9 Fellows, and 19 Scholars. Its undergraduates were (in 1884) 116.

(20) Keble College, built by subscription in memory of John Keble, was incorporated in 1870; it has special regard for economy and Church of England principles. The College is governed by a Warden and a Council of at least 9 members. In 1884 it had 10 Tutors and Lecturers, 12 Scholars, 3 Exhibitioners, and undergraduates to the number of 178.

(21) Hertford College, constituted at first in 1282; reorganized in 1740; dissolved in 1805, and finally re-constituted in 1874; it consists at present of a Principal, 19 Fellows, and 40 Scholars. In 1884 it had 88 undergraduates.

(22) St Mary Hall, established for educationnl purposes in 1333; it possesses a Principal, Vice-Principal, 2 Lecturers and 2 Exhibitioners, and its undergraduate members (1884) amounted to 42.

(23) New Inn Hall, once known as Trilleck's Inn, was used from 1642 to 1646 as a mint for Charles I., where the plate of Colleges and Halls was melted down for his Majesty's gracious use. In 1831 it was restored to the purposes of Academical instruction. It possesses a Principal and an Assistant, and 60 undergraduates.

(24) St Edmund Hall, said to derive its name from the Archbishop of Canterbury under Edward III. In 1557 it came into the possession of Queen's College, which retains the right of appointing the Principal, and admits members to the lectures at Queen's College. It contains a Principal, Vice-principal and 36 undergraduates.

(25) Private Halls: in accordance with a Statute of 1882:

(*a*) Charsley's Hall: Licensed Master. W. H. Charsley, M.A.; undergraduates 38. (*b*) Turrell's Hall: Licensed Master, Rev. H. T. Turrell, M.A., and 5 undergraduates. There are also two Colleges (or rather Halls) for women students, but they are not part of the University; these students are admitted to Lectures at Colleges, and to University Examinations; by special grace of the University they are included in the Honor or Pass Lists of Examinations, but no Degrees are granted to them.

The Students.—Most of the students at the University are members of a College or Hall, but not all. In 1868 persons were first permitted, under certain conditions, to become members of the University without being members of any College or Hall. Such persons keep their statutable residence in houses or licensed lodgings in the town, with the same rights of profiting by Professors' lectures, of competing for University prizes, of attaining distinction in the Public Examinations, and of being admitted to Degrees, and to all the consequent privileges, as are enjoyed by other students.

The reception of students into the University under the prescribed conditions, and the exercise of discipline over them during their residence in Oxford, are committed to a delegacy consisting of the Vice-Chancellor, the Proctors, a Censor, and three members of Convocation nominated by the Vice-Chancellor and Proctors, to hold office for six years. The Censor, who is similarly nominated, holds office for five years. The students are under the supervision of the Censor, who is charged with the care of their conduct and studies. There are also Tutors appointed by the delegates to give instruction to the students. The total number of students at the University (in 1884) amounted to 3,086; of these 269 were non-collegiate (or unattached) students.

Examinations.—There are four terms in each year, and the usual course for students extends over four years, though it may be taken in three years. The average age at which students proceed to the University is nineteen years, as most of the open scholarships at the various Colleges are for persons who have not exceeded their nineteenth year, and the English Public Schools retain pupils till the close of their nineteenth year.

There are three examinations to be passed before the B. A. degree is conferred: (1) Responsions or Matriculation; (2) Moderations (the First Public Examination) or its substitute; (3) Final Schools (the Second Public Examination).

All examinations are of two kinds—Pass or Honor. The Matriculation is only a Pass Examination; that is, it represents a fixed standard to which all students (scholars and commoners) must attain before they can be admitted to other examinations as members of the University; those who fall short of this standard fail; among those who exceed the standard there is no distinction of merit. Moderations and Finals are either Pass or Honor, according to the choice or ability of the candidates; no candidate is debarred from writing on a Pass Examination by previous failures or lapse of time; but it is worthy of special attention that in the Honor Examinations, no candidate can try for Honors more than once, or after a fixed number of terms from the date of his Matriculation; In Moderations, no candidate can secure Honors after his eighth term; In the Final Schools, no candidate can try for Honors after his sixteenth term; unless, having secured Honors in or before that term in one Final School, he desires to secure Honors in a second Final School; in such cases there is an extension of time to the twentieth term.

Moderations (Honors) are held in Mathematics in December and June of every year; in Classics, in March of every year. Those who are not specialising in either of these subjects can either take Pass Moderations (after their fourth term), or avoid Moderations by taking an 'additional' subject at Responsions, provided they intend to take Honors in a Final School.

For those who intend to take Finals in Science or Law, there is, besides the 'additional' subject, a Preliminary

Examination (Pass), which can be taken at any time, and must be taken at some time before they enter for Honors in their Final School.

In Moderations there are three classes of Honors, in order of merit—first, second, or third—but in each class the names are arranged alphabetically, not in order of merit; in the Final Schools there are four classes of Honors, in order of merit, and with the names similarly arranged (alphabetically).

There is no examination or thesis required for the M.A. degree: it is granted as soon as the student has entered on his twenty-seventh term—representing the seven years' term of apprenticeship in the Guilds, before any one could become a Master.

Fees and Dues.—1. At Matriculation (*i. e.*, the formal ceremony before Vice-Chancellor)   £ s. d.   2 10 0

2. On entering a name before a Proctor:

	£	s.	d.
For Responsions (*i. e.*, Matriculation Examination)	2	2	0
For Additional Subject at Responsions	0	10	6
For Preliminary Examinations for Students of Music	1	1	0
For each part of the First Public Examination (Moderations)	1	1	0
For each of the Parts, A (1), A (3), A (4), B (2), B (5), in Pass Finals	1	1	0
For each of the other subjects of the Pass Schools (Finals)	0	10	6
For any Honor School, except Mathematics and Natural Science	2	2	0
For the School of Mathematics	1	11	6

For the School of Natural Science:
  (a) For each of the subjects in the Preliminary Examination 0 10 6
  (b) Final Honor Examination:
    (1) In Physics or Chemistry........ 2 2 0
    (2) In any other subjects.......... 1 1 0
Before each Examination in Civil Law 1 1 0
Before the Examination for the Degree of Master of Surgery.................... 5 0 0
Before Examination in Medicine:
  For each of the subjects, Organic Chemistry and Materia Medica 0 16 0
  For remaining subjects in either Examination for Degree of M.B. 1 11 6
Before each Examination in Music........ 2 0 0
After Examination in Music, before supplicating for degree of Mus. Bac........... 7 0 0
After Examination in Music, before supplicating for Degree of Mus. Doc.......... 2 0 0
Before each Examination in Preventive Medicine............................ 10 0 0

3. Before admission to the Degree of—
  B.A................................ 7 10 0
  M.A. 12 0 0
  B. Mus. 5 0 0
  D. Mus. 10 0 0
  B.C.L. or B.M...................... 6 10 0
  B.D................................ 14 0 0
  D.M., D.C.L., or D.D. 40 0 0

An additional sum of £5 is to be paid for degrees by accumulation, by decree, or in absence; and of £10.10s. for degrees by diploma.

4. To regain the right of voting in Convocation after one's name has been removed from the University Register—

	£	s	d.
Without residence	20	0	0
With 21 days' residence	10	0	0

5. Before incorporation (of Members of other other Universities)—

	£	s	d.
As an Undergraduate	1	0	0
As B.A.	8	0	0
As M.A., B.M., B.C L., or B.D.	15	0	0
As D.M., D.C.L., or D.D.	40	0	0
As B. Mus.	5	0	0
As D. Mus.	10	0	0

6. Besides these fees, every member of the University is charged with the payment of University dues; for each quarter of the first four years from Matriculation (unless the B.A. Degree has been taken before the expiration of this period), 10s.; for every subsequent quarter (or from the time of taking the B.A. Degree), 5s.; but all M.A.'s, or B.C.L.'s may compound by payment of a sum varying from £15 15s. 0d. to £6 9s. 0d., according to his age; this sum is computed by a graduated scale corresponding to periods of five years between the ages of 25 and 70.

Further Fees and Dues have to be paid by students in statu pupillari, as (1) Collegiate, or (2) Non-Collegiate members:

(1) Members of a College or Hall have to pay a deposit (known as caution-money) of nearly £20, at the commencement of their course, while in residence at College or the University (*i. e.*, for 3 or 4 years), they have

terminal bills to pay for board and lodging (either to the College or to their landlord, according as they are in-College or out-College students); for tuition; for building and repairs funds; also terminal College dues, which are heavier than those of the University, and last till the M.A. or an equivalent degree has been taken; also a charge is exacted by the College, nearly equal to that of the University, on the student's taking the degrees of B.A. or M.A.

2. The most economical way (and also the least popular) of attending the University is as a non-Collegiate member; such an unattached student has, besides the University dues and fees to pay, only the following charges, which have the advantage of being clearly defined by statute, viz.:

	£	s.	d.
1. On having his name entered on the books of the Delegacy for unattached students...	2	10	0
2. As caution-money while his name remains on those books	2	0	0
3. For each quarter of the first three years, during which his name is on the books, unless before then he has taken the B.A. degree	0	17	6
4. For every subsequent quarter, while his name is on the books	0	2	6

CHAPTER XVI.

THE UNIVERSITIES OF SCOTLAND.

The Scottish Universities occupy an important place among the great educational institutions of the world, both on account of their long and illustrious history, and of the peculiarly successful manner in which they have at all times kept in touch with the national aspirations and influenced directly the national life, fulfilling the supreme function of a university in reaching and drawing from all classes of the people, rich and poor.

There are four universities in Scotland; St. Andrew's, Glasgow, Aberdeen, and, Edinburgh. The University of St. Andrew's is the oldest of these, and although now the smallest of them all in point of the attendance of students, its past has been singularly brilliant, and being now a federation of colleges, the development of its constitution furnishes useful material for the study of university organization. It is true that the Universities (Scotland) Act, 1889, has brought the universities within the scope of a common, uniform system, and has changed the old systems radically, but to understand the prevailing order of things the better, it will be necessary to give a very brief historical sketch of the institutions concerned.

The University of St. Andrew's.—St. Andrew's has been in existence since 1411, the date of its foundation charter. It had its origin in the efforts of a few partriotic scholars who in 1410 began to lecture on Theology, Canon Law, Philosophy, and Logic. The success of the experiment thus made induced Bishop Henry Wardlaw to grant a charter of foundation, as stated, in 1411. The bulls conveying the Papal sanction were granted by Benedict XIII., the claimant for the Papal throne supported for the time being by Scotland. As no provision for buildings or endowments was made in the charter the work of the University was carried on in churches and in private chambers by the Doctors and Regents. These constituted a faculty with power to confer degrees upon such of their students as the Bishop might, after due examination and advising with the professors, deem worthy of them. The functions and powers of the officers of the University were somewhat curious The Rector could exercise jurisdiction over the citizens, and inflict civil punishment even on the civil magistracy. The members of the University enjoyed special rights and privileges denied to the other citizens. In the earlier days the faculty took a paternal interest in the students in matters beyond the range of their studies. For instance, a rule was laid down compelling the students to live in residence,—" collegialiter "—and for their accommodation hostels were opened by the several masters. The hostels were the cause of many disputes, as students could move from one residence to the other of them, and a rivalry sprang up between the masters. Then a common hall or pedagogy was erected, but some of the masters contended that their private hostels were better than a common hall and the outcome was that the experiment in furnishing a students' residence was practically abandoned for a time.

The University flourished and attracted public attention and bequests. Public spirited men desirous of emulating Bishop Wardlaw arose, and in the course of a period of less than one hundred and thirty years, there were three additional colleges founded in St. Andrew's under the patronage of church and state. These were St. Salvator's College, 1450; St. Leonard's College, 1512; and St. Mary's, 1537. During this period and the years immediately following, the University continued to enjoy public and royal favour and there were not wanting benefactors who lavished money upon it for equipment, bursaries, and buildings.

The relations between the faculty and the students of St. Leonard's College afford a glimpse of the kind of discipline considered necessary in those days. The particulars are taken from the old statutes of the College. "Religious observances played an important part of the students' duties. All were enjoined to speak the Latin tongue, and to express themselves with gravity, modesty, and civility. Menial offices of various kinds fell to the lot of the students. They had to sweep the whole place every Sunday, and engage in a general cleaning twice a year. They were forbidden to frequent the town, to hold nocturnal meetings, to carry knives, or to play football. Women were rigidly excluded from the college precincts." And yet, notwithstanding the severity of its code of rules, it is stated that the College of St Leonard became noted for the "latitude of its teaching and its sympathy with the new learning."

In one sense St. Mary's College is the oldest in the federated University. It represents the ancient St. John's Hall and the *pædagogium*. These old foundations secured the interest of Archbishop Alexander Stewart, the favourite pupil of Erasmus with that of the Beatons and the Melvilles, and they were reconstructed as St. Mary's College, still an integral part of the University.

The colleges drew their support from church benefactions, crown grants, and the transference of tiends from certain parishes to the use of the colleges. There were also endowments by private individuals. The funds were largely under the control of the Archbishop, who was the chief church potentate within the bounds of the ecclesiastical jurisdiction in which the colleges were situated.

The education of Scotland, in all its branches and grades, from the parochial school, the grammar school, to the university, was profoundly influenced by the Reformation. In St. Andrew's, one of the results was the re-organization of the work of the colleges. The colleges of St. Salvator and St. Leonard were restricted to the teaching of Philosophy, Law, and Medicine, and the College of St. Mary to Theology. In 1747 St. Salvator and St. Leonard were united into one corporation, known since then as the United College of St. Salvator and St. Leonard. Since the union until lately the changes have been mainly in the re-arrangement of the chairs and the duties of the professors. As an academical body the University consists of a Chancellor, Rector, Principals (one of the United College, and one of St. Mary's), Professors, Registered Graduates and Alumni, and Matriculated Students.

The University of Glasgow.—This institution also owes its origin to the church. The bull establishing the "*Studium Generale*" was granted by Pope Nicholas V., and is dated 1450. The local movers were headed by the Bishop of Glasgow, who, it seems, had the chief control of its affairs. The University consisted of "a Chancellor, Rector, the masters and doctors in the Faculties of Theology, Canon Law, and the Arts; and of the incorporated students in these faculties," on whom graduation degrees had been conferred. In the early days the University was almost entirely supported by the church, and by fees charged for degrees and for lectures. A residence was provided for the students in Arts, and this house was known as the *Pædagogium* or the College of Arts.

After the Reformation the Crown assumed control, and the form of government was prescribed by the King (James VI), in a charter which, besides the regulations alluded to, contained provisions for an increase of funds. With varying success, but with a gradual advance in usefulness and importance, the present century was reached, and during its course seventeen additional professorships have been founded, the complete list being: Mathematics (1691), Humanity (1706), Oriental Languages (1709), Civil Law (1712), Medicine (1712), Church History (1716), Anatomy (1718) Astromony (1760), Natural History (1807), Surgery (1815), Midwifery (1815), Chemistry (1817), Botany (1818), Materia Medica (1831), Institutes of Medicine (1839), Forensic Medicine (1839), Civil Engineering (1840), Conveyancing (1861), English Language and Literature (1861), Divinity and

Biblical Criticism (1861), Clinical Surgery (1874), Clinical Medicine (1874), Naval Architecture (1883), History (1893), Pathology (1893).

As showing the interest of the Government in the University, and the public spirit of the citizens of Glasgow an incident may be given, taken from a statement published by the University. It was in connection with the removal of the University buildings to a more suitable site than that which it occupied in the centre of the city :—

"The funds at the disposal of the University to carry out the scheme of removal consisted of—(1) £100,000 for sale of the old site ; (2) £17,000 obtained as compensation for a breach of contract with a railway company in a transaction for the sale of the old site ; (3) a sum of £21,400, promised by Government in aid of the scheme of removal, conditionally on a further sum of £24,000 being raised by public subscription, for the erection of a sick hospital in connection with the new University buildings." The amount was found to be inadequate and the Senate made an appeal for more money to the Government and the public. In a short time the citizens subscribed nearly £100,000, and the government realizing the public interest in the case, " announced their intention to ask Parliament for the sum of £120,000, in six annual payments, on condition of a like amount being raised by subscription and expended on the buildings." The sum stated was duly paid, and altogether the large amount of £256,429 was raised for the new buildings and the infirmary for the sick. The new University buildings were designed by Sir G. Gilbert Scott and were erected on Gilmore-hill, where the classes of the University met for the first time in the session of 1870-71.

The University of Aberdeen.—This University comprised two colleges, one founded by Bishop Elphinstone under the authority of a Papal bull dated 1494 at the instance of King James IV. Within this University there was founded in 1505 the College of St. Mary, afterwards known as King's College, the other, or second of the two colleges, was founded in 1593, and was named Marischal College, after its founder, George Keith, fifth Earl Marischal of Scotland, who acted under the authority of an Act of the Scots Parliament. The constitutions, powers, and functions of these colleges differed but slightly from those of the colleges already referred to at St. Andrew's and Glasgow. A fact on which the University prides itself is the success it has attained to in maintaining throughout its long career, a high academic ideal. As it sets forth, "a chief merit appertaining to it in this respect, has been the preservation of the system of graduation as marking the goal of a university course." With respect to this feature the Commission under the Universities Act of 1858, remarks:

"Among the Universities of Scotland a degree in Arts has, in Aberdeen only, continued to be recognized as the proper termination of a student's course. Both in King's and in Marischal College graduation has uniformly prevailed as a general rule, and the effect of the practice in stimulating the exertions of the students has been most beneficial. We are glad to observe from the returns with which we have been furnished, that the importance of graduation as a valuable part of the academical system is now receiving a wider recognition in the other universities also, and we are induced to believe that this is merely the beginning of a still greater advance in the same direction, which will result, we hope, in restoring graduation in arts to its proper position in all the universities."

This quotation is of interest, not only as showing the practice at Aberdeen, but also at the other universities of Scotland, on this important question.

It was not until the year 1860 that the Colleges of King's and Marischal were united and came under the operation of the general Act for the government of universities in Scotland. By ordinance No. 7 of the Commissioners appointed by the Act of 1858, the union was effected and the University constituted a corporate body consisting of a Chancellor, Rector, Principal, Professors, Registered Graduates and Alumni, and Matriculated Students.

The University of Edinburgh.—This institution owes its existence in a peculiar degree to the popular thirst for knowledge which was a distinguishing feature of the latter part of the sixteenth century, in Scotland. It sprang from a small college, called the "Town's College" on account of the latter having been established by the Town Council of Edinburgh, to meet the educational wants of the ratepayers. This was in 1583, and during the long period intervening between that year and 1858, the institution which meanwhile had attained to the full dignity and power of a great University, remained under "the absolute control and patronage of the Town Council of

Edinburgh." Since 1858, its government, has been vested in the Senatus Academicus, subject to the review and control of the University Court, as will be subsequently noticed. It is a corporation consisting of the Chancellor, Rector, Principal, Professors, Registered Graduates and Alumni and Matriculated Students.

It does not seem to have suffered under the management of the Town Council, for the buildings and equipment seem to have kept pace with the world-wide fame of the brilliant Professors who in an unbroken line have occupied its more important chairs. In the additions to its buildings from time to time Government co-operated with the city, and public subscriptions have largely swelled the necessary funds. The necessities of the School of Medicine becoming urgent, an appeal was made to the public in 1873 for subscriptions "for the purpose of purchasing a site for and erecting complete Class Rooms, Theatres, Laboratories, and Museums for the Faculty of Medicine, with the latest scientific improvements; for reorganizing the Class Rooms of the College for the Faculties of Arts, Divinity, and Law; for providing increased and more convenient accommodation for the University Library; for erecting a University Hall for conferring degrees, for holding examinations and other public and academic ceremonials; and for improving to some extent the north front of the College building."

The public subscription amounted to £148,548. The Government contributed £80,000; other sums brought the amount to the sum total of £244,587. The buildings were begun in 1878, partly opened in 1880 and completed for use in 1888. They were designed by R.

Rowand Anderson LL.D., Architect, and in them are placed the "Lecture Rooms, etc., of the Faculty of Medicine (excepting those of Botany and Natural History), the Museums of Practice of Physic, Anatomy, Chemistry, Obstetrics, Materia Medica, and Surgery; a Students' Reading Room, Students' Common Room, Faculty of Medicine Reception Room, and office of the Faculty.

If Glasgow has its "Bute Hall" for conferring degrees, for holding Sunday services, and for general convocation purposes, Edinburgh can boast of its "McEwan Hall" which is a magnificent pile. It is capable of holding 3,000 people. The space is apportioned as follows:—"A flat area, to be occupied by the graduates on ceremonial days; a raised amphitheatre of seats following the sweep of the semi-circle, and two galleries, also semi-circular in form, rising, one above the other. Immediately at the back of the amphitheatre is a vaulted fire-proof corridor and above the latter is the first gallery. The platform is placed on the straight side of the Hall with appropriate seats for the Chancellor, Rector, Principal, University Court, Senatus, Curators, etc." It is exceedingly handsome and worthy of the great University to which it has been donated.

University Government.—The historical notes and other particulars given in the foregoing pages will not only serve as an interesting background to the system of University government now in vogue, but aid in a better understanding of the great revolution effected by recent legislation. Sweeping changes were made in the constitutions of the Scottish Universities by the Universities (Scotland) Act 1858, and an approach made to a uniform system of government for them all. That Act was followed by several others having a bearing more or less upon the Universities, but they scarcely need be mentioned here. The next great step forward was taken in University consolidation when the Act of 1889 was passed. These two Acts (1858 and 1889) with the ordinances depending upon them furnish the constitution of the Scottish Universities of the present day.

The three bodies in which the government of the University is invested are: The University Court, the Senatus Academicus, the General Council. There is also a Universities Committee which shall come into existence as an active body after the expiry of the powers of the Commissioners appointed for the purpose of instituting the recent statutory changes.

The Universities Committee consists of the Lord President of the Privy Council, the Secretary for Scotland, the Lord Justice General, [Scotland], if a member of the Privy Council, the Lord Justice Clerk [Scotland] if a member of the Privy Council, the Lord Advocate [Scotland] if a member of the Privy Council, the Chancellor of each of the Universities, if a member of the Privy Council, the Lord Rector of each of the Universities, if a member of the Privy Council, one member at least of the Judicial Committee of the Privy Council and such other member or members of the Privy Council as Her Majesty may from time to time think fit to appoint.

The powers and duties of the Universities Committee may, subject to any rules or regulations which may from time to time be passed by Her Majesty in Council, be exercised and discharged by any three or more of the committee, one of whom shall be a member of the Judical Committee of the Privy Council, or one of Her Majesty's Senators of the College of Justice in Scotland. Briefly, the Universities Committee is the highest power, in a well-defined limit, in University Government. No new college can be affiliated to, and none affiliated can be withdrawn from, a University without the consent of the Universities Committee. The committee is the judge of the sufficiency of the endowment of any college seeking affiliation. No new professorship can be founded by the University Court without the approval of the Universities Committee.

Scottish University commissioners were appointed by the Act of 1889. Their powers are vast, but as they are not a permanent part of the constitution of the universities, but a temporary element, their work need not be described in detail. On the completion of their labours, they will be virtually succeeded by the University Court and the Universities Committee.

The University Court.—Of the three bodies directly charged with the government of the University, the University Court is the most important, possessing the most extensive powers. Hitherto the Senatus Academicus has had the administration of the property and revenues of the University; under the Act of 1889, the University Court has assumed the entire administration of the real property, and all revenues and endowments which are vested in the University Court by the Act The court reviews the acts of the Senatus, and appoints to all chairs whose patronage is or may in the future be, in the university (the exceptions being such as those appointed by the curators of Edinburgh University, and regius professors). They appoint examiners and lecturers. They define professors' duties (on application and subject to appeal), etc The constitution of the University Court of St. Andrew's differs from those of the other Universities. They are constituted as follows:

In St. Andrew's the Rector, the Principal, the Principal of St. Mary's College (theological), and the Principal of University College, Dundee (affiliated), an assessor nominated by the Chancellor, an assessor nominated by the Rector, the Provost of St. Andrew's for the time being, the Provost of Dundee for the time being, four assessors elected by the General Council, three assessors elected by the Senatus, and such number, not exceeding four in all, of representatives of affiliated colleges.

In Glasgow the Rector, the Principal, the Lord Provost of Glasgow for the time being, an assessor nominated by the Chancellor, an assessor nominated by the Rector, an assessor nominated by the Lord Provost, magistrates and town council of Glasgow, four assessors elected by the General Council, four assessors elected by the Senatus Academicus, such number, not exceeding four in all from affiliated colleges.

The members are drawn from the same sources and in equal numbers, in each section, in the Universities of Aberdeen and Edinburgh as in that of Glasgow.

Seven members of each University Court form a quorum. The Rector, and in his absence the Principal, shall preside at the meetings of the University Court. The University Court is a body corporate, with perpetual succession and a common seal, and in it is vested all the property heritable and moveable pertaining to the University. Its powers which apply alike to the four Scotch Universities are:

To review all decisions of the Senatus Academicus, and to be a Court of Appeal from the Senatus in every case, (except as otherwise provided in the Universities Act of 1858.)

To effect improvements in the internal arrangements of the University, after due communication with the Senatus Academicus, and with the sanction of the Chancellor, provided that all such proposed improvements shall be submitted to the University Council for their consideration.

To require due attention on the part of the professors to regulations as to the mode of teaching, and other duties imposed on the professors.

To fix and regulate, from time to time, the fees in the several classes.

Upon sufficient cause shown, and after due investigation, to censure a Principal or professor, or to suspend him from his office and from the emoluments thereof, in whole or in part, for any period not exceeding one year, or to require him to retire from his office on a retiring allowance, or to deprive him of his office: and during the suspension of any professor, to make due provision for the teaching of his class: Provided always, that no such sentence of censure, suspension, or deprivation, or requisition on a professor to retire from office, shall have any effect until it has been approved by her Majesty in Council.

To inquire into and control the administration by the Senatus Academicus, or Principal and professors of any college, of the revenue, expenditure, and all the pecuniary concerns of the University and of any college therein, including funds mortified for bursaries and other purposes.

In addition to the powers conferred upon it by the Act of 1858, the University Court, under the Act of 1889, has power—

To administer and manage the whole revenue and property of the University, and the college or colleges thereof existing at the passing of this Act, including the share appropriated to such University out of the annual Government grant, and also including funds mortified for bursaries and other purposes, and to appoint factors or collectors, to grant leases, to draw rents, and generally to have all the powers necessary for the management and administration of the said revenue and property.

To review any decision of the Senatus Academicus on a matter within its competency which may be appealed against by a member of the Senatus, or other member of the University having an interest in the decision, and to take into consideration all representations and reports made to it by the Senatus Academicus and by the General Council.

To review, on representation made by any of its members, or by any member of the Senatus Academicus, any decision which the Senatus Academicus may come to in the exercise of its powers in the regulation and superintendence of the teaching and discipline of the University. Provided always, that the University Court shall not review any decision of the Senatus Academicus in a matter of discipline, except upon appeal taken either by a member of the Senatus or by a member of the University directly affected by such decision.

To appoint professors whose chairs are, or may come to be, in the patronage of the University; to appoint examiners and lectures; and to grant recognition to the teaching of any college or individual teacher for the purposes of graduation.

To define on application by any member of the Senatus Academicus the nature and limits of a professor's duties under his commission, subject to appeal to the Universities Committee.

To take proceedings against a Principal or professor, University lecturer, assistant, recognized teacher or examiner, or any other person employed in teaching or examining without the necessity of anyone not a member of the Court appearing as prosecutor, and for the purpose of such proceedings to call before it any member of the University to give evidence, and to require the production of documents, and also to institute and conduct any such inquiries as it may deem necessary.

To appoint from among members of the University or others, not being members of the Senatus Academicus, one-third of the members of any standing committee or committees charged, with the immediate superintendence of any libraries or museums, or the contents thereof, belonging to the University and college or colleges thereof existing at the passing of this Act, and on representation made by any of its members, or by any member of the Senatus Academicus, to review any decision which the Senatus Academicus, in the exercise of its powers, may come to in respect of the recommendations of such committee or committees.

To appoint committees of its own number consisting of not less than five menbers, with powers to report on any business that may be entrusted to them by the University Court, or to carry out special instructions ordered by the University Court.

After the expiration of the powers of the Commission to found new professorships with the approval of the Universities Committee, and after such expiration no new professorship shall be founded except as provided in the Act.

The University Court has power to make such ordinances as it thinks fit, with the approval of Her Majesty in Council: (1) With respect to the appropriation of the sum allotted to the University out of the annual government grant; and (2) with respect to the altering or revoking any of the ordinances affecting the University which have been or may be framed and passed under the Universities (Scotland) Act, 1858, or the Act of 1889, and making new ordinances: Provided that such ordinances, before being submitted to Her Majesty for approval, shall have been communicated by the University Court to the Senatus Academicus and to the General Council, whose opinion thereon, if returned to the University Court within one month, shall have been taken into consideration; Provided also that the said ordinances, when finally adjusted by the University Court, shall have been communicated to the University Courts of the other universities, and that, if notice of dissent to such ordinances shall have been given by any University Court, or by any person directly affected by such ordinance, to the University Court making such ordinances, within one month after the receipt thereof, the dissenting University Court or person may within one month after notifying dissent make a representation in regard thereto to Her Majesty in Council; Provided further that no ordinance made under this section shall be of any validity until it has been approved by Her Majesty in Council, and that it shall be lawful for Her Majesty to refer such ordinances to the Universities Committee, who shall report to Her Majesty thereon ; Provided further, that such ordinances shall be laid before both Houses of Parliament in the manner provided by section twenty of the Act of 1889 ; Provided further, that in computing the period of one month for the purposes of this section, the months of August and September shall not be counted, nor any part thereof.

The Senatus Academicus.—The Senatus Academicus consists of the Principal and the whole of the professors in each University. Their duties are to superintend and regulate the teaching and discipline of the University. The Principal of the University is the President of the Senatus having a deliberative and casting vote. The Senatus appoints two-thirds of the members of any standing committee or committees charged with the immediate superintendence of libraries or museums. It receives in the first instance all reports by such committees and it may confirm, modify or reject the recommendations in such reports, subject to the review of the University Court. One-third of the Senatus constitutes a quorum.

The General Council.—The third body directly charged with a part in the government of the Universities is the General Council. It was instituted in 1858. It is composed of the Chancellor, professors, members of the University Court and all the graduates of the University. This body elects the Chancellor, who presides over its meetings. It also elects four assessors to represent it in the University Court. It is empowered " to take into consideration all questions affecting the well-being and prosperity of the University and to make representations from time to time on such questions to the University ourt, who shall consider the same, and return to the council their deliverance thereon." The Council holds two stated meetings a year, and may hold special meetings at the instance of the Chancellor, who must convene such meetings on a requisition from a quorum of members.

Financial Administration.—On the passing of the Universities Act 1889, Commissioners were appointed with almost absolute powers to construct the university system embodied in the provisions of the said Act. The revenues and funds, bursaries, etc., of the Universities from every source came within the scope of the Commission's sway and in the main passed from them, upon the expiry of their powers, or by their ordinance, in accordance with the statute, to the University Court to which the property was transferred in 1890. The real property is therefore vested in the University Court, and the endowments, bequests and bursaries (with some exceptions) are administered by the University Court, and without exception in accordance with ordinances with which the University Court can deal.

The Appointment of Professors and Examiners.—The appointment of professors and examiners rests with the University Court, with certain limitations, viz:—the chairs must be within the patronage of the University, such professorships as are in the appointment of the curators of the Edinburgh University have not been transferred to the University Court, Regius professors:—so that there is still a want of uniformity in the appointment of professors. In the case of one chair, in the University of Aberdeen, that of systematic theology, the professor is appointed by examination. Assistant professors, and lecturers are appointed by the University Court after consultation with the Senatus Academicus.

Assistants and lecturers shall be in all cases subject to the discipline of the Senatus and University Court.

The examiners for graduation in arts, science, law, divinity, medicine, etc., are the professors of or lecturers on, the subjects which qualify for Degrees and such additional examiners as the University Court may appoint.

Duties of the Chief Officers of the Universities.—The Chancellor is the chief officer of the University. He is elected (for life) by the general council and presides over its meetings. It is through him or his deputy, the vice-chancellor that degrees are conferred on persons found qualified by the Senatus.

The Vice-Chancellor is appointed by the Chancellor, but in no respect can he act for the Chancellor except in so far as the conferring of degrees are concerned.

The Lord Rector is elected by the vote of the Matriculated Students. He is president of the University Court. Before appointing his Assessor in that court he may confer with the Students' Representative Council, with the view of meeting their wishes in making his choice. He is regarded as the students' representative in the University Court, from the fact that he is elected to the position of Lord Rector by their votes.

The Principal is the resident head of the university. He is appointed, by the Crown, and in Edinburgh by the Curators. He is president of the Senatus, and guides its deliberations in the educational side of its work, as well as performing a considerable amount of executive work.

The Dean of Faculties, although still elected in one or two of the Universities by the Senatus, does not seem to have been recognized by the Act of 1889.

The Parliamentary Representative is elected by the General Council. Two University representatives are returned to Parliament from Scotland, Glasgow and Aberdeen from one constituency, and Edinburgh and St Andrew's, for the other.

The duties of the other officials will be sufficiently indicated by the designation of their offices;—Librarian, Curator of museum, Secretary to the University Court, Clerk of Senate, Registrar and Clerk of the General Council.

Bursaries.—The bursaries are administered by the University Court under the ordinances of the Commissioners, the purpose of the founders being kept generally in view.

The Curriculum.—The framing of the Curriculum of studies is under the supervision of the Senatus Academicus, but before entering on the Curriculum each student must pass a preliminary examination in English, Latin or Greek, mathematics, and one of the following:—Latin or Greek (if not already taken), French, German, Italian, Dynamics. The preliminary examinations are held twice each year, at the beginning and at the close of the session. They are conducted by a Joint Board appointed by the University Court, and consisting of four professors or lecturers and eight additional examiners. The standard of the examination and the character of the examination papers will be maintained by the Joint Board, but the examiners at each university will examine candidates for matriculation, and as soon as the answers of the candidates have been marked the examiners send them through the Senatus to the Joint Board. In each university each candidate, before presenting himself for any preliminary examination, must pay to the general fund of the university a fee of half a guinea.

Boards of Studies.—For the purpose of framing the Curriculum for the several departments of study necessary for a degree, the Senatus in each university is empowered to appoint Boards of Studies, corresponding as nearly as may be to the departments of study concerned. Before the end of each Winter Session each Professor and Lecturer in the said Departments of Study shall submit to the proper Board of Studies for its approval a syllabus of the subjects and books proposed for the work of his class for the next academical year. As soon as such approval has been given, the syllabus shall be transmitted to the Faculty of Arts for its consideration. The syllabus, with such observations as the Faculty of Arts may see fit to make thereon, shall then be transmitted to the Senatus for its sanction. Before the end of each winter session each Board of Studies shall prepare a scheme, defining, for the academical year next but one following, the classes which shall be deemed to be Honors classes, and the subjects and courses of reading for Honors in its Department, and shall report the same to the Faculty of Arts for its consideration. The scheme, with such observations as the Faculty of Arts may see fit to make thereon, shall then be transmitted to the Senatus for its sanction. Each Board shall in like manner make recommendations through the

Faculty of Arts to the Senatus in regard to the half courses which may be sanctioned, and the lectures which may be given on special subjects. The Principal and the Dean of Arts are *ex officio* members of each Board of Studies.

Examinations.—There are three classes of examinations:—(1) The preliminary, already described; (2) class examinations, consisting of verbal or oral and written examinations in the work of the class from day to day, which count on the public certificate of attendance on the classes, but not in obtaining a degree; (3) examination for degrees.

Candidates for the ordinary degree of Master of Arts may follow the curriculum and take their degree in the subjects recognized therein, or may vary the curriculum for graduation under specified regulations. In order to graduate with a degree, except Engineering, B.Sc. and B.L. Degree, the preliminary examination must be passed, then attendance on the prescribed courses, after which the examinations in the subjects prescribed for the degree are taken. For the degrees of LL.B. and B.D., candidates must have already passed in Arts. The degree examinations are, in general, conducted by the examiners appointed by the University Court, and consisting of the Professors in the various subjects, in conjunction with non-professional examiners, who are remunerated by the University Court. The standard of the examination in the various subjects is settled by these examiners, professorial and non-professorial, subject to general supervision and regulation by the Senatus. Questions of this kind would not come before the University Court, unless on appeal by a member of the Senatus. Reports from the examiners are submitted to the Senatus. An appeal would lie from the examiners to the Senate and from the Senate to the University Court, in reference to examinations, but this is almost unknown in practice. For degrees, examinations are held twice a year, March, April and October, November. Candidates must attend full courses in at least seven subjects, and be examined on these subjects, in order to qualify for the degree of M.A., of these subjects four must be Latin or Greek, English or a Modern Language or History, Logic and Metaphysics or Moral Philosophy, Mathematics or Natural Philosophy. The departments of study for graduation in Arts in each university includes:—

1. *Language and Literature.*

Latin.	Italian.
Greek.	Sanskrit.
English.	Hebrew.
French.	Arabic or Syriac.
German.	Celtic.

2. *Mental Philosophy.*

Logic and Metaphysics.	Education (Theory, History, and Art of)
Moral Philosophy.	Philosopy of Law.
Political Economy.	

3. *Science.*

Mathematics.	Zoology.
Natural Philosopy.	Botany.
Astronomy.	Geology.
Chemistry.	

4. *History and Law.*

History.	Constitutional Law and History.
Archæology and Art (History f).	Roman Law.
	Public Law.

The Degree of M.A., may be taken with Honors in any of the following groups, in which Honors shall have been established in at least two subjects:—

(a) Classics (i.e., Latin and Greek, with optional subjects, such as Comparative Philology, Ancient Philosophy, and Classical Archæology).
(b) Mental Philosophy.
(c) Mathematics and Natural Philosophy.
(d) Semitic Languages.
(e) Indian Languages.
(f) English (Language, Literature, and British History).
(g) Modern Languages and Literature.
(h) History.

Every Candidate must take up at least two subjects in which he must pass with Honors, and in the remainder secure the necessary standing for the ordinary degree.

Candidates obtaining first or second-class honors may, after a lapse of five years, become candidates for the degree of D. Sc., D. Phil., or D. Litt., according to the departmens in which they may have obtained honors. Such candidates must present a thesis or a published memoir, or work to be approved by the Senatus, and may also be subjected to a further examination if the Senatus think fit.

Candidates for the degree of B. Sc., in pure science or engineering, must attend courses of instruction in seven subjects selected as prescribed, extending over three academical years, and must undergo a first and a final science examination in which the subjects are grouped. Candidates who have taken the B. Sc. degree in pure science or engineering may proceed to the degree of D. Sc., under conditions similar to those described for D. Phil., etc.

The Curriculum in Medicine for the Degrees of M.B., and Ch. B. extends over five years. About twenty main subjects are included, and several shorter courses on special subjects. There are four professional examinations to be taken at various stages of the course. The higher degrees of M.D., and Ch. M. may be separately obtained by those who have previously obtained the double bachelorship. After a certain period passed in further study or in practice, a thesis being required in all cases, and a further examination in Chemical Medicine for M.D., and in Chemical Surgery, Surgical Anatomy, and operations on the dead body, for Ch. M.

A Curriculum of two years is required for the degree of B.L., with a degree examination. If a candidate is not a graduate in Arts he must pass the preliminary examination.

The M.A. Degree and an attendance for three years on a Theological course is necessary to qualify for the degree of B.D. There are two degree examinations, the first embracing Hebrew, New Testament Exegesis, and Apologetics, and the Second Divinity, Church History and Biblical Criticism.

Students' Fees.—Students' Fees are as follows:—For matriculation, £1. 1. 0.; Arts Classes, £3. 3. 0. each, except Natural Philosophy, £4. 4. 0., and Physical Laboratory, £6. 6. 0.; Chemical Laboratory, £10. 10. 0. The other faculties average much the same for classes. So, also, the classes in Queen Margaret's College, for women affiliated with the Glasgow University.

The fees for Degrees are as follows :—

M.A. Degree	£5.	5. 0.
B.Sc. "	3.	3. 0.
D.Litt., D.Sc., D.Phil. Degrees, each	10. 10.	0.
LL.B. Degree	6.	6. 0.
B.L. "	5.	5. 0.
M.B., B.Ch. Degree, total	23.	2. 0.
B.D. Degree	5.	5. 0.

No fees can be charged for Honorary Degrees.
Library Fees, 10s. 6d.. each year.
Graduation, after examination, for membership in General Council (compulsory) £1. 0. 0.

Students' Representative Council.—This is a comparatively new element in Scottish University organization. It is recognized by the Act of 1889 for the first time. The Commissioners, acting under the powers conferred upon them by that Act have issued an Ordinance, providing as follows :—

The Students' Representative Council shall submit to the University Court for approval the regulations under which it exists, and these regulations as approved, or with such alterations as may from time to time be approved by the University Court, shall form the constitution of the Students' Representative Council, and shall, subject to the provisions of this Ordinance, determine the functions thereof, and the mode of election thereto ;

After the University Court has approved of the constitution of a Students' Representative Council, alterations in the said constitution shall be of no effect unless and until they shall receive the approval of the University Court ;

The Students' Representative Council shall be entitled to petition the Senatus Academicus with regard to any matter affecting the teaching and discipline of the University, and the Senatus Academicus shall dispose of the matter of the petition, or shall, if so prayed, forward any such petition to the University Court, with such observations as it may think fit to make thereon ;

The Students' Representative Council shall be entitled to petition the University Court with regard to any matter affecting the Students other than those falling under the immediately preceding sub-section ;

Nothing contained in this Section shall be held to prejudice any right of appeal which may be competent under Section 6, sub-section 2, of the said Act, nor the powers and jurisdiction of the Senatus Academicus with regard to the teaching and discipline of the University.

The Council consists of representatives from the different years of all the different faculties in the University, and its aims are :—(1) To represent the students in matters affecting their interests; (2) to afford a recognized means of communication between the students and the University authorities; and (3) to promote social and academical unity among the students.

Alongside of the Council and working in harmony with it is the University Union. The Council has various sub-committees : an Inter-universities Committee, a Magazine Committee, which conducts a University Magazine, published weekly, fortnightly, or monthly, as the case may be, an Amusement Committee and a Song Book Committee. The consensus of opinion seems to be that the Students' Representative Council has been a useful adjunct to the Universities in the matters of government, and of the social life of the institutions.

The Social Life of the Universities.—Social facilities are increasing from year to year in consonance with the broader ideas which are making themselves felt in University government. Not a remnant of the severe methods of discipline, or restriction noted in connection with St. Leonard's College remains. The social life differs in the different Universities, taking color from local surroundings, yet there is a sameness in many important respects, common to them all. Each for instance has its University Union, its Literary and Debating Society, its magazines, its political clubs, its games, its gymnasium for physical exercise, and its athletic clubs. Taking Glasgow, as an example, we get a typical glance at them all. First, there is the University Union. It originated at a meeting of students and graduates held on February 14th 1885. Its foundation and constitution are as follows :

A sum sufficient to erect a building for this purpose having been offered to the Senate by John M'Intyre, Esq. M.D., Odiham, Hampshire, and the Senate having accepted this gift, Articles of Constitution were drawn up by a Committee of Students and Graduates, and received the approval of the Senate, of the Donor, and of the Students' Representative Council. A further sum of £12,000 was raised by the Union Bazaar of 1889, and devoted to furnishing and endowing the building. In 1893, to meet the increasing membership, the building was largely extended at a cost of £2,800. The Union is governed by a Board of Directors, appointed by the Committee of Management, which is elected annually at the General Meeting of the Members.

The objects of the Union are to provide Students with the comforts and conveniences of a social club, to hold debates, and to form a centre to which the various University societies may be affiliated. The buildings comprise a debating hall, a dinnig hall, reading and news rooms, billiard and smoking rooms, committee rooms, lavatories, etc.

The members of the Union are ordinary members or life members.

Ordinary membership of the Union is open to all matriculated students and all former students of the University, and all medical students of Glasgow whose names are enrolled in the Extra-mural

Album of the University, on payment of an annual subscription of five shillings. Students may join for the summer session only, on payment of three shillings.

All matriculated students and former students of the University may, on payment of the sum of three pounds three shillings, become Life Members of the Union.

The Union has successfully carried out its objects in full, and its handsome building at the northern entrance to the University is the pride of all the students who find it a most convenient and useful centre as well as a place of enjoyment and rest.

Then, there is the Theological Society, where essays are read and debates indulged in on kindred subjects. The ordinary membership is confined to Divinity Students, but students connected with the other faculties of the University may become Associates. Next in order is the Medico-Chirurgical Society, for the prosecution of medical research, and probably the most popular of them all. The Dialectic which meets weekly, during the session for the discussion of literary philosophical, and political subjects. There are also the Oriental Society, for the study of eastern languages, the Alexandrian Society, the members of which discuss questions connected with the literatures of ancient Greece and Rome; the Philosophical Society, the Engineering Society, the Physical Society, the Chemical Society, the Missionary Society, the Christian Association, the Total Abstinence Society, the Athletic Club, the United Presbyterian Students' Society, the Rifle Club, the University Club (Glasgow), the Glasgow University Club (London), and this does not exhaust the list. The University Union Building affords most of them a home and permits of a social intercourse which otherwise would be impossible.

In conducting the affairs of the clubs, societies, etc., the authorities allow the greatest freedom. The students control their own affairs; they have their own building and their own concerns are not interfered with. The influence of the students, Representative Council in the social life of the University is a moderating one. The Council keeps in touch with the Senatus Academicus on the one hand and with the students on the other. There is no restriction placed on the University publications. Members of the Senatus are frequent contributors to the pages of the Students' Magazine. Sometimes the Senatus is severely criticised, but generally the authorities secure the sympathy and support of the periodicals and the best of good feeling generally prevails.

Religious Life in the Universities.—There are Societies for religious purposes. Prayer meetings are held regularly at all the Universities by students whose piety the college gown and trencher cannot hide. There are branches of the Young Men's Christian Association at all the Universities, and they are fairly well supported. Sometimes, there are special evangelistic services held for the students by such celebrated men as Professors Henry Drummond and T. M. Lindsay, D.D., with encouraging results.

Rifle Clubs.—The martial spirit finds an outlet in Rifle Clubs, which are very popular and in volunteer corps, such as the University Company of Artillery Volunteers of St. Andrew's, founded by Professor Scott Lang, now its Honorary Major, and attached to the First Fifeshire Corps of Artillery Volunteers. As its success has drawn attention to it from the other Universities a brief sketch of it from a hand book to the University may be reproduced :—" The Instructor is Brigade, Sergeant Major Brockie, R.A. All the Non-Commissioned officers are at present students, and attention to duty is the principle of promotion. Any student may join, and uniform and accoutrements are supplied free of charge to those who join for three years. There is a Carbine Shooting Club in connection with the Battery, and competitions are held on Saturday forenoon during the session : there are also battery competitions for those who do not join the Shooting Club. Big gun practice is frequently held: the range is a sea one. Every summer, generally in the month of July, four detachments, with officers, take part in the competitions of the Scottish National Artillery Association's Camp at Barry. A preparatory camp is held in the United College quadrangle, some eight days in all being passed under canvas, but in future the preparatory camp will likely be of longer duration. As all expenses in connection with these camps (except that of food at St. Andrew's) are disbursed by the Battery, the camping out is a great incentive to join. In the competitions at Barry the University men have always taken a prominent part and they once carried off the second aggregate badges. The physical training afforded by the drill cannot be over-estimated and the course of gunnery instruction is interesting and profitable. The members enjoy many privileges and had the distinction of forming a guard of honour when Lord Dufferin came to deliver his Rectorial Address. The Battery also sends a representative to the Students' Council.

Students' Residence.—There is no academic provision for residential accommodation in any University. In St. Andrew's, the Professors organize a system of lodgings, while in Edinburgh several Halls of Residence under the supervision of a voluntary Committee provide accommodation for a small proportion of students. In Edinburgh a Hall of Residence for Divinity Students was recently opened, also a voluntary undertaking.

PART III.

UNIVERSITIES OF THE UNITED STATES.

CHAPTER XVII.

HARVARD UNIVERSITY.

The Early History of Harvard.—In 1636, the General Court* of Massachusetts made a grant of four hundred pounds, to which were added in 1640 the ferry receipts between Boston and Charlestown, towards the founding of a college in that colony. Edward Everett in his speech at the second centenary celebration referred to this as the first instance on record of the people's representatives ever giving their own money to found a place of education.

In the following year the General Court appointed twelve of the most eminent men of the colony "to take order for a college at Newtown, shortly afterwards to be called Cambridge." The work was prosecuted with zeal, yet it is doubtful if it could have been carried to a successful issue without the timely bequest of the Rev. John Harvard, who, at his death in 1638, bequeathed to the enterprise one-half of his property, amounting to four hundred pounds and his library, consisting of 320 volumes.

The Act establishing the overseers of Harvard College was passed at a General Court of 1642. These overseers who were granted exclusive powers of control, were the

---
* The name still given to the Legislature of Massachusetts.

Governor, Deputy-Governor, and all the magistrates of the jurisdiction, together with the teaching elders of the six adjoining towns.* This body proving too unwieldly, a corporation with perpetual succession was established by the important charter of 1650, to consist of the president, five fellows, and a treasurer, and to be styled "the President and Fellows of Harvard College." Of this Charter, President Eliot said, "it is in force to-day in every line, having survived in perfect integrity the prodigious political, social, and commercial changes of more than two centuries. This corporation was required to obtain the consent of the large body of overseers to any important step, and to relieve them to some extent of their obligation, an appendix was made to the charter in 1657, granting greater freedom of action to the corporation. In 1672, a new College charter was created at the instance of President Hoar, whereby the name of the corporation was changed to "the President, Fellows and Treasurer;" but the authority of this charter seems never to have been recognized, and in the following year an addition was made to the members of the corporation.

The Colonial Charter.—These modifications were slight compared to the changes introduced in 1692, through the influence of President Mather. In this year a provincial charter was granted to the Colony by William and Mary, and the General Court assembled under that authority granted a new College Charter, whereby a corporation of ten with perpetual succession was granted full powers for the election of officers, and was exempted from all res-

---

*The New England "town" corresponds to the Ontario "township."

ponsibility to the overseers, and from legislative control. This charter never received the Royal sanction, presumably on the ground that no provision was there made for the exercise of the visitatorial power.

In 1697, a new provisional charter modified the powers of President Mather, and increased the number of the Corporation to sixteen. The Vice-President, Governor, and Council were made Visitors. The President and other instructors were required to reside at Cambridge. In 1699 a religious qualification was inserted in the Charter, the visitatorial power was vested in the King, Governor, and Commander-in-Chief, and five of the Council were admitted to the Corporation. Governor Bellamont negatived this on account of the religious clause; this, therefore, was the fourth draft of a charter vetoed on religious grounds, as the Governor was afraid to recognize the ascendency of the Congregational Church.* In 1700, a new charter was drafted by the Legislature, and Governor Bellamont was appointed to present it to the King. Bellamont, however, died before the presentation, and no subsequent attempt was ever made to obtain a College Charter from the Crown. The Legislature of 1707 declared that the Charter of 1650 had never been repealed, and directed the President and Fellows of the College to exercise the powers granted by it. The Corporation was again reduced to seven, and the act thus revised has been ever since recognized as the Charter of the College.

State Legislation.—In 1780, on the adoption† of the

---

* To which the Rev. John Harvard had belonged.
† After the Declaration of Independence, 1776.

State Constitution, official articles were framed, securing to the College the perpetual enjoyment of all its estates. All the rights pertaining to the Overseers were vested in the Lieutenant-Governor, Council, and Senate of the Commonwealth, together with the President of the College, and the ministers of the Congregational churches in the six adjoining towns. Since 1810, various acts have been passed to alter the Constitution of the Board of Overseers. In 1843, clergymen of all denominations were made eligible as Overseers. In 1851, State Senators ceased to be *ex officio* members of the Board, and seats were no longer reserved for the clergy. Thirty members were to be elected by the Senators and Representatives assembled in one room. These thirty members were to be divided into three classes, one of which was to go out of office every year. In 1865, important changes were introduced. The President and Treasurer were made the only *ex officio* members of the Board of Overseers, and the election of the remaining thirty was entrusted to the alumni. A division was made into six classes, one of which should go out of office every year. A peculiar regulation was that no officer of the University was entitled to a vote. In 1880, residents of other States were admitted to election.

Periods in Harvard's History.—President Quincy, in his history of the University,* distinguished four chief periods in the history of Harvard. The first extended from the founding of the College in 1636 to the year 1692, the date of the Colonial Charter. During this period the College was "conducted as a theological

---

* Published in 1840.

institution," and although the Charter had no sectarian bias, the institution was still regarded as an instrument for the promotion of the predominating religious opinions. The second period (1692-1736) was marked by the bitter controversies which sprang up " between those religious parties, into which the Congregational sect divided immediately after the new principle of political power introduced by the provincial charter of William and Mary had deprived it of that supremacy, which the old charter had secured to the Congregational clergy. High Calvinists, indeed, regarded it with diminished favour, but new friends to it arose; its usefulness became acknowledged; and its resources increased.

In the third period, (1736-1780), the divisions of the Congregational sect grew more marked, and Episcopalian influence increased. Still the political troubles of the time suspended controversy, and the College shared in the popularity and financial distress of other patriotic institutions of the day. In the fourth period, from 1780 down, the College, now raised to the rank of a University, partook with the country at large, of the vicissitudes following the war, and subsequently of the prosperity, which ensued upon the adoption of the Federal Constitution and an orderly arrangement of national affairs. This period is further characterized by a strong infusion of physical sciences into the courses of study, and by a waning of theological influences. A new and more prosperous era was opened with the inauguration of President Eliot on May 19th, 1869. At a special meeting of the Faculty of Arts and Sciences in 1894, a minute commemorative of the completion of his twenty-fifth year of office, was adopted and entered upon the records, and the following extracts will show how his services have been appreciated: "The progress which since that time has taken place in the departments of the University is far greater than has been made in any like period since the foundation of Harvard College. That progress has been not merely a growth in numbers, wealth, and intellectual resources; not merely an advance along old and conspicuous lines; but a transformation of nature and spirit, a new birth of university life. The foundation of the progress thus made has been in the development of the elective system.

Organization of the University.—The corporation of which the legal title is "the President and Fellows of Harvard College," consists of the President, Treasurer and five Fellows, all of whom hold office for life. In it is vested the title to the property of the University.

The overseers number thirty-two, including the President and Treasurer of the University, who are *ex officio* members. Five of the overseers go out of office each year, their places being filled on Commencement Day by an election in which alumni of the College of five years' standing, Masters of Arts, and holders of honorary degrees are entitled to vote, if present in person.

Appointments of members of the teaching staff are made by the Corporation with the approval of the Overseers. Professorships are held without express limitation of time. Assistant professorships are held for five years, and tutorships for not more than three years. At the end of the term of an Assistant Professor or Tutor, his connection with the University ceases, unless he is re-appointed.

Lecturers are appointed for not more than one year. Instructors are appointed for such terms as convenience may require. Proctors are appointed for not more than one year, to assist the Faculties in the conduct of examinations, and in the preservation of order. All officers of instruction and government are subject to removal for inadequate performance of duty, or for misconduct.

The revenues of the University are derived from permanent endowments, gifts for immediate use, and students' fees. The University has no income from the State, and has not received any gift from the State since 1810. Undergraduates pay $150 per annum for tuition. The following items from the Treasurer's Report will indicate the nature of the resources :—

EXTRACT FROM TREASURER'S REPORT

Capital.

Separate Investments	$1,845,516 81
General	208,000 00
Railroad Bonds	1,161,941 37
Sundry "	686,642 50
Sundry Stocks	287,009 79
Real Estate	2,434,502 98
Sundries	282,072 39
Cash	401,582 88
Total	$8,367,268 72

Revenue

Receipts from Term Bills in the whole University	$ 524,550 32
Gifts for immediate use	58,846 22

Every candidate must furnish a testimonial of honorable dismissal from the school last attended, and must also refer to two persons from whom information about him may be obtained. A certificate of preparation is also required of every candidate for a Preliminary Examination.

Requirements for admission.—The examinations for admission embrace two classes of studies, *Elementary* and *Advanced*. A candidate must pass an examination in one of the following :

(a) All the elementary studies, and at least two advanced studies.

(b) All the elementary studies, except either German or French, and at least three advanced studies

(c) All the elementary studies, except either Greek or Latin, and at least four advanced studies.

(d) All the elementary studies except either Greek or Latin and either German or French, and at least five advanced studies.

ELEMENTARY STUDIES.—1. *English.*—Works prescribed (a) for general knowledge as a basis for composition (b) for special knowledge.

2. *Greek.*—The translation at sight of simple Attic prose with grammatical questions.

3. *Latin.*—The translation at sight of ordinary prose, and questions as in Greek.

4. *German.*—The translation at sight of simple prose

5. *French*—The translation at sight of simple prose.

6. *History and Historical Geography.*—Either (a) History of Greece and Rome or (b) History of United States and England.

7. *Mathematics.*—Algebra and Geometry.

8. *Physical Sciences.*

ADVANCED STUDIES.—The number of necessary advanced studies has been specified above. There are nine in all distributed through the following subjects:—

1. *Greek.*—Sight translation from Homer, Herodotus, with questions.

2. *Latin.*—Translation at sight from Cicero and Virgil, with questions.

3. *Greek aad Latin Composition.*—

4. *German.*—Translation at sight of modern German prose, and a general knowledge of portions of six prescribed authors as the basis of a composition.

5. *French.*—Translation at sight of standard French, and a composition based on prescribed authors.

6. Plane Trigonometry and Logarithms, Solid Geometry.

7. The Elements of Analytic Geometry, Advanced Algebra. Certain books are recommended, but none prescribed.

8. *Physical Science.*—Experimental Physics.
9. "   "   "   Chemistry.

In these two subjects, both a written and laboratory examination.

The candidate may take the entire examination at one time, or divide it (a) between two years or (b) between June and September of the same year.

I. ANTICIPATION OF COLLEGE STUDIES.—A candidate may present himself for examination in any of the advanced studies not offered by him for admission, and thus qualify himself to pursue more advanced courses in those subjects in College.

II. Certain studies may be anticipated by examination.

The advantages attached to these examinations are:—

(1) If the studies anticipated amount to one-half the work of the Freshman year, the student may be admitted to the Sophomore class, on making up the deficiency in his Freshman studies.

(2) In any case the studies anticipated are placed to the student's credit towards his degree, and a reduction

may be made in the number of courses regularly required in the Junior and Senior years.

ADVANCED STANDING. — Admission to any year is granted on fulfilling certain examination requirements. *Ad eundem* is not granted without examination.

SPECIAL STUDENTS.—Special students are admitted to the College without examination, but are not candidates for a degree.

Undergraduate Courses.—The course leading to the degree of A B. is of three or four years' duration.

For the Freshman year are prescribed :—

1. *Rhetoric and English Composition.*—Hill's Rhetoric, and part of his Foundations of Rhetoric. Three times a week.

2. *German or French.*—Prescribed for those only who have not presented both German and French for admission.

German.—An elementary course for those who have not presented German for admission, and more advanced courses with specified authors for students who are not beginning the subject.

French.—As in German.

ELECTIVE STUDIES.—Every Freshman is required to submit his choice of studies to an adviser. Courses must be selected from the following to make up five full courses in all, and not more than two courses in the same department may be elected without permission :—

Greek.—Six half courses. The most advanced course of these requires a study of portions of Homer, Lysias, Plato and Euripides. Students are placed in this course according to their proficiency and must not elect it in the first instance. Certain of the half courses are parallel, though not identical.

Latin.—Six half courses. The arrangement is similar to that in Greek. The most advanced course requires a study of portions of Cicero, Livy, Terence and Plautus.

English.—One-half course in the history of English Literature.

German.—Seven full courses, two half courses, and one equivalent to a course and a half. These are of various degrees of difficulty. The three advanced courses treat respectively of Lessing and the German Drama, Schiller and his contemporaries, and Goethe and his time.

French.—Four full courses, two half courses and an elementary full course. Practice in speaking and writing French, and the reading of difficult modern French are the features of the higher courses.

Italian or Spanish.—Elementary. One course in either subject.

History.—One course. Mediæval and Modern European History.

Government and Laws.—One-half course in Constitutional Government.

Fine Arts.—One course in the principles of Delineation, Colour and Chiaroscuro.

Music.—One course in Harmony for students proficient in piano or organ playing.

Mathematics.—Two courses and four half courses of varying difficulty.

Engineering.—Two courses.

Physics.—Two courses and one half course. Experimental and Descriptive Physics.

Chemistry, Botany, Zoology, Geology.—Four courses and four half courses.

Higher courses in the studies named above and courses in other departments are open to such Freshman as obtain written permission from the instructors. The prescribed work for the Sophomore and Junior years consists of Themes and Forensics. No studies are prescribed for the Senior year. Every Sophomore, Junior and Senior is required to take four elective courses, or an equivalent amount of courses and half courses. Many courses in each of the following departments are offered for choice:—

Semitic Languages and History, Indo-Iranian Languages, Classical Philology, English, German, Germanic Philology, (comprising Gothic, Old Saxon, etc.) French, Italian, Spanish, Romance Philology, (primarily for graduates), Comparative Literature, Philosophy, Education and Teaching, History and Political Science, the Fine Arts, Architecture, Music, Mathematics, Engineering, Physics, Chemistry, Botany, Zoology, Geology, Anatomy, Physiology and Physical Training, Military Science.

Conditions of Election.—The scope of the elective studies is outlined in the above general synopsis. The student's choice is limited to those studies which his previous training qualifies him to pursue; and he must observe any restrictions that may be attached to the particular courses he wishes to select. He is further required to avoid any conflict of recitation hours or of examinations.

An undergraduate who wishes to take a graduate course is required to consult the Instructor in advance. It will be seen that students who prefer a course like that usually prescribed by American colleges may secure it by a corresponding choice of studies; while others who have decided tastes, or think it wiser to concentrate their study on a few subjects, obtain every facility for doing so.

For the professional degrees, including the degree in applied science, the options are much less wide; but they are still important.

Degrees—The ninth statute of the University enumerates the degrees granted and the mode of conferring them. The ordinary degrees of Bachelor of Arts,

Bachelor of Science, Master of Arts, Civil Engineer, Doctor of Philosophy, Doctor of Science, Bachelor of Divinity, Bachelor of Laws, Doctor of Medicine, Doctor of Dental Medicine, Doctor of Veterinary Medicine, and Bachelor of Agricultural Science are conferred, after recommendation by the several Faculties, by vote of the Corporation, with the consent of the Overseers.

There are four grades of the degrees of Bachelor of Arts and Bachelor of Science, and two grades of the degrees of Bachelor of Laws and Doctor of Medicine. Honorary degrees are conferred by vote of the Corporation with the consent of the Overseers.

Examinations.—The Examinations are conducted by the Faculties, and are mid-year and final. Examinations may also at the discretion of the Professor be given to a student at any time merely as a means of estimating his proficiency.

CHAPTER XVIII.

YALE UNIVERSITY.

Historical Sketch of Yale College.—The reasons which led to the foundation of the original Collegiate School were the inconvenient distance of Harvard, and the consequent expense of sending students there, combined with the growing suspicion of the laxity of Harvard in matters of religion. In 1701, the General Court of Connecticut met at New Haven and granted a charter to erect a Collegiate School. Ten clergymen were appointed trustees, and the sum of £60 granted annually until the Court should order otherwise. The College was temporarily located at Saybrook, but on the appointment of Abraham Pearson as Rector, his home at Killingworth (now Clinton) was made its headquarters and it remained so till his death in 1707. Rector Andrew, who succeeded to the post, lived at Milford. This seriously impaired the organization of the School, for the classes were now for some years divided by the forty miles which lay between Milford and Saybrook. This state of affairs induced the trustees to remove the school in 1716 to New Haven. But a serious split still existed, for in 1717, Rector Andrew granted four degrees at New Haven, and one degree was conferred by Mr. Woodbridge at Wethersfield. This anomalous state of affairs still prevailed in the following year, and the Legislature decided to divide its yearly grant among the several instructors at Wethersfield, New Haven, and Saybrook.

At this critical time news came from England which fixed the College firmly at New Haven, and gave it the name it now bears. This news was the announcement of Governor Yale's gift of "three bales of valuable goods, a portrait of George I., the Royal coat of arms, and a case of books," the estimated value of the whole being £800. In honor of this gift the Collegiate School received the name of Yale College, and became firmly established at New Haven. In 1719, the General Court made an annual grant to the College of £300. A great sensation was caused in 1722 by Rector Cutler's adherence to the Episcopalian heresy, and he was forthwith requested to resign. An interregnum ensued which lasted until 1726. The Trustees resided at the College, each in turn, for a month, and attempted to fulfil the duties of a College President.

In the year 1745 a new charter was granted to Yale College, whereby the Rector and ten other trustees, then in office, were made a body corporate and politic, hereafter to be known as "The President and Fellows of Yale College in New Haven," with perpetual succession and the customary corporation privileges. Thus the Rector and Trustees became the President and Fellows with paramount control of the affairs of the College with power to make laws and ordinances as they might see fit, and with authority to make all appointments. No qualifications for trustees were mentioned and no provisions were made for ecclesiastical government. In 1753, the Corporation imposed a religious test which remained in force for over twenty years. In 1756, Professorships of Divinity were established, and in 1757, the College was formed into a separate Church. President Stiles made it a stipulation on receiving office in 1777 that the religious test should be abolished. During his administration, a committee was appointed in 1791 by the Legislature to confer with the Corporation of the College, with the result that the arrearages on certain State taxes were paid on condition that the Governor, Lieutenant-Governor, and the six oldest assistants, should be added to the Corporation.

President Timothy Dwight administered the affairs of the College from 1795 to 1817. In 1801 a Professorship of Law was established, and in 1813, the Yale Medical School. Under President Day, from 1817 to 1846, the influence of the Faculty constantly increased, and a Theological School was founded as a distinct department. The new State Constitution confirmed in 1818 the privileges enjoyed by the Corporation. The Yale Law School was established in 1824. President Theodore Woolsey, who held the office from 1846 to 1871, has been called the greatest of Yale's Presidents. The foundation of the Sheffield Scientific School in the second year of his administration was one of the most important educational events of the century. It is impossible to dwell in detail on the fruitful development of the various departments of this period.

President Porter succeeded to office in 1871. On March 23rd, 1872, the Corporation voted that Yale College " be recognized as comprising the four departments of which a University is commonly understood to consist," and an Act was subsequently passed by the State Legislature giving the alumni of the institution representation in its governing body. In 1870, Classics became optional after the beginning of the junior year. In 1876 the elective system was extended so as to cover the afternoon exercises of the junior and senior years, and in the same year entrance examinations were permitted outside of New Haven. The present system of options was introduced in 1884.

The Rev. Timothy Dwight has held the office of President since 1886, and his administration has been an era of prosperity and advancement. An Act legalizing the use of the title, "Yale University," by the Corporation existing under the name of "The President and Fellows of Yale College," was approved by the Governor on March 8, 1887. At the same time the old name Yale College was limited by the Corporation to the Academical Department, which it had originally denoted.

Organization of the University.—The trustees partly fill their own vacancies, and are partly elected by the Alumni, the six chosen by the latter being in addition to the number fixed by the charter of 1745. The Governor and Lieut.-Governor of the State are members of the Board *ex officio*.

Professors and Instructors are appointed by the President and Fellows, generally on nominations made by the Faculties. Assistant Professors are usually appointed for five years. Professors have usually permanent appointments.

The revenues are derived from various sources. The University enjoys the interest on many private endowments, and individual gifts of land continually add to the revenues. The Government for many years devoted the proceeds of the Congressional land grant of Connecticut to the Sheffield Scientific School, but that fund has latterly been applied to another institution in the State. At present, therefore, there is no State aid. Undergraduates in Yale College and the Sheffield Scientific School pay $125 a year for instruction. The fees vary in the other departments of the University.

Requirements for admission.—No one is admitted to the Academical Department of Yale College until the completion of his fifteenth year, and testimonials of good moral character must also be presented. A bond, executed by parent or guardian for five hundred dollars must be given to the Treasurer as security. Candidates for admission to standing in any year of the undergraduate course are examined, in addition to the preparatory studies, in those subjects which have already been pursued by the class which they wish to enter. The following subjects are required:

Latin.—Grammar, sight, prose and selections from Cicero, Virgil, and Ovid, the latter at sight.

Greek.—Grammar, prose, prosody, sight, selections from Xenophon and Homer,

History.—Roman and Greek.

Algebra and Geometry.—

French or German.—No authors specified.

English.—

The above examinations may be divided, with not less than a year between the two parts.

The Undergraduate Courses.—The length of the undergraduate course in Yale College is four years. The following is a synopsis of the courses:—

First Year.—Fifteen hours a week prescribed. No options except between French and German.

Greek, Latin and Mathematics occupy eleven hours per week ; Modern Languages three hours and English one hour.

The Mathematics of this year consist of Geometry, Trigonometry and Mathematics.

Greek.—Selected portions of Homer, Herodotus, Thucydides and Plato.

Latin.—Livy, Cicero and Horace in prescribed selections

English Literature. —Brooke's Primer. Three plays from Shakespeare and Milton's Minor Poems.

French or German.

Second Year.—There are six courses offered of three hours each per week in Greek, Latin, Mathematics, Modern Languages, English and Physics. This year is optional in so far as five courses are demanded out of six offered, and in the Modern Language course, either French or German may be taken, but not both. There is also an optional course of one hour a week in Elocution. The courses in the above subjects are extended developments of First Year's work.

Note.—If a student can pass a satisfactory examination in any of the Freshman or Sophomore courses for the work of one year in advance, he may be allowed to choose from the list of electives some other course covering the same number of hours.

Third Year and Fourth Year.—The prescribed studies in the third year occupy three hours per week in Logic, Psychology and Ethics. Jevons and Fowler's Logic. Ladd's Psychology and Porter's Elements of Moral Science. There is for the first term an optional course of one hour in Advanced Oratorical Speaking. Every member of the Junior Class must take 15 to 18 hours per week of Class Room work, and thirty hours must be covered between the last two years. The prescribed studies in the senior year consist of one course in Philosophy chosen from a list of four more courses.

Elective Courses are offered in :—

I. *Psychology, Ethics, Philosophy.*—Eight undergraduate courses, and six graduate courses, which latter are open to seniors making a specialty of the study.

II. *Political Science and Law.*—Nine courses. Suggestions are made as to choice and certain courses are especially for Seniors.

III. *History.*—Seven courses, of which some are particularly for Seniors.

IV. *Romance Languages.*—Ten courses in French, Italian and Spanish.

V. *Germanic Languages.*—Ten courses in Modern German, Scientific German, Gothic, Old High German, and old Saxon, etc. Occasionally, courses are given in Swedish, Norwegian, Danish and Old Norse.

VI. *English.*—Ten courses Old, Middle and Modern English, approached both from the literary and more purely philological point of view. Some of the courses are particularly for Juniors, and others for Seniors,

VII. *Ancient Languages.*—Greek, six courses. Latin, nine courses. Sanskrit, one course. Linguistics, one course.

VIII. *Biblical Literature.*—Hebrew, Arabic, Assyrian, Greek, ten courses.

IX. *The Fine Arts.*—Four courses.

X. *Physical and Natural Science.*—
  Physics.—Three courses.
  Chemistry.—Four courses, with directions as to choice.
  Geology.—Three courses.
  Mineralogy.—Two courses.
  Physical Geography and Botany.—Three courses. Two for Juniors.
  Biology.—One course for Juniors and three for Seniors.

These courses are open only to those who pursue the entire course.

XI. *Mathematics.*—Eleven courses, four of which are particularly for Seniors.

XII. *Music.*—Seven courses.

XIII. *Physical Culture.*—Three courses, of which one is particularly for Seniors.

Options.—The system of options has been outlined in the above synopsis. For the first two years the work is almost entirely prescribed. In the Junior and Senior years over four-fifths of the work is elective. The whole number of elective courses open to the two classes is at the present time one hundred and twenty-nine; and in addition, there are several courses of lectures, attendance on which is optional. To promote the rational choice of elective courses, Special Honours are awarded in various groups. (Catalogue, p. 104.)

Degrees.—Degrees are voted and conferred by the Corporation, on the recommendation of the Faculties. The following degrees are granted :

For the Undergraduate courses.—Bachelor of Arts, Bachelor of Laws, Bachelor of Civil Law, Bachelor of Divinity, Bachelor of Fine Arts, Bachelor of Philosophy, Bachelor of Music, Doctor of Medicine.

Note.—The degree of Bachelor of Arts is the only undergraduate degree conferred by the Faculty of Yale College proper.

Examinations.—Examinations are under the charge of the Faculties, and are conducted by them.

CHAPTER XIX.

THE COLLEGE OF NEW JERSEY.

Historical Sketch.—The College originated in the plan of Jonathan Dickinson, John Pierson, Ebenezer Pemberton, Aaron Burr, with others, to found an institution " in which ample provision should be made for the intellectual and religious culture of youth desirous to obtain a liberal education, and more especially for the thorough training of such as were candidates for the holy ministry." Its first charter was granted in 1746 by the Hon. John Hamilton, President of His Majesty's Council, and is noteworthy as the first College Charter ever given in this country by a Governor or acting Governor with simply the consent of his Council.

A second and more ample charter was granted September 14th, 1748, by the " trusty and well-beloved " Jonathan Belcher, Esquire, Governor and Commander-in-chief of the Province of New Jersey. After the war of the Revolution, the charter was confirmed and renewed by the Legislature of New Jersey. In response to the earnest desire of the petitioners for this charter, that " those of every religious denomination may have free and equal liberty and advantage of education in the said college any different sentiments in religion notwithstanding," it was expressly provided that no " person of any religious denomination whatsoever" should be excluded " from free and equal liberty and advantage of education or from any of the liberties, privileges or immunities of the said college on account of his or their being of a religious profession differing from the said trustees of the said college."

In 1754, the college having, meanwhile, been removed from its old site at Newark, the first building was erected for instruction in Princeton. It was proposed to name this building " Belcher Hall " in recognition of Governor Belcher's devoted services. At his request the Trustees ordered " that the said edifice be in all time to come called and known by the name of Nassau Hall."

The College of New Jersey, as now constituted, includes the " John C. Green School of Science." This institution, which has its own professors and instructors, was founded in 1873 upon an endowment of Mr. John C. Green. The instruction given falls in three departments, General Science, Civil Engineering and Electrical Engineering. Its design is to furnish more extended and special instruction in the natural sciences, providing several scientific courses leading to the degree of Bachelor of Science and also various graduate courses. The Department of Civil Engineering was added in 1875, by further endowment from the residuary legatees of Mr. Green. The Department of Electrical Engineering was added in 1889 by the same donors.

Organization of the University.—In the confirmation of the charter of 1748 by the New Jersey Legislature after the Revolutionary War, the corporation was styled " the Trustees of the College of New Jersey ;" they were empowered to hold and administer the property of the College, make laws for the government of the institution, choose its President and Faculty and confer degrees.

This board is a self-perpetuating body, composed of twenty-seven members, with the Governor of the State as President *ex officio,* or in his absence, the President of the College. The Professors and Faculty are appointed by the Board of Trustees.

Revenues.—The Revenues are derived from private endowments and fees from students. Tuition and public room fee $150 per annum.

Requirements for admission.—All candidates for admission to any class must bring with them testimonials of good moral character and attainments. The minimum requirements which are expected of all candidates are:—

English.—Composition based upon specified books and authors, with questions as to the subject matter, structure and style of the books.

Latin.—Grammar, Latin Composition (continuous prose), specified portions of Cæsar, Virgil and Cicero.

Greek.—Grammar and Composition, Xenophon, Herodotus (portions of Book VII) or Homer's Iliad I-III.

Elementary French or Elementary German.

Mathematics.

The additional requirements for advanced standing are:—

Latin.—Five subjects offered of which two or more must be chosen. Portions of Ovid, Sallust, Virgil, Sight-translation, Roman History and Geography.

Greek.—As in Latin.

French.—Dumas, La Tulipe Noire, Daudet, Lettres de mon Moulin, Prose.

German.—Goethe, Hermann and Dorothea (3 cantos). Composition and easy extracts.

Mathematics. — Either (*a*) Solid and Spherical Geometry, or (*b*) Logarithms and Plane Trigonometry.

The examination may be divided with an interval of a year.

Special courses are offered in which certificates of proficiency are granted at the completion. A separate entrance examination is required. Candidates from other approved colleges are admitted into the Sophomore, Junior, and Senior years upon an examination covering the work of the preceding year.

Undergraduate Courses.—FIRST YEAR.—Latin, Greek, Mathematics, English, History, and an option between French or German.

Latin.—Livy, 4 books ; Cicero; De Senectute ; Terence, 1 play ; Gellius ; selections, Composition, History ; Sight-reading optional.

Greek.—Xenophon, Hellenica I-II, Symposium, Memorabilia ; Herodotus, Selections for Sight-reading, Grammar, Prose, History.

English.—Elocution, Rhetoric, two essays and an oration.

German.—Four elective courses of different grades. In the most advanced :—Grammar, Composition, Chamisso, Peter Schlemihl, Schiller, Maria Stuart.

French.—Two elective courses.

Mathematics.—Four required courses and one elective.

Required.—First Term.—Latin 4, Greek 4, Mathematics 4, Bible 1. Total 13 hours, Second Term.—Latin 4, Greek 4, Mathematics, 4, Bible 1. Total 13.

Elective.—German or French, 2 hours. Total, 15 hours. English also is required outside of schedule hours.

SECOND YEAR.

A continuation of the first year's work, and, in addition, General History, Mechanics, Chemistry, Zoology and Botany. Options may be taken in any two of the following subjects : Latin, Greek, Mathematics, French, German.

Latin.—Five required courses. Prescribed work in Cicero, Horace and Catullus. Four elective courses, and one purely optional. In these courses there is a more advanced study of authors, largely in connection with the history of definite periods. 2 hours per week.

Greek.—Two required courses, and one elective. Required are : Demosthenes, his life, etc. The Olynthiacs and Philippics ; Plato : Apology and Crito ; Xenophon : Memorabilia and Symposium ; Lysias : Orations, Composition

Mathematics.—Required. Conic Sections (3 hours in first term).
Elective.—Differential and Integral Calculus.
English.—The work is based on Hunt's Studies in Literature and Style; Principles of Discourse, and Champney's History of English.
History.—On the basis of Freeman's General Sketch.
Zoology and Botany, Chemistry and Mechanics.
First Term.—Required. Latin, 2; Greek, 2; Mathematics, 2; History, 2; Zoology and Botany, 2. Total, 11 hours.
Elective.—Two only to be taken (four hours) from the following: Latin, 2; Greek, 2; Mathematics, 2; French, 2; German, 2. Total, 15 hours.
Second Term.—Latin, 2; Greek, 2; English, 2; Chemistry, 2; Mechanics, 2. Total, 10 hours. Electives as in first term. Total, 14 hours.

THIRD YEAR. Required. Physics, Psychology, Logic, Political Economy.
First Term.—Required. Physics, 3; Psychology, 2. 5 hours. Five electives, 10 hours. Total, 15 hours.
Second Term.—Required. Logic, 3; Political Economy, 2. 5 hours. Electives, 10 hours. Total, 15 hours.

Numerous elective courses are offered in History of Philosophy, Plato, Experimental Psychology, History, Public Law, Constitutional Law, Art, Aristophanes, Juvenal, Plato, Seneca, Plautus, English, Old English, Middle English, German, French, Italian, Spanish, Mathematics, Anal. Mech., Astronomy, Theoretical Chemistry, Physics, Biology, Geology, Histology, Vert. Anatomy.

FOURTH YEAR.—Required are: *First Term.*—Ethics, 2. Six electives, 12 hours. Total, 14 hours.
Second Term.—Required. Evidence of Christianity, 1 hour. Electives, 12 hours. Total, 13 hours.

Elective Courses.

In addition to the italicized courses above, which are identical in the junior and senior years, there are electives offered especially for the seniors in Advanced Logic, Physiology, Psychology, Aristotle, Theism, Metaphysics, Experimental Psychology, General Psychology, Lucretius, Science and Religion, Outlines of Philosophy, History,

Jurisprudence, Roman Law, Finance, History and Politics, History of Political Economy, Art, Sanskrit, Greek, Latin, Roman Law, Hebrew, English Literature, Gothic, Old English, Poetics, Prose Fiction, American Literature, German, Mid. High German, Old High German, Old Norse, Old French, Italian, Mathematics, Astronomy, Practical Astronomy, Physics, Practical Physics, Laboratory Chemistry, Physical Geography, Physiology, Embryology, Comparative Osteology, Histology, Mammalian Anatomy, Palæontology.

Degrees.—The Faculty recommends students for the degrees of Bachelor of Arts, Bachelor of Science, Civil Engineer, Electrical Engineer. The higher degrees are also conferred of Master of Arts, Master of Science, Doctor of Philosophy, Doctor of Science, Bachelor of Divinity.

Examinations.—At the end of each term each class is ordinarily examined in the studies of that term. At the close of the second term the examination in certain subjects may embrace not only the work of that term, but the course of the entire year. In addition to the regular examinations, partial examinations or written recitations are held from time to time during the term. In the Freshman class, special examinations are held early in the first term, the results of which determine the distribution of the class into graded divisions. These are re-organized at the beginning of the second term according to the results of the last preceding regular examinations. Examinations are for the most part conducted in writing, but in certain subjects are oral in whole or in part. Private examinations are not allowed except in extreme cases and by special permission of the Faculty. Absence from an examination, except for reasons of absolute necessity, will be regarded as a serious delinquency.

CHAPTER XX.

COLUMBIA COLLEGE.

Historical Sketch.—The charter of King's College was granted October 31st, 1754, from which day the college dates its official existence. One of its provisions was that no one should be excluded from its privileges on religious grounds. The Trustees had in possession at this time some seventeen thousand dollars, being the proceeds of a series of public lotteries. This sum, together with a grant of land by Trinity Church on condition that the President should be an Episcopalian, constituted the capital of the college for some years to come. Early in 1776, the college building was converted into a military hospital, and the College remained in abeyance for eight years, during the revolutionary period. It was revived in 1784 by Act of the Legislature, and, under the name of Columbia College, was placed under the temporary control of the Regents of the University of the State of New York. It may be stated here that on the 13th April, 1887, the Legislature of the State of New York passed an Act reviving the original charter with amendments.

For seventy years after the revival of the charter in 1787 the income of the College was too meagre to admit of much extension of the system. A committee, however, was appointed in 1853 in anticipation of a favourable disposal of college property to inquire into the best method for liberalizing the course of instruction. A full execution of the scheme they proposed was not attempted for want of the requisite funds. In November, 1858, a University course was opened, but was relinquished for lack of encouragement after one year's trial. This tentative University course, however, resulted in the establishment in 1858 of the present Law School, for thirty-three years under the able management of Professor Theodore W. Bright. The Medical Faculty had been in abeyance since 1810, when in June, 1860, by agreement, the College of Physicians and Surgeons became the Medical Department of Columbia College. This connection, a merely nominal one, continued until 1891, when the College of Physicians and Surgeons surrendered its separate charter and became an integral part of Columbia College. The continuous development of the College was signified by the establishment in 1864 of the School of Mines; in 1880 of the School of Political Science; and in 1883 of a course of collegiate study for women to be pursued under the general direction of the Faculty of the College. In 1889 Barnard College was established for women studying for the Columbia degrees, and there they now receive instruction from the Faculty and other officers of instruction of Columbia College.

Hon. Seth Low was installed President of Columbia College on February 3rd, 1890. Under his administration it has steadily grown in power and influence. One of the first official acts of President Low was to arrange a scheme of proper university organization. As a result, the College has now University Faculties of Law, Medicine, Mines (or applied Science), Political Science, Philosophy, and Pure Science, each with its own special function, and each sending two delegates to a body denominated the University Council, which is charged with the general supervision of University work as a whole.

Columbia College now consists of the School of Arts, (the original college founded in 1754); the School of Law; the College of Physicians and Surgeons to which all students are admitted; and the above mentioned Faculties which conduct all courses leading to the University degrees of Master of Arts and Doctor of Philosophy.

Organization of the University.—By the provisions of the above Act, the Trustees were, in the first instance, appointed by the State Legislature. Their term of office is for life, and they are a self-perpetuating body. The title to all the property of the College is vested in the Trustees, who appoint the President and all officers of instruction and administration, and are the ultimate source of authority in all matters pertaining to the College.

The Professors and Faculty are appointed by the trustees. Their relative rank is as follows :—Professor, Adjunct Professor, Instructor, Tutor, Assistant, Lecturers have only a temporary or non-continuous connection with the College. Appointments of all officers of instruction, other than professors and adjunct-professors are made by the Faculties of the Schools in which such officers are to serve, subject to confirmation by the Trustees.

The receipts for the year ending June 30th, 1894, amounted to $747,635.62, chiefly made up of receipts from rents $386,276.14, and fees from students 276,606,-

38. The fee for matriculation is $5.00, and for Tuition in the School of Arts $150 per annum. There is no State Tax.

Requirements for Admission.—The candidate must be at least fifteen years of age and of good moral character. A satisfactory examination must be passed in the following seventeen subjects :—

English.—Two sections. 1. Grammar, 2. Composition, based on prescribed works.

Latin and Greek.—Five sections, including four books of Xenophon and three books of Homer.

Ancient History—and Geography.

Mathematics.—Three sections.

French or German.—Two sections.

A preliminary examination on certain portions of the foregoing subjects is offered in the May or June preceding the autumn term.

There is also an admission of special students by arrangement with the Dean, and an admission to advanced standing on examination.

The Undergraduate Course.—The Revised Statutes, adopted June 6th, 1892, provide that four years are required to complete the courses leading to degrees in the School of Arts. The following table offers a synopsis of the courses with information as to the various options allowed. Special attention should be directed to the system of options that obtains in the senior year. The studies of the senior year are all elective, and may be taken at the choice of the student in the courses that are open to them in the University Departments of Law, Medicine, Mines, Political Science, Philosophy and Pure Science. In the department of Law the first year course of 13 hours a week may be taken in part preparation for the degree of A.B., to which two hours must be added from other University Courses. In the department of Medicine the first year's course occupies the whole fifteen hours required for the A.B. degree. From this arrangement it will be seen that the senior year in the School of Arts is the point of contract between the College and the University:—

Freshmen and Sophomore Classes.—The studies of the freshmen class occupy fifteen hours a week and are all obligatory, except that a freshman must choose French or German (that one of them upon which he was examined for admission), but is not required to take both. The studies of the sophomore class require sixteen hours a week, and are all obligatory; a student may, however, substitute chemistry, three hours a week, for any language, ancient or modern, except English. The required studies are:—

In the freshman year:

	Hours a week.		Hours a week.
Greek	3	Mathematics	3
Latin	3	French or German	3
Rhetoric	3		

In the sophomore year:

	Hours a week.		Hours a week.
Greek	3	Mathematics	2
Latin	3	History	2
Literature	3	French and German	3

Chemistry (in place of Greek, Latin, French, or German) 3 hours.

A freshman or a sophomore who shall pass satisfactory examinations in the French and German of the first and second years, may substitute an elective course in French, German, Italian or Spanish, on the recommendation of the head of the department.

Junior Class.—For the studies of the junior class fifteen hours a week are required ; of these, four are for obligatory studies and eleven for elective courses.

The required studies are :

	Hours a week.
History and Political Economy	2
Logic and Psychology	2

Written work in English, under the direction of the Professor of Rhetoric, is required of each junior.

The elective courses open to the juniors are :

	Hours a week.		Hours a week.
Astronomy	2	English, Laws of Prose Composition	2
Biology, Elementary, with laboratory work	3	English, Shakespeare, Language, Versification, etc	2
Botany, Elementary, with laboratory work	3	English, Spencer and the Elizabethan Poets	1
Botany, with laboratory work	2	English, Milton and the Caroline Poets	
Chemistry, Inorganic, with laboratory work	3	English, 19th Century Literature	2
Chemistry, Applied Chemistry	3	Greek, Sophocles and Thucydides	3
Geology, General	2	Greek, Æschylus and Isocrates	2
German, Goethe's Faust	2	Greek, Lectures on the Greek Drama	1
German, History of German Literature	2	Greek, Lectures on Greek Art	1
German, Se'ect Historical Prose	2	Language, General Introduction	3
German, History or German Language	2		
German, Middle High German	2		

	Hours a week.		Hours a week.
Latin, Juvenal and Cicero de Officiis	2	Romance Languages:	
Latin, Terence, Andria and Phormio, and Lucretius de Rerum Natura	2	French, French Rhetoric.	3
		French, French Literature in the 17th Century	3
Mathematics, Analytical Geometry	3	Italian, Elementary	3
Mathematics, Projective Geometry	2	Italian, Prose and Poetry of the 16th Century	3
		Italian, Prose and Poetry of the 14th Century	3
Mechanics, with experiments	2	Spanish, Elementary	3
Physics, Elementary, with laboratory work	5	Spanish, Modern Prose and Poetry	3
Physics, Elementary — minor course — with laboratory work	3	Spanish, Literature of the Golden Age	3
Rhetoric, Lectures and Essays	2	Semitic Languages:	
		Hebrew, Biblical Hebrew, Elementary Course	2

Senior Class. — Seniors are required to take fifteen hours of elective courses, the following being open to them:

- English, Laws of Prose Composition in English.
- English, Shakespeare, Language, Versification, etc.
- English, Chaucer, Language, Versification, etc.
- English, The Poetry of Tennyson, Browning, and Matthew Arnold.
- English, Anglo-Saxon Poetry and Early English.

- English, Anglo-Saxon and English Historical Grammar.
- English, Spencer and Milton.
- English, 19th Century Literature.
- English, American Literature.
- English, English Versification.

Germanic Languages:
- German, Goethe's Faust.
- German History of German Literature.
- German Selected Historical Prose.
- German History of the German Language.
- German, Danish and Norwegian Literature.

- Greek, Æschylus and Isocrates.
- Greek, Lectures on the Greek Drama.
- Greek, Pindar and Demosthenes.
- Greek, Lectures on Elegiac, Iambic, and Melic Poets.
- Greek, New Testament, Epistles.
- Greek, New Testament, Gospels and Acts.
- Greek, Greek Art.
- Greek, Typography, Mythology and Monuments of Ancient Greece.

Language, General Introduction.

- Latin, Juvenal and Cicero de Officis.
- Latin, Lucretius.
- Latin Roman History, Tacitus, Suetonius, Velleius Paterculus.
- Latin, Plautus.
- Latin, Horace, rapid reading of all the poems.

- Literature, History and Theory of Criticism.
- Literature, History of Modern Fiction.
- Literature, Epochs of the Drama.

Oriental Languages:
- Sanskrit, Elementary.
- Semitic, Biblical Hebrew.
- Semitic, Semitic Epigraphy.
- Semitic, Arabic.

Pedagogy, Principles of Teaching.

- Philosophy, Ethics.
- Philosophy, General History of Philosophy.
- Philosophy, Philosophy of Kant and his Successors.
- Philosophy, Experimental Psychology.

Romance Languages:
- French, French Literature in the 17th Century.
- French, French Literature in the 18th Century.
- French, Victor Hugo.
- Spanish, Composition, Modern Prose and Poetry.

Constitutional History of Europe and the United States.

Constitutional History of England.

History of Political Theories.

Political Economy.

- Astronomy, General.
- Astronomy, Practical Astronomy and Navigation.
- Biology, Elementary, with laboratory work.
- Biology, General Zoology.
- Botany, Elementary with laboratory work.
- Botany, General Botany.
- Botany, Economic Botany.
- Chemistry, Inorganic with laboratory work.
- Chemistry, Applied Chemistry.
- Chemistry, Qualitative Analysis with laboratory work.
- Geology, General Geology.
- Geology, Economic Geology.
- Mathematics, Determinants, and Modern Geometry.
- Mathematics, Differential and Integral Calculus.
- Mechanics with experiments.
- Physics, Elementary—major course—with laboratory work.
- Physics, Elementary Physics—minor course—with laboratory work.
- Physics, Light and Heat.
- Physics, Higher Physics.

In addition to the above, first-year courses in the School of Law, School of Mines, and the College of Physicians and Surgeons are open to them; and such as may desire to do so can prepare themselves for advanced standing in those schools by electing these first year courses as a whole or in part, and counting them for the degree of Bachelor of Arts.

Degrees.—The President confers the following degrees:

—(a) In the College proper, commonly known as the School of Arts, the degree of Bachelor of Arts on the recommendation of the Faculty of Arts.

(b) The professional and technical degrees of Bachelor of Laws, upon the recommendation of the Faculty of Law; Doctor of Medicine upon the recommendation of the Faculty of Medicine; Bachelor of Science, Engineer of

Mines, Civil Engineer, Metallurgical Engineer, Electrical Engineer and Sanitary Engineer, upon the recommendation of the Faculty of the School of Mines, and

(c) The purely University degrees of Master of Arts, Master of Laws, and Doctor of Philosophy, upon the recommendation of the University Council. The degrees of Doctor of Laws, Doctor of Sacred Theology, and Doctor of Letters are conferred *honoris causa* by the Trustees at their discretion.

Examinations.—Two examinations are held every year, one commencing on the last Monday in January, and the other on the Monday of the third week preceding Commencement. It is the privilege of any department to announce that in some or all of its courses the result of the mid-year examination will be tentative only, the grade given after the final examination applying to the whole year. Absence from more than ten per cent. of the exercises in any course during a single term disqualifies from examination in that course. A third failure in any course involves exclusion from the College. At the close of every term students are classified in five grades according to merit, A, B, C, D, E. Students in grade E, are required to pass a supplemental examination. Honors are awarded at the end of the second year, at the end of the third year, and at the end of the course. A graduation Thesis is required prior to the granting of a degree.

CHAPTER XXI.

THE UNIVERSITY OF MICHIGAN.

Historical Sketch.—Although the University of Michigan, as now constituted, derives its origin from a provision in the Constitution of Michigan enacted in 1837, still the beginning of the university idea must be sought in the fantastic Act of 1817 to establish the "Catholepistemiad" or "University of Michigania." By the law of April 30th, 1821, the Catholepistemiad became the University of Michigan with Detroit still as its site. The Act gave into the hands of a new board composed of twenty-one Trustees, including the Governor, the control of the funds in the possession of its predecessor, and entrusted to them also the management of a Congressional land grant made in 1804 for educational purposes, and the disposal of the land derived from the treaty at Fort Meigs in 1817. In 1826, Congress gave to Michigan for a 'Seminary of Learning' two townships of land in lieu of the one given in the Act of 1804.

In 1837, Michigan was admitted into the Union, and the University then was finally established on its present basis as a State Institution. The Government of the University was vested in a Board of Regents to consist of twelve members and a Chancellor, who was *ex officio* President of the Board; the members were to be appointed by the Governor on the advice and with the consent of the Senate. The Governor, Lieutenant-Governor,

Judges of the Supreme Court, and Chancellor of the State were *ex officio* members of the Board. The Regents were empowered to regulate the courses of instruction, and to remove any professor or tutor in the best interests of the University. The Regents with the Superintendent of public instruction were authorized to establish branches of the University, and it was incumbent on them to establish in connection with every such branch, an institution for the education of females in the higher branches of knowledge. By an amended Act the Board was authorized to elect a Chancellor not a member of the Board, and to prescribe his duties. The Governor of the State was made *ex officio* President of the Board, and the Board was allowed to establish branches without obtaining further authority from the Legislature. The University eventually established nine of the prescribed branches throughout the State, but when it was discovered that their establishment hampered the central organization they were in 1849 discontinued.

On March 20th, an Act locating the University at Ann Arbor was approved. In 1838, the Regents, having large expectations from the proceeds of land sales, obtained from the Legislature a loan of $100,000 for building purposes, and in September, 1841, the doors of the University at Ann Arbor were opened to six students. The fortunes of the University until the appointment of its first President in 1852, were precarious in the extreme. The revenues were seriously impaired by a mismanagement of the landed property, and there was much friction in the internal organization. Nearly all the small income received was used in paying interest on the $100,000 indebtedness, and during those years until 1849 the branches were also supported by the University. In the latter years of the decade, the faculty by the efforts to crush out Secret Societies caused the disturbance commonly known as the "Society War." A report, drawn up as early as 1840, strongly urged a transfer of authority from the Legislature to the Regents and a freedom of action for the Faculty in their proper domain. As a result of this feeling, a constitution adopted by the people in 1851, provided that the Regents should be elected from the judicial districts with power to appoint a President of the University and to exercise a general supervision over affairs.

On account of internal friction it was decided to free the hands of the incoming board by dismissing the entire Faculty, which extreme measure was forthwith carried into execution. The University therefore entered upon a fresh era, when in 1852 the new Board of Regents assumed the duties of office. Dr. Henry Tappan was elected President and immediately the prospects brightened. During Dr. Tappan's administration the faculty was materially strengthened, and students in every department increased. But a serious error in the mode of electing the Board of Regents, whereby all passed out of office at the same time, led to numberless complications, resulting finally in the arbitrary dismissal of the President, despite the acknowledged ability and succees of his administration. A new Board, only two of whose members were College graduates, took office in 1858. Shortly before the lapse of their authority in 1863, they summarily dismissed President Tappan, and made many other changes in the faculty. This injustice bore some good fruit at least, for in 1863 the rotary system of electing the Regents which is still in vogue was established.

In 1866, an Act was passed granting a permanent tax to the University of 1-20 of a mill on the assessed value of property in the State. In 1868, an annuity of $15,000 was granted, thereby establishing the principle of State aid. In 1870, co-education was established, and the Prussian system of admission to the University from effective preparatory schools in Michigan without examination was introduced. In 1883, the same privilege was extended to other States.

Dr. James B. Angell, who is still the President of the University, took office in 1871. His administration has been an unqualified success, and his innovations have invariably resulted in the advantage of the University. New departments of instruction have been established and the old ones strengthened and extended. A free elective system was introduced, which would enable a capable student to complete his course in less than four years, or which would permit such a student to pursue more studies and accomplish more work in the four years of his collegiate career. Special students over twenty-one years of age were admitted to the courses of the University without an entrance examination. The 'University System' was established or in 1882, and ten years earlier seminary methods of study were first introduced.

U

Organization of the University.—The University derives its origin from a provision in the Constitution * of Michigan, the effect of which is to make the Regents of the University a branch of the State Government. The article in the constitution provides for the election of these Regents, authorizes them to elect a President of the University, and gives them supervision of the institution and the direction and control of all expenditures from the University interest fund, which is a fund created by the gift of two townships of land by the Federal Government to the State of Michigan for the endowment of a University.

The Regents, eight in number, are now elected by popular vote, for a term of eight years. Two are elected every second year, and have entire control of the University in every particular.

The professors and other teachers are appointed by the Regents, who have the power of removing them at any time. The younger members of the faculty are generally appointed first for a limited period, one year or three years. Professors are appointed permanently, though sometimes the first appointment is only for a year.

The revenue of the University is derived from three sources :—(a) The endowment, above referred to, by the National Government, which yields about $38,000 annually ; (b) By a State tax of one-sixth of a mill on all the taxable property of the State, which yields at present $188,300 ; (c) Fees from students, which usually yield about $125,000.

---

*Adopted in 1837.

Requirements for Admission.—Candidates for admission must be at least sixteen years of age, present evidence of good character, and bring credentials. There are three alternatives for examination :

(a) Admission on diploma is granted to the graduates of 144 approved preparatory schools.

(b) *Ad eundem* admission to advanced standing. Note.—When candidates for advanced standing have not passed a year at an approved college the must pass an entrance examination.

(c) Persons over twenty-one years of age who do not desire to take a degree are admitted to the courses without examination.

When admission is by examination the subjects are divided into groups, and the candidate is examined in that group which is determined by the character of the work he intends to pursue, and the degree he desires to take.

FOR THE DEGREE OF BACHELOR OF ARTS.

1. English Grammar, Composition and Rhetoric. Subjects of composition are selected from prescribed works.
2. History—including ancient history.
3. Mathematics—Algebra, Geometry.
4. Physics—an amount represented by Carhart and Chute's Elements.
5. Botany.
6. Latin—Grammar, Compositiın, and general reading.
7. Greek—Grammar, Composition, and three books of Xenophon's Anabasis.

FOR THE DEGREE OF BACHALOR OF PHILOSOPHY.

As in the above course, except that French or German is substituted for Greek and Grecian History.

FOR THE DEGREE OF BACHELOR OF SCIENCE.

Two groups are distinguished.

(a) For graduation in General Science, Chemistry and Biology.

(b) For graduation in Civil, Mechanical, Mining or Electrical Engineering.

The subjects for (a) are :—

1. English Language, Composition, Rhetoric, and Mathematics, as for Arts.

2. History.

3. French, German, Latin. Any two of these two languages may be offered.

In French and German, special works are not prescribed, although for the latter Schiller's Tell is recommended.

In Latin—Some introductory text-book.

Four books of Cæsar, and one of Cicero.

4. Physics and Botany.

5. Chemistry, Geology, Zoology, Physiology, Physical Geography, Astronomy.

The candidate may offer any two of these subjects.

The subjects for (b) are—

1 and 2 as in (a) with Trigonometry in addition.

3. Physics.

4. English Literature. Stopford Brook's Primer as a basis.

5. As in (a).

6. French, German, Latin. An examination in any one of these languages.

For the Degree of Bachelor of Letters.

1. English and Mathematics as in Arts, with English Literature in addition.

2. Physics and Botany as in Arts.

3. As in 5. of Science, except that three of the subjects are prescribed.

4. History—general, English and American.

5. Civil Government—Fisk's Civil Government, Hinsdale's American Government (I. and II.)

6. French, German or Latin.

Instead of English History, and three of the optional sciences in 3, French, German or Latin may be offered as in the Science group.

The Undergraduate Courses.—Nominally the courses are four years in length, but some students are able to graduate in a shorter time. Degrees are earned either on the credit system, or on the university system In the former a student must secure a stated number of hours of credit, generally 120, an hour of credit being the equivalent of one exercise a week for one semester Nothing, therefore, prevents a student from graduating when his hours of credit have been earned to the satisfaction of the faculty.

The University system is open to undergraduates who have completed their second year, and have also secured at least sixty hours of credit, including all the prescribed work. Students under this system must pursue three distinct lines of study, one major course and two minors, and pass a special examination on each. Examinations for degrees may be granted to a candidate who has been enrolled under the university system for at least three semesters, or in other words has attended the University for three and a half years. The following is a synopsis of the undergraduate course :—

1. FOR GRADUATION ON THE CREDIT SYSTEM.

For the Degree of Bachelor of Arts.—120 hours of credit work.
The prescribed work is as follows :
1 Greek. Sixteen hours in five prescribed courses. A specified selection of works in prose and verse and the history of Greek Literature. Eight hours are recommended for the first year. After the completion of the first three courses in Greek (amounting to eight hours), a candidate may discontinue the subject, but from among the other courses he must select enough to secure 120 hours of credit There are eighteen courses in all offered for study in Greek, thus affording thirteen purely optional courses.

2. Latin. Fifteen hours in four prescribed courses. This is of the same nature as the Greek course. After the completion of courses 1 and 2 (amounting to seven hours) the study may be discontinued under the same conditions as in Greek. Seven hours are recommended for the first year. There are twenty-five courses in all, some few of which are open to graduate students only.

3. French. Eight hours in two courses. These courses are elementary. There are besides twenty-six more advanced optional courses, covering a wide field.

It is recommended that the eight hours prescribed be taken in the first year.

4. English. Five hours in two prescribed courses.

Paragraph-writing and Rhetoric.

Two hours are recommended for the first year.

Twenty optional courses besides are open to undergraduates.

5. Philosophy. Two or three hours in one of two courses prescribed. Logic or Psychology.

This course is not recommended for the first year.

Twenty-four optional courses besides are open to undergraduates.

6. Mathematics. Fifteen hours in four prescribed courses—Plane Trigonometry and Algebra, Plane Analytic Geometry, and two courses of Calculus.

Instead of these some other equivalent in mathematics may be taken. Seven hours are recommended for the first year. After the completion of the first two courses, or their equivalent, a candidate may discontinue the study, provided that he makes up the required number of hours of credit from the optional courses. Twenty-seven optional courses besides are open to undergraduates.

It will be noticed that approximately half the work (sixty hours) is prescribed.

THE DEGREE OF BACHELOR OF PHILOSOPHY.

(120 hours.)

1. English as in Arts.
2. Philosophy as in Arts.
3. Mathematics as in Arts.
4. Latin as in Arts,

5. French. (a) For those who entered without French, sixteen hours, which are optional with the exception of the same prescribed work as in Arts. After the completion of the prescribed two courses (eight hours) French may be discontinued, provided that an equivalent number of optional hours is taken.

(b) For those who entered with French, eight hours of advanced work are necessary.

6. German. (a) For those who entered without German, sixteen hours including course 1, elementary and oppositions, in courses 2, 3, 4 (Calendar, pp. 61-62). After the completion of eight hours of German, the subject may be discontinued, on the same conditions as in French.

(b) For those who entered with German, eight hours taken optionally in courses 3 and 4.

(pp. 61-62.)

There are twenty-seven elective courses besides, open to undergraduates.

In French and German sixteen hours in all are recommended in the first year. For this degree from fifty-three to seventy hours are more on less prescribed out of 120 hours.

THE DEGREE OF BACHELOR OF SCIENCE.

(120 hours.)

1. French as in Philosophy.
2. German as in Philosophy.
3. English as in Philosophy.
4. Philosophy as in Arts.
5. Mathematics. Seven hours in two prescribed courses or their equivalent.

Plane Trigonometry, Algebra, Plane Analytic Geometry.

6. Physics. Five hours in one prescribed course. Mechanics, Sound, Light.

There are also twenty optional courses for undergraduates.

.7 General Chemistry. Seven hours in two prescribed courses. Inorganic Chemistry, Descriptive and Experimental.

There are also ten optional courses in General Chemistry.

8. Zoology, Botany or General Biology. Five hours are required of optional work.

The courses in these subjects will be found on pp. 89-94 of the calendar.

9. Physical or Biological Sciences. Twenty-five hours are required of optional work in these courses.

It is desirable for the student in this course, as in others, to put to his credit fifteen hours a week for each semester (sometimes sixteen) which amounts to thirty hours a year, or the required number of credit hours—120—in four years. Mathematics, French, German and English should occupy twenty-five hours out of thirty-two in the first year. In this course 72-89 hours are more or less prescribed out of 120 hours.

For special degrees in Science, see calendar p. 102.

THE DEGREE OF BACHELOR OF LETTERS.

(120 hours.)

1. French. Sixteen hours, including the two prescribed courses as in Arts. After concluding these two prescribed courses, French may be discontinued on the ordinary conditions.

2. German. Sixteen hours—one elementary prescribed course, and options in three prescribed courses. After the completion of eight hours of German, the subject may be discontinued under the ordinary conditions.

3. English. Nine hours in four prescribed courses, two of which are as in Arts. The other two courses comprise elementary work in Old and Middle English.

4. History. Six hours in two prescribed courses. General History of Europe from the fall of the Roman Empire to the outbreak of the French Revolution.

5. Philosophy as in Arts.

6. Mathematics. Three hours in one prescribed course. Plane Trigonometry and Algebra.

For the first year are recommended three hours in Mathematics; eight hours in French; eight hours in German; two hours in English; History, or other studies, eleven hours, or in all sixteen hours a week for each semester.

II. FOR GRADUATION ON THE UNIVERSITY SYSTEM.

Other courses in the University are offered in Sanskrit, Hellenistic Greek, Hebrew, Assyrian, Arabic, Italian, Spanish, Portuguese, Gothic, Swedish, Danish-Norwegian, Elocution and Oratory. The Science and Art of Teaching, Political Economy and Sociology, International Law, Music, Bibliography, Natural Science, Drawing, Surveying, Civil Engineering (pp. 96-97), Mechanical Engineering (pp. 97-98), Marine Engineering, Mining Engineering and Metallurgy. For further account of the Engineering Courses see calendar, pp. 104-114 and p. 124 for the work prescribed in the first year.

The Nature of the Options.—As a rule, from fifty to seventy hours, rarely more, are practically prescribed, that is to say, certain general courses of study amounting to that number of hours are prescribed, but there is an option exercised within certain of these specified courses. The student's choice for the rest is unhampered whether he graduate under the University or the Credit System.

The Degrees.—The University grants the following degrees at the conclusion of the undergraduate courses:

Bachelor of Arts, Bachelor of Philosophy, Bachelor of Science (in general), Bachelor of Letters.

The degree of Bachelor of Science may also be given in Chemistry, Biology, or Engineering.

Examinations, Etc.—Examinations are conducted by the members of the Faculty. There are no special examiners appointed from outside. These examinations are partly oral and partly in writing, as the examiner may choose to make them.

CHAPTER XXII.

CORNELL UNIVERSITY.

Historical Sketch.—Cornell University was incorporated by the Legislature of the State of New York on the 27th of April, 1865. The Congress of 1862 had granted public lands to the several States, from the sale of which there should be established a perpetual fund, the interest of which should be inviolably appropriated by each State claiming the benefit of the act to the endowment and maintenance of at least one college, where the leading object should be, not to the exclusion of other scientific and classical studies, to give instruction in agriculture, military tactics, and the mechanic arts.

After $64,440 had been realized on the New York scrip, the sales entirely ceased. Ezra Cornell, who had long been dreaming of charitably bestowing his fortune now saw his opportunity at hand. By way of a direct donation he gave $500,000 to the University, 200 acres of land with useful buildings, and some smaller gifts for special purposes. His largest gift, however, came later in the shape of profits made by the University on the sale of the land scrip which he purchased from the State.

On the cessation of sales the Legislature had authorized the sale of the remaining scrip to the Trustees of the

University or "to any person or persons" at a price of not less than thirty cents per acre, sales having originally been as high as eighty-five cents. Cornell purchased the scrip at thirty cents, and agreed to allow from the profits thirty cents more to the original College Land Scrip Fund, on condition that all profits above that figure should be placed to the credit of the Cornell Endowment Fund, and exempted from the conditions governing the agricultural College grant.

The utmost sum which the State of New York could have realized on the whole of the scrip at the decreased market price, would have been less than $600,000. The College Land Scrip Fund now amounts to nearly $500,000 and will ultimately reach over $600,000. The Cornell-Endowment Fund, owing to Ezra Cornell's successful location of the scrip, and the unexpectedly large profits, has already realized a net return of nearly $4,000,000. This sum has further been supplemented by numerous large donations from other sources. In an agreement with the Legislature, August, 1866, it was stipulated that the Cornell Endowment Fund should be the property of the University, while the College Land Scrip Fund, on the other hand, was held by the State in trust, subject to all the conditions imposed by Congress.

In March, 1895, two important laws were enacted in the Legislature. The Legislature consented to absorb the College Land Grant Fund into the Treasury of the State, and to issue to the University certificates of indebtedness bearing interest at the rate of five per cent.

This relieves the University of the responsibility of ultimately investing $600,000, and of the danger of obtaining ruinously low rates of interest. On petition from the Board it was enacted that the number of elective trustees should be thirty instead of fifteen as formerly.

Organization of the University.—Cornell University derived its charter from the State of New York (Laws of New York, 1865, chapter 585). The charter leaves the trustees free to make provision, in the planning of instruction and investigations, for all branches of science and knowledge. But as the University received a certain portion of congressional lands, which were donated to the State of New York for the establishment of an institution which should teach the sciences related to agriculture and the mechanic arts, including military tactics, these subjects must always remain an unalterable part of the curriculum.

The University has thirty-eight trustees; of these, eight are trustees *ex officio*, including, besides the President and Librarian of the University, the Hon. Alonzo B. Cornell and the high State officials, namely, the Governor of New York, the Lieutenant-Governor, the Speaker of the Assembly, the Superintendent of Public Instruction and the President of the State Agricultural Society. The remaining thirty are elected in groups of six for a term of five years. Of the six, four are elected by the Board of Trustees, and two by the Alumni of the University. As the Board of Trustees is the only legal corporation, it has, therefore, all authority under the law. It delegates, however, the educational work of the institution to the Faculty; but all important changes must be submitted to the Board for their approval.

All members of the instructing staff in Cornell are appointed by the Board of Trustees on the nomination of the President of the University. Professors are appointed without limit as to term, personal?y therefore, during good behavior. Assistant professors are appointed for a term of three years, which in the president's opinion should be raised to five years. Instructors, assistants, etc., are appointed for one year. Those members of the instructing staff who are appointed for a term are, as a rule reappointed at its expiration.

University Finances.—The Revenue is derived from the Cornell Endowment Fund now amounting to nearly four million dollars, and from the College Land Scrip Fund now amounting to $473,402.87. The History of these endowments has already been outlined. Gifts from individuals now amount to $1,983,548. The remaining revenue is derived from the fees of students.

The following tables give a fair idea of the rate at which the Endowment of Cornell is increasing, also the rate of increase of the total revenue and of the income from students' fees:

THE ENDOWMENT.

1881-82	$ 964,503
1882-83	3,539,283
1883-84	3,583,274
1884-85	3,642,304
1885-86	3,699,994
1886-87	4,282,042

1887-88	$4,528,350
1888-89	4,678,729
1889-90	4,719,505
1890-91	5,070,101
1891-92	5,728,452
1892-93	6,095,219
1893-94	6,078,019
1894-95	6,187,965

THE ANNUAL REVENUE.

	Total Income.	Income from Fees.
1881-82	$ 142,371	$ 13,940
1882-83	211,367	13,502
1883-84	217,273	17,395
1884-85	240,071	20,980
1885-86	245,320	22,575
1886-87	251,620	30,304
1887-88	329,811	39,448
1888-89	362,164	47,208
1889-90	375,298	53,587
1890-91	416,267	90,401
1891-92	464,426	96,894
1892-93	469,467	106,568
1893-94	496,352	114,093
1894-95	515,412	114,420

The following table gives the total expenditure for salaries of the instructing staff, and also the number of instructors of all grades during the years 1881-95:—

	Aggregate of Salaries.	No. of Instructors.
1881-82	$ 96,073	49
1882-83	99,622	50
1883-84	104,047	52
1884-85	113,150	56
1885-86	118,950	61
1886-87	132,294	80
1887-88	151,550	90
1888-89	175,250	101
1889-90	178,383	106
1890-91	204,400	116
1891-92	228,566	128
1892-93	241,075	147
1893-94	249,300	149
1894-95	260,827	162

There is no State tax in support of the University; but the State has recently established a State veterinary college, making an appropriation of $150,000 for buildings, and this will be maintained by the State.

Five hundred and twelve students from New York State are educated free on State scholarships, from which source the University derives no revenue. The annual tuition fee in the School of Law, in the Medical Preparatory Course and in Arts, Philosophy and Science is $100. In all other courses it is $125.

Free tuition is also given to students intending to complete the course in Agriculture, and to special students in Agriculture. There are also certain special fees in the departments for materials consumed etc., which add nothing to the real income of the University.

Requirments for Admission.—Candidates must be at least sixteen years of age, or, if women, seventeen. The examinations are held in Ithaca only, and twice in the year. There are three alternatives for examinations as a means of entering the University:

(1) Diplomas issued by the Regents of the University of the State of New York, and pass cards presented as supplementary, are accepted for all subjects covered by such diplomas. In the case of French and German, a statement by the teacher of the work done must accompany the diploma. To secure exemption from the primary examination in English, the diploma must cover six academic counts, including English Composition.

(2) The application from the Principal of a school, accompanied by full information regarding the work

done by the applicant, is sometimes accepted in lieu of examinations. But no school certificate exempts from the primary examination in English.

(3) Persons at least twenty-one years of age (in the case of students in Agriculture eighteen) may on recommendation of a Professor be exempted from entrance examinations, provided that they give evidence of ability to do special work. They may graduate in any course, on condition of passing the required examinations, including the entrance examinations.

The examinations for admission consist of two divisions. The first, a primary examination, is required for all courses, but is not sufficient without an advanced examination. The following are the requirements :—

The Primary Examination embraces the following subjects :— English, geography, physiology and hygiene, arithmetic, plane geometry, algebra, American history. In English, the candidate must write three essays based on certain works of authors prescribed, and further, show a satisfactory knowledge of these works. No student markedly deficient in English is admitted to the University. Sufficiently elementary work is prescribed in the remaining subjects.

The advanced examinations for admission differ with the various courses to which admission is sought.

1. Bachelor of Arts :—For this course examinations are demanded in (1) Greek (facility in translation of simple attic prose and Homer, a knowledge of Greek accidence and the outlines of syntax, and some command of Greek prose composition); (2) Latin. (Sight-translation, Latin prose, and a detailed examination on assigned portions of Cæsar, Virgil, and Cicero); (3) Grecian and Roman history, and outlines of ancient geography, Fyffe's primer of Greece, Creighton's primer of Rome, and Tozer's primer of classical geography.

2. Philosophy :—(1) Latin—as above ; (2) Grecian and Roman history—as above ; (3) French or German. No special authors or works are designated. In the case of French, candidates are

expected to able to read easy French at sight, and to translate readily simple English into French. Pronunciation, and translation and writing of French from dictation are included. Candidates are expected to present a statement from their teachers of the amount of French previously read, the text-books used and proficiency attained. Similarly in German.

3. Science and Agriculture :—(1) French—as in preceding course; (2) German—as in preceding course; (3) Mathematics—Solid geometry—(Newcomb's elements or the equivalent), advanced algebra; plane trigonometry—(Well's treatise or the equivalent); (4) Latin—(Four books of Cæsar or the equivalent and good knowledge of the grammar.)

In place of a modern language requirement an equivalent amount of an ancient classical language may be accepted, provided that the work omitted is made up in the subsequent course.

4. Mechanical engineering, electrical engineering, and architecture :—(1) Mathematics as in the preceding course; (2) French or German as in course 1 and 2.

5. Civil Engineering :—(1) Mathematics—(Solid Geometry); (2) French or German as in 1 and 2.

6. Medicine :—(1) Latin—(four books of Cæsar and grammatical knowledge); (2) Greek (enough to enable the student to recognize and analyze scientific terms); (3) Plane trigonometry as in 3; (4) French or German as in 1 and 2.

The Undergraduate Course.—The length of all undergraduate courses is four years, except the law course, which is three years. The following is a synopsis of those leading to the various degrees :—

BACHELOR OF ARTS.

First year :—Greek. 3 hours a week through the year of three terms; Latin, 3 hours; French, 3 hours; English, 2 hours. (Rhetoric).

Mathematics, 3 hours; (Solid geometry, algebra Trigonometry.) Grecian History; Roman History; Hygiene.

Second year:—Greek, 3 hours; Latin, 3 hours; German, 3 hours; English, (Rhetoric); physiology, psychology, logic, 3 hours; Military drill; Elective, 0 to 4 hours each term.

Third year;—Entirely elective, provided that the major part of the work is in literary, historical, philosophical and mathematical subjects.

Fourth year:—As in third year, but 2 hours a week devoted to theses.

BACHELOR OF PHILOSOPHY.

Students in this course who in the last two years elect continuously not less that nine hours of studies in history and political science, will receive the degree of Ph. B, in history and political science.

First year:—As in the first year of the arts course, only substituting German (as in second year of arts) for Greek.

Second year:—As in second year of arts, substituting history for Greek, and with a choice between French and German.

Third and Fourth years:—as in the preceding course.

BACHELOR OF SCIENCE.

First year:—Mathematics—5 hours; French—3 hours as in arts; German—3 hours as in second year of arts; English (Rhetoric), Chemistry—3 hours (General Inorganic Chemistry); elementary—or for more advanced students qualitative and quantitative analysis): Hygiene.

Second year:—French or German, 3 hours devoted to three prescribed works in either language also 3 hours of elective work in either language; English—2 hours (Rhetoric); Physics, 3 hours: Mechanics and Heat; Electricity and Magnetism; Acoustics and Optics; (A more advanced course for those taking elective works in Physics); Botany, 2 hours.

Physiology, Psychology and Logic as in preceding courses, elective, 1 to 5 hours each term.

Third year:—Entirely elective, but that a majority of the work must be in Natural Science or Mathematics.

Fourth year:—As in third year, except that 2 hours must be devoted to theses.

Degree of M.E.

First year :—Elementary Mathematics, French or German, Chemistry, Drawing.

Second year :—Mathematics, designing, experimental mechanics and heat, shop work, electricity, chemistry, acoustics and optics.

Third and Fourth years :—More specialized work with options in the fourth year.

Bachelor of Science in Agriculture.

First year :—French or German or Mathematics, Zoology and Entomology, English, Drawing, Chemistry, Hygiene, Drill.

Second year :—English, Physics Agricultural Chemistry, Political Economy, Physiology, Microscopy, applied Mathematics. Elective 0 to 2 hours each term.

Third year :—Elective ; but 12 hours to be devoted to agricultural subjects.

Fourth year :—Seven prescribed hours in agriculture. The rest elective, except that five hours must be devoted to agricultural subjects.

Optional Courses.—As will be seen from the preceding synopsis, the courses in the third and fourth years are almost entirely elective, with the restrictions that have been noted. The Sophomore year also contains certain electives. The lectures are arranged to satisfy all the different degrees of proficiency, and there are special courses adapted to the needs of prospective teachers, etc.

University Degrees.—The degrees of Cornell Univer- are granted by the Board of Trustees on the recommendation of the faculties. They are as follows :—

Bachelor of Arts.

Bachelor of Philosophy.

Bachelor of Letters (to be abolished in 1896).

Bachelor of Science or Bachelor of Science in Natural History.

Bachelor of Science in Agriculture.
Bachelor of Science in Architecture.
Bachelor of Laws.
Civil Engineer.
Mechanical Engineer.
Also the advanced degrees of—
Master of Arts.
Master of Philosophy.
Master of Letters.
Master of Science.
Master of Laws.
Master of Science in Architecture.
Master of Civil Engineering.
Master of Mechanical Engineering.
Master of Science in Agriculture.
Doctor of Philosophy.
Doctor of Science.

Examinations.—Examinations are conducted by the members of the instructing corps. The heads of departments are responsible therefor, though in making out the questions they may be aided by the assistant professors, instructors, etc.

CHAPTER XXIII.

THE JOHNS HOPKINS UNIVERSITY.

The establishment of this University marks an epoch in the development of the system of higher education in the United States. Prior to that event the chief work of all the universities had been the education of undergraduates; since then an increasing part of the work of many of them and all the work of others, has been the further education of those who have already completed an ordinary university course. This change has been the result to a large extent of the policy deliberately adopted by the management of the Johns Hopkins University.

Historical Sketch.—The location of the University was no doubt determined by the fact that Mr. Hopkins, who furnished the original endowment, was a citizen of Baltimore, but the selection was in every way a fortunate one. Baltimore is sufficiently near Washington for the University to be beneficially affected by the political life of the national capital, without the inevitable distraction from work that would be caused by constant and immediate contact with it. The foundation of the University is a bequest of one-half of the founder's estate of seven million dollars, the other half having been devoted to the establishment of a Hospital with a view to the ultimate development of a teaching medical department. At Mr. Hopkins' request an incorporation was in 1867 formed under a general statute, "for the promotion of education in the State of Maryland," but very little was done during his life to give practical effect to his intentions. In 1874 the Board of Trustees began an elaborate investigation of existing university constitutions in the United States and elsewhere, and after obtaining the advice of such experienced educators as President Eliot of Harvard, President White of Cornell, and President Angell of Michigan, they placed at the head of the proposed University, Daniel C. Gilman, then President of the University of California, and formerly a Professor of Yale College. For some months he continued in Europe his inquiries into the constitution and working of universities, and on his return the character to be given to the new institution was outlined in his inaugural address delivered early in 1876. Its aims were to be, "an enduring foundation; a slow development; first local, then regional, then national influence; the most liberal promotion of all useful knowledge; the special provision of such departments as are elsewhere neglected in the country; a generous affiliation with all other institutions, avoiding interferences and engaging in no rivalry; the encouragement of research; the promotion of young men, and the advancement of individual scholars, who by their excellence will advocate the sciences they pursue, and the society where they dwell." The University was opened for students in October, 1876, in buildings erected in a densely-peopled part of the City of Baltimore. It was not the settled purpose of the management that the academical work should always be carried on there, but as time passed, old buildings were improved and new ones erected to meet the demand for accommodation, until the series was crowned by the completion in 1894 of the noble edifice called "McCoy Hall," after the devisor of the fund which enabled the trustees to erect and equip it. As the new buildings have all been constructed in the most substantial manner it seems quite unlikely that the work of the University will ever be removed from where it is now carried on. The construction of the Johns Hopkins' Hospital was delayed for some time by the loss of a part of the capital of the endowment, but it was completed a few years ago and in the fall of 1893 the Medical School in connection with it was opened for the reception of students. Johns Hopkins' University seems to have reached a period in its history when the stream of private donations may be expected to be virtually continuous, and each year the list of benefactions is increased by several additions.

Organization of the University.—The first trustees were selected by the founder of the University in 1867. They were twelve in number, and as vacancies have occurred they have been filled by the exercise of co-optation. The President is a member of the Board, *ex officio*. The Trustees are invested with full control over the property and management of the University. They make all appointments and promotions of members of the teaching staff, and of other officials, and they regulate all salaries and other expenditures. The policy has been adopted with respect to the new Medical faculty of placing the members of it on the same footing as that occupied by members of the Arts faculty. In this way the medical teachers do not depend at all for remuneration on the earnings of the faculty of which they are members, but are paid their salaries out of the revenues of the University. The instructors in the Arts faculty are classified as follows: associates, associate professors, and professors, and some of those now in the highest grade have passed through all the inferior ranks. Some of the eminent men who held professorship at the organization of the University have taken similar positions in other institutions, but a few of them remain still on the list. The policy has from the first prevailed of distinguishing between the "University" and the "College," the latter name being given to the body made up of undergraduates in the Arts faculty, and the former including those who take post-graduate or professional courses.

Requirements for Matriculation :

1. Mathematics.—Arithmetic, Algebra, Plane and Solid Geometry, Plane Trigonometry, Analytic Geometry.

    NOTE. Elementary Mechanics may be substituted for Analytical Geometry by students selecting groups which do not include Minor Mathematics or Major Physics.

2. Latin.—Certain specified works, or an equivalent amount. Accidence, Syntax, Prosody.
3. Greek.—As in Latin.
4. German.
5. French.
   Candidates not offering Greek must offer both French and German, with a choice between two groups: (*a*) Advanced German and Elementary French, or (*b*) Advanced French and Elementary German.
6. English.—(*a*) A general knowledge of the substance of certain specified books as the basis for a composition.

    (*b*) A detailed knowledge of the subject-matter, form, and structure of specified books.

7. History.—England and the United States, or Greece and Rome, and the outlines of Geography.

8. Science.—The elements of Chemistry, Botany, or Physical Geography.

The matriculation examination may be divided with the interval of a year.

Candidates from approved schools are excepted from a portion of the examination.

Undergraduate Courses.—The course for the degree of A.B. occupies three years. The following courses are prescribed for all undergraduates: Rhetoric; English Literature; Economics and History; Philosophy; Minor French; Minor German; English Composition; Drawing; Physical and Vocal Culture.

A student must select one of the following groups of study:

I. THE CLASSICAL GROUP.

Consisting of (*a*) The prescribed courses; (*b*) Latin, Greek, a Laboratory course, Comparative Philology, and an Elective course of two hours weekly in the Third Year.

II. THE MATHEMATICAL-PHYSICAL GROUP.

The same course as in the Classical group, except that two years of Mathematics and Physics are substituted for Latin and Greek, and one year of Chemistry is added.

III. THE CHEMICAL-BIOLOGICAL OR PRELIMINARY MEDICAL GROUP.

(*a*) The prescribed courses; (*b*) Physics, Chemistry, and Biology, with laboratory practice.

IV. THE PHYSICAL-CHEMICAL GROUP.

The same as group II., except that two years are devoted to Chemistry and one year to Mathematics.

V. THE LATIN-MATHEMATICAL GROUP.

This differs from group I. only in substituting Mathematics for Greek.

VI. THE HISTORICAL-POLITICAL GROUP.

This group omits Greek and retains but one year of Latin, providing two years of History and two years of Political Science.

VII. THE MODERN LANGUAGE GROUP.

This group substitutes for Greek two years of English, and, retaining one year of Latin, substitutes for the other an additional year of either French or German. A year of Spanish or Italian may be substituted for the latter.

ELECTIVE COURSES.

Two hours a week in the Third Year may be devoted to subjects from among the following:—Differential Equations, Astronomy, Zoology, Hebrew, Latin, Greek, German, Italian, English Literature, History of Philosophy.

With the approval of his adviser a student may also substitute other studies for two, or occasionally three of the courses laid down in his group

The Graduate Courses.—The relative importance of the graduate courses to the undergraduate courses in Johns Hopkins University cannot be estimated alone by a comparison of numbers. Still the numbers have a certain significance, and a reference to the register will show that the usual excess of the graduate students over the undergradutes is as three to one. But a truer insight into the real greatness of Johns Hopkins University is obtained when we realize that this University has become the type upon which other universities have sought to model their courses of graduate instruction, and the general system of their post-graduate work. President Low, of Columbia College, in a late address, recognized fully the value of the work that this University has accomplished. "It is the glory of Johns Hopkins University that, being a type new to American experience, its methods and ideals have been largely adopted by both the older and the new institutions of the higher learning in the United States. . . . When, therefore, (in 1874) President Gilman was called to the duty of organizing the Johns Hopkins University, the man and the opportunity for a university of a new type met in America for the first time."

The degree of Doctor of Philosophy is offered to those who continue their University studies for three years or more after having attained the degree of Bachelor of Arts. Their attention must be given to studies which are included in the faculty of philosophy and the liberal arts, and not in the professional faculties of law, medicine, and theology. Students who have graduated in other institutions of repute may offer themselves as candidates for this degree. The student must show his proficiency in one principal subject and in two that are secondary, and must submit himself to rigid examinations, first written, and then oral. He has also to present a thesis which must receive the written approval of the special committee to which it may be referred, with the concurrence of the entire faculty, and must subsequently be printed. These requirements are enforced by an academic body known as the Board of University Studies. As an indication of the possible combination which may be made by those who are studying for the degree of Ph. D. the following schedule is presented:—

1. Physics, Mathematics, and Chemistry.
2. Animal Physiology, Animal Morphology, and Chemistry.
3. Chemistry, Mineralogy, and Geology.
4. Mathematics, Astronomy, and Physics.
5. Sanskrit, Greek, and Latin.
6. History, Political Economy, and International Law.

7. Greek, Sanskrit, and Latin.
8. French, Italian, and German.
9. Latin, Sanskrit, and Roman Law.
10. Latin, Sanskrit, and German.
11. Assyriology, Ethiopic and Arabic, and Greek.
12. Political Economy, History, and Administration.
13. English, German, and Old Norse.
14. Inorganic Geology and Petrography, Mineralogy, and Chemistry.
15. Geology, Chemistry, and Physics.
16. Romance Languages, German, and English.
17. Latin, Greek, and Sanskrit.
18. German, English, and Sanskrit.

CHAPTER XXIV.

CLARK UNIVERSITY.

Historical Sketch.—Clark University was founded by the munificence of Mr. Jonas G. Clark of Worcester County, Massachusetts. His desire was "that special opportunities and inducements be offered to research, that to this end the instructors be not overburdened with teaching or examinations; that new measures, and even innovations, if really helpful to the highest needs of modern science and culture, be freely adopted." Eight University Graduates accepted Mr. Clark's invitation to constitute with himself a Board of Trustees. A petition for a Charter was at once made by this Board, and it was obtained from the Legislature of Massachusetts on January 18th, 1887.

On May 1st, 1888, Dr. G. Stanley Hall accepted the Presidency, and was at once granted one year's leave of absence, with full salary, to visit the Universities of Europe. The opening exercises were held in the University on October 2nd, 1889. The founder, in outlining his aims, said,—" We propose to go on to further and higher achievements. We propose to put into the hands of those who are members of the University every facility which money can command—to the extent of our ability—in the way of apparatus and appliances that can in any way promote our object in this direction." After consideration, it was decided to begin with graduate work only and in the five departments of Mathematics, Physics,

Chemistry, Biology, and Psychology. In addition to these, modern languages are taught in order to meet the practical needs of students. As new departments are established they will be chosen in so far as they are scientifically most closely related to those already existing; so that the body of sciences may be kept vigorous and compact, and that the strength of the University may always rest not upon the number of subjects, nor the breadth nor length of its curriculum, but upon its thoroughness and its unity. "Clark University is exclusively what is called in Europe a Philosophical Faculty, devoted to a group of the *pure sciences* which underlie technology and medicine, but not yet applying its work to these professional fields." Instead of a dissipation of energies in University extensions, the opposite course is followed of university concentration, as in the Ecole Pratique of France.

Organization of the University.—By the Act of Incorporation the trustees were made a corporation by the name of "The Trustees of Clark University," to be located in Worcester, for the purpose of establishing and maintaining an institution for the promotion of education, and investigation in science, literature and art, to be called Clark University.

Other sections of the Act provided that the corporation should be permitted to receive and hold real or personal estate, that they should possess all the privileges of similarly incorporated institutions in the Commonwealth, and that they should have complete control of the organization of the University, and supervision over its affairs.

The original board was nominated by Mr. Clark. The Act of Incorporation ordered that the number of the Trustees should not be less than seven, nor more than nine. The Act further defines the scope of their authority as above stated. Vacancies are filled by election of the Trustees at a meeting duly called for that purpose.

The Faculty are appointed by the Board of Trustees, upon the nomination of the President, generally for one, three or five years, or to continue during the pleasure of the Board.

Revenues.—The revenues are interest upon its endowment. The fees from students are small, and there is no State Tax.

Requirements for Admission.—The degree of B.A. or its equivalent, is required for matriculation. There is no undergraduate course, and so far, only the degree of Ph. D. has been conferred, by the Board on recommendation of the Faculty.

Examinations.—These are (1) a preliminary examination a year beforehand for admission to candidacy and (2), a final examination before a jury, which must consist of at least four, must include the chief instructors of the candidate, and often includes an additional Professor from the same department of another university, who is invited by the President.

CHAPTER XXV.

THE UNIVERSITY OF CHICAGO.

Historical Sketch.—The first University of Chicago closed its work in 1886. Within a few months thereafter, Mr. John D. Rockefeller took into consideration the founding of a new institution of learning in that city. In the fall of 1888 he conferred with Professor Wm. R. Harper in regard to it, and finally entered into communication on the subject with Rev. F. T. Gates, Secretary of the American Baptist Education Society. In December, 1888, Mr. Gates brought the matter before the Board of the Society, which instructed the Secretary to use every means in his power to originate and encourage the movement. At the anniversary of the Education Society, held in Boston, in May, 1889, the Society formally resolved to take immediate steps towards the founding of a well equipped college in the city of Chicago. To make it possible to carry out this purpose, Mr. Rockefeller at once made a subscription of $600,000, toward an endowment fund, conditioned on the pledging of $400,000 before June 1st, 1890. This money was obtained, and in addition Mr. Marshall Field donated a block and a half of ground, valued at $125,000 as a site for the new institution. Two and a half blocks were afterwards purchased, thus providing a site of four blocks, or about twenty-four acres. On September 10th, 1890, the University was incorporated, and in the spring of 1891, Professor William Rainey Harper, of Yale University accepted the position of President. By the generosity of Mr. John D. Rockefeller, the founder, and others the endowment of the University has rapidly increased until the present time, when the aggregate endowment is estimated at $4,500,000.

Organization of the University.—The University of Chicago is incorporated under the laws of the State of Illinois. The certificate of Incorporation was filed September 10th, 1890, and recorded in Cook county, September 20th, 1890. The objects for which the corporation was formed, are stated in the second section of the certificate as follows:—To provide opportunities for all departments of higher education to persons of both sexes on equal terms; to establish, conduct and maintain academies, preparatory schools, or departments, and manual training schools in connection therewith; to establish and maintain one or more colleges, and to provide instruction therein; to establish and maintain a University in which may be taught all branches of higher learning; and to provide and maintain courses of instruction in all its departments, to prescribe the courses of study, employ professors, etc.; and to control the government and discipline in said University, and in each of the institutions subordinate thereto. The Corporation was further granted the customary privileges of similar corporations, such as the power to receive and invest funds, etc., in the use of the University.

The number of the trustees was fixed at twenty-one, and directions given as to the manner of their selection. They were appointed originally by the Board of the American Baptist Education Society. Two-thirds of the Trustees, and also the President of the University, must be members of regular Baptist churches. They are arranged in three equal classes, and annually on the retirement of one class, they elect by ballot seven successors. The trustees make by-laws for the government of the corporation, and of its several departments, and of the several institutions of learning under its care and control, and for the proper management of the educational, fiscal, and other affairs of the corporation.

The members of the Faculty are appointed by the Board of Trustees. The classification is as follows:—The Head Professor, Professor, Associate Professor, Assistant Professor, Instructor, Tutor, Assistant, Reader, Docent and Fellow. The tenure of office of Assistant Professors is four years; of Instructors, three years; of Tutors, two years; of Assistants, Readers, Docents, and Fellows one year. At the end of their term the connection ceases from the rank of Assistant Professor downward, unless there is re-appointment. All officers of Instruction and government are subject to removal for inadequate performance of duty, or for misconduct.

The revenue is derived from endowments, and fees of the students. On January 1st, 1896, the endowments will aggregate $4,500,000. The fees from students amount to something over $100,000. The matriculation fee is $5; the fee for instruction, $40 a quarter; and the fee for a diploma, $10. There is a special fee besides for science students. Private donations are also made for current expenses. There is no State tax.

Requirements for Admission.—The undergraduate portion of the University of Chicago is divided into what are known as the various Colleges with respect to the curriculum of study and the degree desired, and each College is further subdivided into what is termed an Academic College covering the first and second years of the course, and a University College embracing the work of the two final years.

The University gives examinations for admission in the following subjects, but not all of these subjects will be required for admission from any one candidate.

1. *Greek.*—Four examinations are offered. Sight translation of Attic prose, and an average passage of Homer. Questions on grammar, prosody, etc., Greek prose.

2. *Latin.*—Five examinations. Sight translations of Cæsareun and Ciceronian Latin. Questions on prosody, literature, grammar, etc., Latin prose.

3. *History.*—The candidate must prepare specially some topic chosen from a given list of nine historical subjects.

There are also three optional examinations on Grecian, Roman, and Mediæval and Modern History, with a compulsory examination on the history of the United States, for which no separate credit is given.

4. *Mathematics.*—Three examinations. Algebra, Plane Geometry and Solid Geometry.

5. *English.*—The examination consists of two parts, which, however, cannot be taken separately. The candidate is required,—First to write a paragraph or two on each of the several topics chosen by him from a considerable number of prescribed works (perhaps ten or fifteen). The candidate is expected to read intelligently all the books prescribed, and to have freshly in mind their most important details. Second—A certain number of prescribed books must be minutely studied.

6. *German.*—Three examinations.

(1) Proficiency in the elements of the language commensurate with the reading of 100-200 duodecimo pages of easy German prose and lyrical poems.

(2) A thorough knowledge of accidence, and the essentials of syntax. Translation of ordinary German at sight, presupposing the reading of two hundred pages of modern comedy, and various prescribed works. The writing in German of a paragraph upon one of several subjects selected from the prescribed works. Ability to follow a recitation conducted in German, and to answer in that language.

(3) The translation of continuous English prose into idiomatic German

7. *French.*—Three examinations of a similar character to those in German, except that each of these examinations is partly written, partly oral; the latter being employed as a test of grammatical knowledge and ability in pronunciation. In the second examination the equivalent of 1000 duodecimo pages, at least, of standard French is required, including certain prescribed works. In the third examination, among other things, there is an examination on French literature since the Renaissance conducted orally in French.

8. *Physics.*—Mechanics, sound, heat, light.

9. *Chemistry.*—A course of fifty experiments performed by the student. The record of these experiments to be presented to the examiner. Also certain experiments during the examination. A written examination on some text-book, such as Remson, or Roscoe.

10. *Biology.*—The candidate must submit to the Examiner a note-book of drawings, descriptions, etc., must perform satisfactory work under supervision in the College laboratory, and pass a written examination on certain general questions.

11. *Physiography.*
12. *Geology.*
13. *Astronomy.*

The system of units is employed in the admission examination as follows:—

The four examinations in Greek are held to be worth 7 units; Latin, five examinations, 10 units; History, 2 units in all; Mathematics 2 units, English 1 unit, German 3 units, French 3 units, Physics 1 unit, Chemistry 1 unit, Biology 1 unit, and one unit for any two of the following: Physiography, Geology, Astronomy.

For admission to an Academic College, a candidate must pass in subjects representing 13 of the above units, which must include the History of the United States, one unit in English, and two in Mathematics. If a student is admitted without Latin he shall within a year and a half make up privately the minimum of Latin required (2 units). Students who offer Latin shall offer either two or four units; and those who offer Greek shall offer at least two units. In view of the fact that in order to graduate from the Academic College to the University College, it is necessary to have completed: (1) The group of studies for admission appropriate to the degree sought, and (2) The course of study in the Academic College appropriate to the same degree, (as will be indicated), therefore the subjects for admission are arranged into the groups appropriate to the various degrees of A.B., Ph.B., and S.B. For example, the admission group for the A.B.

course is: Latin 4 units, Greek 3 units, Mathematics 2 units, English 1 unit, History 1 unit, Physics 1 unit, German or French 1 unit.

Undergraduate Courses.—The work of any Academic College is eighteen Majors. Each quarter is divided into two terms of six weeks each. In the Academic Colleges a Major calls for ten, and a Minor for five hours a week of class-room work for one term. A Double Major or Double Minor calls for the corresponding number of hours a week for one quarter The courses of study below are Double Minors, unless otherwise designated, each of which is equivalent to a Major. In addition to the eighteen Majors there are required a series of themes in English, Elocution for three quarters, and Physical Culture. Double Minors require five hours a week for a quarter. The following is the scheme of work in the Academic College of Liberal Arts for the degree of A.B.:—

Latin.—Three Majors required. Three Double-Minor courses, comprising selections from Cicero, Livy, Terence, Tacitus, Horace; translation at sight and hearing; prose; literature. Each course may be taken in any quarter.

Greek.—Three Majors. There are five courses, of which one only is prescribed, and two to be chosen.

Xenophon, Memorabilia, Plato, Apology, Homer, Lysias, Isocrates, Euripides.

Mathematics.—Two Majors in two courses. Plane Trigonometry, the elements of the Analytic Geometry of the conic sections, and the elementary theory of finite and infinite Algebraic and Trigonometric series.

History.—Two Majors in two courses. Mediæval and Modern History.

English.—Two Majors. One initial course in Rhetoric and English Composition, and an advanced course in the same which is optional. A course in English Literature. Themes in English for all who do not elect the advanced course in Composition.

French.—Three Majors in six courses. The first three are elementary, and intended for those who have entered or without French.

German.—Three Majors. One Double Major elementary course, followed by an intermediate course for those who have entered without German. For those who have entered with one unit in German, three courses in specified modern prose authors, German Comedies and German Lyrics. For those admitted with two units, three courses in Modern prose, Goethe and Schiller. Students admitted with three units elect their courses from those offered in the University Colleges.

Science—Candidates who offered no science at admission must take two Majors of Science from among the following: Physics, Chemistry, Biology, Geology. The two Majors should be confined to one department.

Philosophy.—Two Majors. Psychology, Ethics. Either after the completion of twelve Majors in the Academic College, or, if that is impracticable, early in the University College.

Elective.—One Major.

For the courses in the other Academic Colleges of Literature and Science, see Circular, p. 22 and pp. 25 ff.

A student is admitted to the University College, when he is credited with full work in the Academic Colleges. The work of any University College is eighteen Majors. In the University Colleges a Major calls for eight hours a week and a Minor for four hours a week for one term. Most of the courses are Double Minors, calling for four hours a week for a quarter. The courses are purely elective within the following limits:

(1) If two Majors of Philosophy have not been completed in the Academic Colleges, they must be elected as a part of the work in the University Colleges.

(2) Class work in Physical Culture is required.

(3) A student may not select more than one-half his courses during any three consecutive quarters of College work from any one Department.

(4) A student may not select his courses during any three consecutive quarters of College work from more than four Departments.

(5) Students for the degrees of A.B., Ph.B. or S.B. shall select one-third of their work from certain departments specified.

For the degree of A.B., one-third of the work must be selected from the following departments, which have numerous courses open to graduate students and students of the University Colleges:—

1. Philosophy and Pedagogy.
2. Political Economy.
3. Political Science.
4. History.
5. Archæology.
6. Sociology and Anthropology.
7. Comparative Religion.
8. Semitic Languages and Literatures.
9. Biblical and Patriotic Greek.
10. Sanskrit and Indo-European Comparative Philology.
11. Greek Language and Literature.
12. Latin Language and Literature.
13. Romance Languages and Literatures.
14. Germanic Languages and Literatures.
15. English Language, Literature and Rhetoric.
16. Biblical Literature in English.
17. Mathematics.

Other departments from which one-third of the work for the A.B. degree may be chosen are Astronomy, Physics, Chemistry, Geology, Zoology, Anatomy and Histology, Physiology, Neurology, Palæontology, Botany, Elocution, Physical Culture.

Degrees.—The degrees of Bachelor of Arts, Bachelor of Philosophy, Bachelor of Sciences, Master of Arts, Master of Science,

Doctor of Philosophy, Bachelor of Theology, Bachelor of Divinity are conferred upon the recommendation of the several Faculties, confirmed by the University Senate. No honorary degrees are conferred by the University.

Examinations.—Examinations are partly oral, and partly written. They are conducted every quarter. The University Examiner has charge of admission to the University, of all examinations, whether regular or special, of the record of courses taken by each student, and the rank attained in them, of diplomas, certificates of work, and letters of admission.

APPENDIX A.

KING'S COLLEGE CHARTER.

GEORGE THE FOURTH, by the Grace of God, of the United Kingdom of Great Britain and Ireland, King, Defender of the Faith, and so forth :

To all to whom these Presents shall come—GREETING :

Whereas the establishment of a College within our Province of Upper Canada, in North America, for the education of youth in the principles of Christian religion, and for their instruction in the various branches of science and literature, which are taught in our Universities in this Kingdom, would greatly conduce to the welfare of our said Province ; and whereas, humble application hath been made to us by many of our loving subjects in our said Province, that we would be pleased to grant our Royal Charter for the more perfect establishment of a College therein, and for incorporating the members thereof for the purpose aforesaid :

Now know ye, that We, having taken the premises into our Royal consideration, and duly weighing the great utility and importance of such an institution, have, of our special grace, certain knowledge, and mere motion, ordained and granted, and do by these presents for us, our heirs, and successors, ordain and grant, that there shall be established at or near our Town of York, in our said Province of Upper Canada, from this time, one College with the style and privileges of an university, as hereinafter directed, for the education and instruction of youth and students in arts and faculties, to continue for ever, to be called King's College ;

And We do hereby declare and grant that our trusty and well-beloved, the Right Reverend Father in God, Charles James, Bishop of the Diocese of Quebec, or the Bishop for the time being of the Diocese in which the said Town of York may be situate, on any future division or alteration of the said present Diocese of Quebec, shall for us, and on our behalf, be Visitor of the said College, and that our trusty and well-beloved Sir Peregrine Maitland, our Lieutenant-Governor of our said Province, or the Governor, Lieutenant-Governor, or person administering the Government of our said Province, for the time being, shall be the Chancellor of our said College ;

And We do hereby declare, ordain, and grant, that there shall at all times be one President of our said College, who shall be a clergyman in holy orders of the United Church of England and Ireland, and there shall be such and so many professors in different arts and faculties within our said College, as from time to time shall be deemed necessary or expedient, and as shall be appointed by us or by the Chancellor of our said College, in our behalf and during our pleasure ;

And We do hereby grant and ordain, that the Reverend John Strachan, Doctor in Divinity, Archdeacon of York, in our said Province of Upper Canada, shall be the first President of our said College, and the Archdeacon of York, in our said Province, for the time being, shall, by virtue of such his office, be at all times the President of the said College ;

And We do hereby for us, our heirs, and successors, will, ordain, and grant that the said Chancellor and President, and the said professors in our said College, and all persons who shall be duly matriculated into and admitted as scholars of our said College, and their successors, for ever, shall be one distinct and separate body politic and corporate, in deed and in name, by the name and style of " The Chancellor, President, and Scholars of King's College, at York, in the Province of Upper Canada," and that by the same name they shall have perpetual succession and a common seal; and that they and their successors shall, from time to time have full power to alter, renew, or change such common seal at their will and pleasure, and as shall be found convenient ; and that by the same name they, the said Chancellor, President, and Scholars, and their successors from time to time, and at all times hereafter, shall be able and capable to have, take, receive, purchase, acquire, hold, possess, enjoy, and maintain, to and for the use of the said College any messuages, lands, tenements, and hereditaments, of what kind, nature, or quality soever, situate, and being within our said Province of Upper Canada, so as the same do not exceed in yearly value the sum of fifteen thousand pounds sterling above all charges, and moreover to take, purchase, acquire, have, hold, enjoy, receive, possess, and retain, all or any goods, chattels, charitable or other contributions, gifts or benefactions whatsoever ;

And we do hereby declare and grant that the said Chancellor, President, and Scholars, and their successors by the same name, shall and may be able and capable in law to sue and be sued, implead and be impleaded, answer and be answered in all or any court or courts of record within our United Kingdom of Great Britain and Ireland, and our said Province of Upper Canada, and other our dominions, in all and singular actions, causes, pleas, suits, matters, and demands whatsoever, of what nature or kind soever, in as large, ample, and beneficial a manner and form as any other body politic and corporate, or any other our liege subjects, being persons able and capable in law, may or can sue, implead, or answer, or be sued, impleaded, or answered, in any manner whatsoever ;

And We do hereby declare, ordain, and grant that there shall be within our said College or Corporation a Council, to be called and known by the name of the "College Council ; "

And We do, will, and ordain that the said Council shall consist of the Chancellor and President for the time being, and of seven of the professors in arts and faculties of our said College, and that such seven professors shall be members of the Established United Church of England and Ireland, and shall previously to their admission into the said College Council, severally sign and subscribe the Thirty-nine Articles of religion as declared and set forth in the Book of Common Prayer ; and in case at any time there should not be within our said College seven professors of arts and faculties, being members of the Established Church aforesaid, then our will and pleasure is, and we do hereby grant and ordain, that the said College Council shall be filled up to the requisite number of seven, exclusive of the Chancellor and President for the time being, by such persons, being graduates of our said College and being members of the Established Church aforesaid, as shall for that purpose be appointed by the Chancellor for the time being of our said College, and which members of Council shall in like manner subscribe the Thirty-nine Articles aforesaid, previously to their admission into the said College Council:

And Whereas it is necessary to make provision for the completion and filling up of the said Council at the first institution of our said College, and previously to the appointment of any professors or the conferring of any degrees therein, now we do further ordain and declare that the Chancellor of our said College for the time being, shall, upon or immediately after the first institution thereof, by warrant under his hand, nominate and appoint seven discreet and proper persons, resident within our said Province of Upper Canada, to constitute jointly with him, the said Chancellor and the President of our said College for the time being, the first or original Council of our said College, which first original members of the said Council shall in like manner respectively subscribe the Thirty-Nine Articles aforesaid, previously to their admission into the said Council;

And We do further declare and grant that the members of the said College Council, holding within our said College the offices of Chancellor, President, or professor in any art or faculty, shall respectively hold their seats in the said Council, so long as they and each of them shall retain such their offices as aforesaid, and no longer, and that the members of the said Council, not holding offices in our said College, shall, from time to time vacate their seats in the said Council when and so soon as there shall be an adequate number of professors in our said College, being members of the Established Church aforesaid, to fill up the said Council to the requisite number before mentioned:

And We do hereby authorize and empower the Chancellor for the time being of our said College to decide in each case what particular member of the said Council not holding any such office as aforesaid, shall vacate his seat in the said Council, upon the admission of any new member of Council holding any such office:

And We do hereby declare and grant that the Chancellor for the time being of our said College, shall preside at all meetings of the said College Council which he may deem it proper and convenient to attend, and that in his absence the President of our said College shall preside at all such meetings; and that in the absence of the said President the senior member of the said Council present at any such meeting shall preside thereat, and that the seniority of the members of the said Council, other than the Chancellor and President, shall be regulated according to the date of their respective appointments: Provided always that the members of the said Council being professors in our said College, shall in the said Council take precedence over and be considered as seniors to the members thereof, not being professors in our said College:

And We do ordain and declare that no meeting of the said Council shall be, or be held to be, a lawful meeting thereof, unless five members at the least be present during the whole of every such meeting, and that all questions and resolutions proposed for the decision of the said College Council, shall be determined by the majority of the votes of the members of the Council present, including the vote of the presiding member, and that in the event of an equal division of such votes, the member presiding at any such meeting shall give an additional or casting vote:

And We do further declare that if any member of the said Council shall die or resign his seat in the said Council, or shall be suspended or removed from the same, or shall, by reason of any bodily or mental infirmity, or by reason of his absence from the said Province, become incapable for three calendar months, or upwards, of attending the meetings of the said Council, then, and in every such case a fit and proper person shall be appointed by the said Chancellor, to act as and be a member of the said Council in the place and stead of the member so dying or resigning, or so suspended or removed or incapacitated as aforesaid, and such new member, succeeding to any member so suspended or incapacitated, shall vacate such his office on the removal of any such suspension or at the termination of any such incapacity aforesaid, of his immediate predecessor in the said Council:

And We do further ordain and grant, that it shall and may be competent to and for the Chancellor for the time being of our said College to suspend from his seat in the said Council any member thereof, for any just and reasonable cause, to the said

Chancellor appearing: Provided that the grounds of every such suspension shall be entered and recorded, at length, by the said Chancellor in the books of the said Council and signed by him: and every person so suspended shall thereupon cease to be a member of the said Council, unless and until he shall be restored to, and re-established in such his station, therein by any order to be made in the premises by us, or by the said Visitor of our said College acting on our behalf and in pursuance of any special reference from us:

And We do further declare, that any member of the said Council, who, without sufficient cause, to be allowed by the said Chancellor by an order, entered for that purpose on the books of the said Council, shall absent himself from all the meetings thereof which may be held within any six successive calendar months, shall thereupon vacate such his seat in the said Council:

And We do by these presents for us, our Heirs and successors, will, ordain, and grant, that the said Council of our said College shall have power and authority to frame and make statutes, rules, and ordinances, touching and conerning the good government of the said College, the performance of Divine service therein, the studies, lectures, exercises, degrees in arts and faculties, and all matters regarding the same; the residence and duties of the President of our said College; the number, residence, and duties of the professors thereof; the management of the revenues and property of our said College; the salaries, stipends, provision, and emoluments of and for the President, professors, scholars, officers and servants thereof; the number and duties of such officers and servants; and also touching and concerning any other matter or thing which to them shall seem good, fit, and useful for the well-being and advancement of our said College, and agreeable to this our Charter; and also from time to time by any new statutes, rules, or ordinances to revoke, renew, augment, or alter all, every, or any of the said statutes, rules, and ordinances, as to them shall seem meet and expedient: Provided always, that the said statutes, rules, and ordinances, or any of them shall not be repugnant to the laws and statutes of the United Kingdom of Great Britain and Ireland, or of our said Province of Upper Canada, or to this our Charter: Provided also that the said statutes, rules, and ordinances shall be subject to the approbation of the said Visitor of our said College for the time being, and shall be forthwith transmitted to the said Visitor for that purpose ; and that in case the said Visitor shall for us and on our behalf in writing signify his disapprobation thereof within two years of the time of their being so made and framed, the same or such part thereof as shall be so disapproved of by the said Visitor, shall from the time of such disapprobation being made known to the said Chancellor of our said College, be utterly void and of no effect ; but otherwise, shall be and remain in full force and virtue : Provided nevertheless, and we do hereby expressly save and reserve to us, our heirs, and successors the power of reviewing, confirming, or reversing by any order or orders to be by us or them made, in our or their Privy Council, all or any of the decisions, sentences, or orders, so to be made as aforesaid by the said Visitor, for us and on our behalf, in reference to the said statutes, rules, and ordinances or any of them ;

And we do further ordain and declare that no statute, rule, or ordinance shall be framed or made by the said College Council touching the matters aforesaid, or any of them, excepting only such as shall be proposed for the consideration of the said Council by the Chancellor for the time being of our said College ;

And We do require and enjoin the said Chancellor thereof to consult with the President of our said College and the next senior member of the said College Council respecting all statutes, rules, and ordinances, to be proposed by him to the said Council for their consideration ;

And We do hereby for us, our heirs and successors, charge and command that the statutes, rules, or ordinances aforesaid, subject to the said provisions, shall be strictly and inviolably observed, kept, and performed from time to time in full vigour and effect under the penalties to be thereby or therein imposed or contained ;

And We do further will, ordain, and grant that the said College shall be deemed and taken to be an University, and shall have and enjoy all such and the like privileges as are enjoyed by our Universities of our United Kingdom of Great Britain and Ireland, as far as the same are capable of being had or enjoyed by virtue of these our letters patent ; and that the students in the said College shall have liberty and faculty of taking the degree of Bachelor, Master, and Doctor in the several arts and faculties at the appointed times, and shall have liberty within themselves of performing all scholastic exercises for the conferring such degrees in such manner as shall be directed by the statutes, rules, and ordinances of the said College;

And We do further will, ordain, and appoint, that no religious test or qualification shall be required of or appointed for any persons admitted or matriculated as scholars within our said College, or of persons admitted to any degree in any art or faculty therein, save only that all persons admitted within our said College to any degree in Divinity shall make such and the same declarations and subscriptions, and take such and the same oaths as are required of persons admitted to any degree of Divinity in our University of Oxford;

And We do further will, and direct, and ordain that the Chancellor, President, and professors of our said College, and all persons admitted therein to the degree of Master of Arts or to any degree in Divinity, Law, or Medicine, and who from the time of such their admission to such degree, shall pay the annual sum of twenty shillings, sterling money, for and towards the support and maintenance of the said College, shall be and be deemed, taken, and reputed to be members of the Convocation of the said University, and, as such members of the said Convocation, shall have, exercise, and enjoy all such and the like privileges as are enjoyed by the members of the Convocation of our University of Oxford, so far as the same are capable of being had and enjoyed by virtue of these our letters patent, and consistently with the provisions thereof;

And We will and by these presents for us, our heirs, and successors, do grant and declare that these our letters patent, or the enrolment or exemplification thereof, shall and may be good, firm, valid, sufficient, and effectual, in the law according to the true intent and meaning of the same, and shall be taken, construed, and adjudged in the most favourable and beneficial sense for the best advantage of the said Chancellor, President, and Scholars of our said College, as well in our courts of record as elsewhere, and by all and singular judges, justices, officers, ministers and other subjects whatsoever of us, our heirs, and successors, any mis-recital, non-recital, omissions, imperfection, defect, matt r, cause, or thing whatsoever to the contrary thereof in any wise notwithstanding.

In witness whereof We have caused these Our Letters to be made Patent. Witness Ourself at Westminster, the fifteenth day of March, in the eighth year of Our Reign.

By writ of Privy Seal,

(Signed) BATHURST.

KING'S COLLEGE LAND ENDOWMENT.

George the Fourth, by the Grace of God, of the United Kingdom of Great Britain and Ireland, King, Defender of the Faith, &c.

To all to whom these Presents shall come—GREETING :—

Whereas by our letters patent, made under the Great Seal of our United Kingdom of Great Britain and Ireland, and bearing date at Westminster the fifteenth day of March, one thousand, eight hundred and twenty-seven, in the eighth year of our reign, We of our special grace, certain knowledge, and mere motion, did for us, our heirs, and successors, ordain and grant that there shall be established at or near our Town of York, in our said Province of Upper Canada, from this time one College with the style and privileges of an University, as in the said letters patent directed, for the education and instruction of youth and students in arts and faculties, to continue for ever to be called King's College, and we did thereby for us, our heirs, and successors, will, ordain, and grant that the Chancellor, President, and Professors of our said College, and all persons who shall be duly matriculated and admitted as Scholars of our said College, and their successors for ever, shall be one distinct and separate body politic and corporate in deed and in name, by the name and style of "The Chancellor, President, and Scholars of King's College at York, in the Province of Upper Canada," and that by the same name they shall have perpetual succession and a common seal, and that they and their successors shall from time to time have full power to alter, renew, or change such common seal at their will and pleasure, and as shall be found convenient ; and that by the same name they, the said Chancellor, President, and Scholars, and their successors from time to time, and at all times hereafter, shall be able and capable to have, take, receive, purchase acquire, hold, possess, enjoy, and maintain to and for the use of the said College any messuages, lands, tenements, and hereditaments of what kind, nature, or quality soever, situate and being within our said Province of Upper Canada, so as the same do not exceed in yearly value the sum of fifteen thousand pounds sterling above all charges ; and moreover to take, purchase, acquire, have, hold, enjoy, receive, possess, and retain all or any goods, chattels, or other contributions, gifts, or benefactions whatsoever : And Whereas by order of His late Most Excellent Majesty, King George the Third, certain large tracts of land were reserved and set apart for the purpose of promoting education, and for the foundation of an University in our said Province, and it hath been represented to us that by exchanging certain other tracts of land belonging to us in our said Province, called "Crown Reserves," for an equal portion of the lands which have been so set apart for the purpose of promoting education and the foundation of an University as aforesaid, a fund may the more easily and certainly be procured for the immediate establishment of the said University—to be called King's College, conformable to the provisions contained in our said letters patent ;

Now therefore know ye that in the place and stead of two hundred and twenty-five thousand, nine hundred and forty-four acres, part of the tracts of land so reserved and set apart by his said late Majesty as hath been heretofore mentioned, and which we have reserved to us, our heirs and successors, as no longer to be reserved or set apart, for the purposes aforesaid, We of our special grace, certain knowledge, and mere motion have given and granted, and by these presents do give and grant unto the Chancellor, President, and Scholars of King's College at York in the Province of Upper Canada, and to their successors for ever, all those several parcels or tracts of land situate in our said Province, and containing together by admeasurement two hundred and twenty-five thousand, nine hundred and forty-four acres, be the same more or less, being (here follow details of lots).

Given under the Great Seal of our said Province,

Witness our trusty and well beloved Sir Peregrine Maitland, K.C.B., Lieutenant-Governor of our said Province, and Major-General commanding our Forces therein at York, this third day of January, in the year of our Lord one thousand eight hundred and twenty-eight, and in the eighth year of our reign.

Entered with the Auditor, tenth day of January, one thousand eight hundred and twenty-eight.

By Command of His Excellency in Council.

P. M.   J. B. ROBINSON,
Attorney-General.

D. CAMERON,
Secretary.

APPENDIX B.

UPPER CANADA COLLEGE.

This institution was established in 1829 by Order-in-Council, at the instance of Sir John Colborne, who was then the Lieutenant-Governor of Upper Canada. The effect of the order was to suspend the Home District Grammar School,* to appropriate its site as a means of creating a building fund, and to grant to the proposed institution a new site on "Russell Square." This endowment was increased by the addition of a land grant of 63,268 acres,† which also was made on the strength of an Order-in-Council. The organization of the "Upper Canada College and Royal Grammar School" appears to have been of a somewhat vague kind during the first few years of its existence, its government being vested in a board of managers designated‡ the "President, Directors, and Trustees." For some years, the Legislative Assembly, prompted by a desire to defeat the plan of the promoters of a sectarian University, endeavored to convert Upper Canada College into a non-sectarian one, and when a compromise was effected in 1837 it included a settlement of the Upper Canada College question in its terms. The University Act of that year§ provides that "the Minor or Upper Canada College shall be incorporated with, and form an appendage of, the University of King's College, and be subject to its jurisdiction and control." The Principal was to be appointed by the Crown during pleasure; the Vice-Principal and tutors were to be nominated by

---

*Established under the Act of 1807 (see above p. 23).
†Afterwards increased to 63,996 acres.
‡ See Report of King's College Commission, 1852, p. 339.
§ 7 William IV., cap. 16.

the Chancellor* of King's College, subject to the approval of its Council ; and the Chancellor was to have authority to suspend or remove the Vice-Principal or tutors.

For some years the financial affairs of King's College and of Upper Canada College were very much complicated, and each institution was made a subject of investigation by the King's College Commission,† appointed in 1848. The result of the inquiry was to show (1) that the accounts of the two institutions had been "so mixed up in the Kings College books as to preclude the possibility of a clear exposition of them," and (2) that before King's College had been organized at all, advances had been made out of its endowment to Upper Canada College, amounting‡ to $137,639. An attempt was made in the University Act§ of 1849 to improve the position of the College by (1) cancelling its entire indebtedness to the University, and (2) conferring on it a quasi-autonomous constitution. Under that statute it was retained as an "appendage" of the University, but it was created a corporation under the name of "the Principal, Masters and Scholars of Upper Canada College and Royal Grammar School." The Governor-General of Canada was made Visitor *ex officio* ; the Principal was to be appointed by the Crown on the nomination of the University Senate, which had also a right to suspend him from the exercise of his functions. The Act created a "Council" of which the Principal was to be a member *ex officio*, the other four members to be appointed‖ by the Crown during its pleasure. The administration of its finances was entrusted to the University "Endowment Board," which was composed of one member appointed by the Crown, one by the Univer-

---

*At that time the Lieutenant-Governor of Upper Canada *ex officio*.

†Composed of the Hon. Justice Burns, Joseph Workman, M.D., and John Wetenhall, Esq.

‡See King's College Report, 1852, p. 341. On p. 53, the aggregate of advances, with accrued interest to date, is given as £75,506 ($302,024.)

§12 Vict , cap. 82.

‖It was made a condition of eligibility that appointees should be graduates of the University and should not be ecclesiastics.

sity Senate, one by the University Caput, one by the Council of Upper Canada College, and one by the members of its staff.

The University Act* of 1853 dissolved the corporation of the College, and provided that the "institution and all its affairs and business" should be placed "under the control, management, and direction of the Chancellor, Vice-Chancellor, and members of the Senate of the University of Toronto." The Governor-General was continued as Visitor, and the Senate was authorized to make statutory provision for its government, and to fix the number, duties, and emoluments of all the members of its teaching staff, who were to be appointed by the Crown. The financial management, like that of the University, was handed over to the Bursar as an independent Crown officers.

Under this constitution Upper Canada College continued to perform its work till 1887, in which year an Act† was passed by the Ontario Legislature removing it entirely from the control of the University Senate, and placing it under the management of a Board of five trustees appointed by the Lieutenant-Governor during pleasure. The Board was authorized to make regulations for the admission and promotion of pupils, for the collection of fees, for the care of the property, and for the moral training and religious instruction of the pupils. It was provided that all the members of the teaching staff should have the qualifications of High School masters or assistants, and that the College should be subject to the "same inspection as the High Schools generally." By another Act‡ all the property of the College was vested in the Crown, which was authorized to provide a new site, to erect new buildings upon it, and to sell the old site for the common advantage of Upper Canada College and the University, the Crown to receive out of the proceeds $120,000 for the erection of new buildings, exclusive of site, and $100,000 as an endowment. By an Act§ passed in the following year authority was given to transfer the original site to the University subject to the above charges ; and by an Act‖ passed

---

*16 Vict. cap. 89.
†50 Vict., cap. 42.
‡ 50 Vict. cap. 44.
§ 51 Vict. cap. 38.
‖ 55 Vict. cap. 63.

in 1892 it was actually made part of the University endowment, subject to the same liens, and also to expenses of management and municipal local improvement rates.

In 1894 an important change was made in the organization of the College by an Act* which is also a consolidation of the previous statutes. The number of trustees was raised to nine the additional four being made elective by the members of the " Upper Canada Old Boys' Association." The Board was entrusted with the management of the endowment and other permanent funds, and the College was provided with a Bursar of its own. In 1895 the financial separation of the College from the Provincial University was completed by the passage of an Act† which authorized the University management to pay off the lien of $100,000 at the then value of a capital sum of that amount due in seven years, with discount at four and a half per cent. per annum. What is left of the value of the old site of Upper Canada College becomes an un-encumbered addition to the endowment of the University.

* 57 Vict., cap. 60.
† 58 Vict., cap 58.

APPENDIX C.

THE ORGANIZATION OF KING'S COLLEGE.

On the 10th of June, 1837, the College Council adopted, after consideration and amendment, a report on organization, which had at its request been drafted by Dr. Strachan, then President of the University. The essential portions of this scheme* are as follows:—

I. CURRICULUM.†

1. *Classical and Modern Literature.* — This embraces the Greek and Latin Languages; Ancient History; Ancient and Modern Geography; Chronology and Antiquities; Modern Literature, English and Foreign; Modern History; Rhetoric; Grammar; Composition and Style.—Two Professors

2. *Physics* — Application of Science to the Arts; Astronomy; Modern Geography, etc.—Two Professors.

3. *Mental Philosophy* — Moral and Intellectual Philosophy; Christian Ethics; Political Economy.—The President.

4. *Theology.* — Hebrew and Oriental Languages; Natural and Revealed Religion, etc.—(This Department may remain at present in abeyance.)

5. *Jurisprudence* — Law of Nature, and of Nations; Civil, English, and Constitutional Law; History and Principles of the British Constitution.—One Lecturer.

6. *Medicine* — Chemistry, with Geology and Mineralogy; Anatomy and Physiology; Theory and Practice of Physics; Principles and Practice of Surgery; Materia Medica, Therapeutics, and Botany, with Midwifery and Diseases of Women and Children.—One Professor and three Lecturers.

---

*The full text of the report, taken from the Council's Minutes, is printed in Hodgins' "Documentary History," Vol. III., pp. 93-96.

†This course of study is avowedly based on that of King's College, London, which is affiliated to the University of London.

II. Finances.

Estimated Expenditure:

1. The President, till enabled by an adequate remuneration to resign his parish, to receive only the small remuneration allowed him in April, 1827, by Lord Bathurst, for superintendence of the University.... £ 250
2. The five Professors residing within the College, and devoting themselves entirely to the duties of their Departments, each £450 2,250
3. Add to the salary of the Senior Professor............ 50
4. The Lecturer on Jurisprudence...
5. The Lecturer on Anatomy.......
6. The Lecturer on Theory and Practice of Physic and the Principles and Practice of Surgery, etc.......................... } As only a portion of their time will be required, £200 each 800
7. The Lecturer on Materia Medica, etc.........................
8. Librarian.. 100
9. Gardener 100
10. Library, annually 200
11. Philosophical and Chemical apparatus, and formation of a Museum, per annum...................... 250
12. Servants and Contingencies 600

                                    £4,600

13. To this expenditure must be added the aid annually necessary to support the Minor or Upper Canada College 800
14. The Bursar's and Registrar's Office............ 600

    Total annual expense (sterling) £6,000

Ways and Means;

1. Interest accruing, directly or indirectly, on the sum of £70,000 due upon land sold...................... £4,200
2. Average rents 1,200
3. Interest on £30,000 due by the Minor or Upper Canada College 1,800

    Halifax currency................................ £7,500
    Or Sterling..................................... 6,400

    Surplus (exclusive of fees from students) .... £ 400

III. REGULATIONS.*

The academical year of the London University may be adopted with a slight alteration, so as to shorten by a fortnight the long vacation. It consists of three terms: (1) From the beginning of October to the week before Christmas; (2) from the beginning of the second week in January to the week before Easter; (3) from Easter to the third Friday in July.

Students to be received will be of three descriptions: (1) King's College Classical Students, admitted to a regular and prescribed course of general study, but allowed to attend any particular lectures not comprised in that course; (2) King's College Medical Students, who enter upon a course of medical study, but are allowed to attend any particular lectures not comprised in the course; (3) Occasional Students, namely, all persons who are desirous of attending any separate course or courses of lectures, or private instruction given in the College.

It shall be the duty of the President and Professors to submit to the College Council such an arrangement of the various branches of knowledge to be taught as may seem best calculated to insure the full efficiency of each of the six departments.

The Professors, under whose care any department is placed, being responsible for its management, shall constitute a subsidiary Board, at which the Senior Professor shall preside, in order to consult from time to time, how they may distribute their respective labours to the best advantage, so as to give unity and system to the studies embraced by their respective departments, and what improvements may be conveniently introduced, subject, nevertheless, to the consideration and confirmation, in all respects, of the College Council.

The reports from each Department, with such observations and recommendations respecting studies and discipline as may appear useful, shall be made to the President at the end of each term, to be laid before the College Council.

The Professors employed shall be wholly devoted to their duties as Members of the University.

---

*Extracts from the Minutes of the College Council.

THE INAUGURATION OF KING'S COLLEGE.

The formal opening of the College for the admission of students took place in the Parliament Building,* on the 8th of June, 1843. After Divine service in the Chapel, the doors of the Hall,† were thrown open to those who had received tickets of admission. The Mayor and members of the Council of the City of Toronto were invited guests. The academic procession included : (1) The members of staff, the pupils, and the officials of Upper Cannada College ; (2) the members of staff, the students and the officials of King's College ; and (3) graduates not members of the University. The Chancellor, Governor-General Metcalfe, was absent on account of "pressure of public business," and the President, Bishop Strachan, conducted the proceedings in his stead. "On His Lordship's right and left hand were ranged stalls for the Professors," as follows :—

Rev. John McCaul, LL.D.,
    Professor of Classical Literature, Belles Lettres, Rhetoric and Logic.
Rev. James Beaven, D.D.,
    Professor of Divinity, Metaphysics, and Moral Philosophy.
Richard Potter, Esq., M.A.,
    Professor of Mathematics and Natural Philosophy.
Henry H. Croft, Esq.,
    Professor of Chemistry and Experimental Philosophy.
Wm. C. Gwynne, Esq., M.B.,
    Professor of Anatomy and Physiology.
John King, Esq., M.D.,
    Professor of Theory and Practice of Medicine.
Wm. H. Blake, Esq., M.A.,
    Professor of Law.
Wm. Beaumont, Esq., M.R., C.S.L.,
    Professor of Principles and Practice of Surgery.

---

*Pending the completion of the College building, the corner stone of which had been laid by the Governor-General, Sir Charles Bagot, on the 23rd of April, 1842.

†Formerly the Legislative Assembly Chamber. The Parliament of the United Provinces of Upper and Lower Canada then sat in Kingston.

The Registrar of the University, Henry Boys, Esq., M. D., "called up the Students, and they subscribed the declaration of obedience to the Statutes, Rules, and Ordinances, each, when he had signed, withdrawing to the robing-room, where he put on the academic costume,* and then returned to the hall." The following are the names of those who, on this occasion, subscribed the declaration :†

Mr. Barron (Fredk. W.)	Mr. Jones (Edward C.)
(Incorporated from Queen's College, Cambridge.)	Mr. Lyons (Wm. M.)
	Mr. Macaulay (John J.)
Mr. Baldwin (Edmund.)	Mr. McDonell (Samuel S.)
Mr. Bethune (Norman.)	Mr. McLean (Thomas A.)
Mr. Boulton (Chas. K.)	Mr. Moule (Arthur D.)
Mr. Cathcart (Joseph A.)	Mr. Patton (James.)
Mr. Crookshank (George.)	Mr. Roaf (John.)
Mr. Draper (W. G.)	Mr. Robinson (Christopher.)
Mr. Grassett (Elliott.)	Mr. Sharpe (Alfred.)
Mr. Hagerman (James T.)	Mr. Smith (Larratt W.)
Mr. Halliwell (John.)	Mr. Stanton (James.)
Mr. Jarvis (Wm. P.)	Mr. Stennett (Walter.)
Mr. Jessop (Henry B.)	

Inaugural addresses were then delivered by the President, Bishop Strachan ; the Vice-President, Dr. McCaul ; and two of the Visitors, Chief Justice Robinson and Mr. Justice Hagerman.

---

*" The gown of the Undergraduates was the same as that worn by the Pensioners of Clare Hall, Cambridge—the society of which the Rev. Dr. Harris, the first Principle of Upper Canada College, had been a member."

†" Of the students admitted on this occasion, twenty-two were members of the United Church of England and Ireland ; one a member of the Church of Rome ; one of the Church of Scotland ; one a Congregationalist; and one a Baptist."

APPENDIX D.

KING'S COLLEGE COMMISSIONS.

The management of the finances of King's College was always a subject of anxiety to the Legislature and the Governor of the Province, and various attempts were made from time to time to disentangle the accounts of the University corporation, which had become complicated with those of Upper Canada College. One method resorted to was the appointment of Commissions, and two of these are worthy of a brief notice.

I. THE EDUCATIONAL COMMISSION OF 1839.

Sir George Arthur, Lieutenant-Governor of Upper Canada and *ex officio* Chancellor of the University of King's College, at the instance of the Legislative Assembly of the Province, required* of King's College Council in April, 1839, an account of the state of the finances of the corporation. An investigation by a Committee of the Council brought to light the fact that the Bursar of the College was a defaulter to the amount of over $25,000, and that advances had been made to Upper Canada College amounting in the aggregate to over $130,000. The Legislative Assembly requested that the matter be further enquired into, and Sir George Arthur issued a commission to the Rev. John McCaul, the Rev. Henry James Grasett, and Mr. Samuel Bealy Harrison† authorizing them to report on the state of the Province educationally, and on the constitution and endowment of King's College in par-

---

* Hodgins' "Documentary History," vol iii., p. 187.

†Rev. John McCaul afterward became President of the University of Toronto, and the Rev. H. J. Grasett became Dean of Toronto. Mr. Harrison was subsequently appointed Judge of the Home District. All these became members afterwards of the Council of Public Instruction.

ticular.* As King's College had not at that time been organized, and as Upper Canada College had already absorbed a large amount of the capital which had accrued from the sale of University lands, the Commission reported the details of a plan† by which the College might be made to serve as a temporary university. The assets of King's College were given in the report as amounting to £246,845 ($987,380) on the 30th of November, 1839, and the annual expenditure at £1,032 ($4,128).

King's College Commission, 1848-1850.

On the 20th of July, 1848, after King's College had been five years in operation, a statute was passed by its Council, with the approval of Lord Elgin, who was then Governor-General of the province and *ex officio* Chancellor of the University, appointing "John Wetenhall of Nelson, in the county of Halton, Joseph Workman of the city of Toronto, and Robert Easton Burns of the same place," as Commissioners, with power to "examine into and report upon the financial affairs" of King's College and Upper Canada College. After Mr. Wetenhall's death the inquiry was conducted by his surviving colleagues, and most of its duties were discharged by Dr. Workman, who had been appointed "Visiting Commissioner." The report and accompanying appendices make a voluminous document, which was printed by order of the Legislative Assembly in 1852. A few extracts will give a fair idea of the character of the investigation and of the condition into which the affairs of King's College had fallen :—

"The account books kept in the College office were from the very foundation defective, confused, and totally unsuited to the requirements of a correct business establishment. No regular balance had ever been struck, by which their accuracy might have been tested or their inaccuracy detected. Indeed, balancing was quite foreign to the character and structure of such books. The

---

* These men were a committee of a larger commission appointed to investigate the state of business in the several public departments.

† See Hodgin's "Documentary History," vol. iii., pp. 261-265. This scheme was never carried out. It was authorized by Act of Parliament (2 Vict., cap. 10).

want of it was not felt, because the system (if such a term be applicable to uniformity of confusion) pursued in the office admitted of no such process of comparison. * * * The first element of all business accountancy, a cash-book, was not found in the institution, and the want of it seems to have been unfelt by either the Bursar or the Council, until the unexpected discovery of that officer's default, after an incumbency of over twelve years, brought out the fact that he had not kept any separate, or at least instructive record of his own private cash and that of the University.

"An endowment, consisting of nearly a quarter of a million of acres of the choice lands of the province, nearly all in occupancy under lease, and valued by the Council, at its first meeting, as worth no less than one pound per acre, was thus (after many years of previous mismanagement by the servants of the Crown) at the outset subjected to defective administration. No proper rent-roll accounts were opened or compiled, showing the pecuniary relations existing between the tenants and the proprietor. Rents were received, when offered ; lands were sold when sought for ; purchase money was taken when brought in ; interest was accepted when tendered ; and such occurrences gave introduction to the names of the respective parties to the account of the University. But the reappearance of such names in the accounts depended partly on the parties' own choice, or on their own conceptions of moral or business obligations."

The commissioners, in drawing up their report, divided the whole interval between 1827 and 1850 into two periods, one extending to July, 1839, and the other from that date to the date of the inquiry. In dealing with the earlier period, they give a clear account of the losses caused by default of the then Bursar, and running through both periods there is a current of animadversion directed against losses of the most serious kind, caused by gross mismanagement of the University endowment and the persistent practice of paying annual expenses out of capital. In a different vein are the remarks made about the purchase of the present University grounds, consisting originally of over 150 acres.

"The entire cost of these grounds, including the price of the land and expenditure thereon down to the first of January, 1850, has been about £13,993 ; the average expense of management has been nearly £350 a year. The College grounds are, perhaps, at present the most beautiful public enclosure in British America. No investment ever made by the University could be regarded as equal to this, either in present or prospective value. This property may be regarded as a reliable and available asset of the University, which would at any time produce three or four times the total cost. In the event of the reduced state of the general endowment, conjointly with the continuance of the present excess of expenditure over income, rendering necessary a further recourse to the fixed system of replenishing the funds by fresh sales of marketable property, the College grounds will be found well suited to the future wants of the University."

In the general financial summary appended to the report for the purpose of exhibiting the then state of the University's affairs, the total amount of capital which should have been at the command of the University authorities is estimated at nearly £336,930, of which there had by that time been " alienated in current expenditure and losses " no less a sum than £166,319. This includes £75,506 of principal and accrued interest owing by Upper Canada College. The following table, covering the seven years during which King's College had been in operation, shows the rapidity with which the capital of the endowment was diminished to meet the annual outlay :—

	Income.	Expenditure.	Deficit.
1843	£6,405	£6,987	£ 582
1844	7,154	12,139	4,985
1845	8,981	10,623	1,642
1846	8,591	11,428	2,836
1847	7,307	10,136	2,829
1848	7,749	10,810	3,060
1849	7,966	11,362	3,896
Total deficit.			£19,830

APPENDIX E.

TORONTO UNIVERSITY COMMISSIONS.

By the University Act* of 1849 the Governor-General of Canada was declared to be the "Visitor" of the University of Toronto, and since 1867 the Visitatorial function has been vested in the Lieutenant-Governor of Ontario. That the Visitor's powers are not merely nominal has béen shown by the issue of two Commissions of investigation, one by the Governor-General of Canada in 1861, the other by the Lieutenant-Governor of Ontario in 1895.

THE UNIVERSITY COMMISSION OF 1861.

The occasion of the issue of this commission was the agitation kept up for several years by various religious denominations, with a view to securing a share of the revenue from the endowment of the University of Toronto. During the session of 1860 the matter was brought before Parliament by petitions which were referred to a special committee for inquiry and report. As Parliament was then sitting in Quebec it was inconvenient, if not impossible, to make a thorough investigation of the financial condition of the University of Toronto, and in October, 1861, Lord Monck appointed as Commissioners to "enquire as to the affairs and financial condition" of the institution, James Patton of Toronto, John Beatty of Cobourg, and John Paton of Kingston. The report of this Commission was completed in May, 1862, and was printed as a public document by order of the Legislative Assembly in the session of 1863. A perusal of it shows that there was no longer any ground for complaint, on the score either of mismanagement of the endowment by the Bursar, or of a chronic excess of annual expenditure over annual income. During the interval since the report† of 1848-50 the sum of $355,907 has been expended out of capital

---

*12 Vict., cap. 82.
†See appendix D.

on the University building, and $65,569 on the library and museums, and this reduction of the endowment had resulted in a corresponding decrease of revenue. The commissioners note that prior to 1861 no revenue had been derived from fees, as matriculated students received their tuition free, and the fees paid by those who had not matriculated were assigned as perquisites to the several professors. At the date of the report the capital of the endowment was estimated to be $963,567, and the following table gives the income and expenditure for the years that had elapsed since the passing of the Act* of 1853 :

	Income.	Expenditure.	Surplus.	Deficit.
1853	$67,076	$54,928	$12,148	
1854	52,928	49,453	13,475	
1855	57,476	56,779	696	
1856	66,577	65,206	1,370	
1857	60,182	60,917		$ 785
1858	55,733	55,386	347	
1859	51,585	70,154		18,569
1860	54,375	63,153		8,777
1861	50,355	61,829		11,473

The Commissioners drew attention to the fact that the former University building, with the land around it had been taken into the possession of the Government of Canada in 1853, and had from that time been appropriated to the public service without any compensation of any kind to the University.

*16 Vict., cap. 89.

The object in view in the appointment of the Commission made it necessary for its members to suggest, if possible, some plan by which the expenditure on the University of Toronto and on University College might be so reduced as to leave a portion of the revenue from the endowment to be devoted to the promotion of higher education elsewhere, under the provisions of the University Act of 1853. The scheme embodied in the report is partly academic and partly financial. Under the former aspect provision is made in it (1) for the affiliation of teaching arts colleges to the University, and (2) for the reconstitution of the Senate, with equitable recognition of affiliated institutions ; under the latter an outline is given of a financial plan which would enable all affiliated colleges to participate in the aid given by the Province for the advancement of higher education. As no legislation was ever enacted for the purpose of giving effect to the scheme, the latter has now only an historical value in relation to the evolution of the Provincial University.

THE UNIVERSITY COMMISSION OF 1895.

Owing to the development of a certain amount of friction in the University of Toronto between the students and the University Council, a Commission of investigation was in 1895 issued to Chief Justice Taylor of Manitoba, Judge Senkler of the County of Lincoln, J. J. Kingsmill, Q.C., of Toronto, B. M. Britton, Q.C., of Kingston, and Professor Campbell of the Montreal Presbyterian College. As the matters inquired into were purely questions of discipline, and as the report of the Commission has not yet led to any legislative change in the constitution of the University it is unnecessary in this connection to make any further reference to it.

APPENDIX F.

PROPOSED BASIS OF UNIVERSITY FEDERATION, 1885.

1. It is proposed to form a confederation of Colleges, carrying on, in Toronto, work embraced in the Arts curriculum of the Provincial University, and in connection therewith the following institutions, namely : Queen's University, Victoria University, and Trinity University, Knox College, St. Michael's College, Wycliffe College, and Toronto Baptist College, shall have the right to enter into the proposed confederation, provided always that each of such institutions shall, so long as it remains in the confederation, keep in abeyance any powers it may possess of conferring degrees other than degrees in Divinity, such powers remaining intact, though not exercised. It shall be lawful for the Senate, from time to time, to provide by statute for the admission of other institutions into the confederation under the limitations above prescribed. Nothing herein contained shall be held to repeal any of the provisions for affiliation of institutions as contained in R. S. O., cap. 210, sec. 61.

2. The head of each confederating college shall be *ex officio* a member of the Senate of the Provincial University, and in addition thereto the governing body of each confederating college shall be entitled to appoint one other member of the Senate. The University professoriate shall be represented by two of their members on the Senate, and the Council of University College by one of its members, in addition to the President.

3. The undergraduates of any confederating University shall be admitted *ad eundem statum*, and the graduates in Law and Arts of any confederating university shall be admitted *ad eundem gradum* in the Provincial University. Such of the graduates in Medicine of any confederating University as shall have actually passed their examinations within the limits of the Province of Ontario, shall be admitted *ad eundem gradum* in the Provincial University.

4. During the continuance of such confederation, but no longer, all graduates in Medicine and Law so admitted shall have the same rights, powers, and privileges as are at present enjoyed by the like graduates of the Provincial University, except as herein otherwise provided.

5. All graduates in Medicine, including such admitted graduates, shall vote as one body, and be entitled to elect four members of the Senate. All graduates in Law, including such admitted graduates, shall vote as one body, and be entitled to elect two members of the Senate.

6. The graduates in Arts of the several Universities entering into the confederation shall, for the period of six years after the requisite legislation shall have been obtained, be entitled to the following representation on the Senate, namely : those of Queen's University to elect four members ; those of Victoria University to elect four members ; and those of Trinity University to elect four members. The graduates in Arts of the Provincial University, other than those admitted *ad eundem gradum* under this scheme, shall be entitled to elect twelve members of Senate. After the said period of six years, separate representation shall cease, and the entire body of graduates shall unite in electing a number of representatives equal to those previously elected by the several Universities in confederation.

7. (*a*) University College shall afford to all students, who desire to avail themselves thereof, the requisite facilities for obtaining adequate instruction in the following subjects in the curriculum of the Provincial University, viz. :· Latin, Greek, Ancient History, French, German, English, Oriental Languages, and Moral Philosophy, provided that it shall be competent to the governing body of University College to institute additional chairs which do not exist in the University.

(*b*) Attendance on instruction provided in any of the confederating colleges, including University College, shall be accorded equal value as a condition of proceeding to any degree with attendance on the work of the University Professoriate.

8. There shall be established another teaching faculty in connection with the Provincial University, to be called the University

Professoriate, which shall afford to all students of the Provincial University who desire to avail themselves thereof, the requisite facilities for obtaining adequate instruc ion in the following subjects, in accordance with the curriculum of such University, namely: Pure Mathematics, Physics, Astronomy, Geology, Mineralogy, Chemistry, Zoology, Botany, Physiology, Ethnology (including Comparative Philology), History, Logic, Metaphysics, History of Philosophy, Italian and Spanish, Political Economy and Civil Polity, Jurisprudence, Constitutional Law, Engineering, and such other Sciences, Arts, and branches of knowledge as the Senate of the Provincial University may from time to time determine, except such subjects as are prohibited from being taught by Revised Statutes of Ontario, cap. 209, sec. 9.

9. The Professors in such University Faculty shall be a corporation presided over by a chairman. The same person shall be President of University College and chairman of the Faculty of the University Professoriate. University College and the Faculty of the University Professoriate shall be complementary the one to the other, and afford to all University students the requisite facilities for obtaining adequate ins'ruction in all subjects prescribed in the curriculum of the Provincial University. If, in the interests of the general objects of the confederation it shall be found advantageous to have any subject transferred from University College to the University, or from the University to University College, it shall be competent to the governing bodies of the College and University to arrange for such transfer.

10. Every graduate's or student's diploma or certificate of standing, issued by the Provincial University, in addition to being signed by the proper University authorities in that behalf, shall indicate the College or Colleges in which such student attended lectures, and shall be signed by such professors, teachers, and officers of such College or Colleges as its or their governing body or bodies may from time to time determine.

11. With a view to the advantageous working out of this scheme, representatives of the various colleges and the University Faculty, shall from time to time meet in Committee and arrange time-tables for lectures and other College and University work.

12. The Senate of the Provincial University may, of its own motion, enquire into the conduct, teaching, and efficiency of any professor or teacher in the University Faculty, and report to the Lieutenant-Governor the result of such enquiry, and may make such recommendations as the Senate may think the circumstances of the case require.

13. All students, except in cases specially provided for by the Senate, shall enroll themselves in one of the Colleges and place themselves under its discipline. The authority of the several Colleges over their students shall remain intact. The University Professoriate shall have entire responsibility of discipline in regard to students, if any, enrolled in the University alone ; in regard to students entering in one or other of the Colleges, its powers of discipline shall be limited to the conduct of students in relation to University work and duties. All other matters of discipline affecting the University standing of students shall be dealt with by the Senate of the Provincial University.

14. The University Endowment and all additions thereto shall be applied to the maintenance of the Provincial University, the University Faculty, and University College.

15. There shall be the following staff in University College:

One Professor of Greek,
" " Latin,
" " French,
" " German,
" " English,
" " Oriental Languages,
" " Moral Philosophy,

One Lecturer in Ancient History,

One Tutor in Greek,
" " Latin,
" " French,
" " German,
" " Oriental Languages,
" " English,

One Fellow in Greek,
" " Latin,
" " French,
" " German,
" " English.

Additional assistance in the above subjects to be provided so that no Honor Class shall exceed twelve, or Pass Class thirty.

16. There shall be a University Professoriate adequate to give instruction in each of the following subjects, namely: Pure Mathematics, Physics, Astronomy, Geology, Mineralogy, Chemistry, Applied Chemistry, Zoology, Botany, Ethnology, History, Italian and Spanish, Logic and Metaphysics, History and Philosophy, Political Economy and Civil Polity, Constitutional Law, Jurisprudence, Engineering. As regards Tutors and Fellows, assistance shall be provided to the University Faculty similar to that mentioned above for the College, as may be required.

17. The University Professoriate lectures shall be free of charge to all students matriculated in the University, who are members of a confederating College, but in the case of students (if any) who do not belong to any College, the Senate shall determine the fees which shall be charged for the several courses of lectures in the University. But such laboratory fees, as may be fixed from time to time by the Senate, shall be paid by all students.

18. The various Colleges which are at present affiliated to any of the universities entering into the confederation, shall have the right to be affiliated to the Provincial University.

19. The curriculum in Arts of the Provincial University shall include the subjects of Biblical Greek, Biblical Literature, Christian Ethics, Apologetics or the Evidences of Natural and Revealed Religion, and Church History, but provision shall be made by a system of options to prevent such subjects being made compulsory by the University upon any candidate for a Degree.

20. No College student shall be allowed to present himself for any University examination subsequent to matriculation without producing a certificate, under the hand and seal of his College, that he has complied with all the requirements of his College affecting his admission to such an examination.

21. The University College work shall continue to be carried on as at present, in the College buildings, and the University work shall be carried on in the same buildings, in the School of Practical Science, and in such other buildings as may hereafter be erected on the present University grounds, in the City of Toronto. A building suitable for a University Examination Hall, Senate rooms, Registrar's and other offices shall be erected on said grounds. Additions to be made to the School of Science sufficient to afford proper accommodation for students in Mineralogy, Botany, and other subjects, and for the accommodation of the Museum, which should be removed from its present quarters, in order to be more serviceable for Science students.

22. The following also to be considered : Completion of the Collection of Physical Apparatus ; Physiological Laboratory and Apparatus ; Astronomical Observatory and Instruments, and provision for the Education of Women.

APPENDIX G.

VICTORIA COLLEGE CHARTER.

WILLIAM THE FOURTH by the Grace of God, of the United Kingdom of Great Britain and Ireland, King, Defender of the Faith, &c.

To all to whom these Presents shall come—GREETING:

Whereas divers of our loving subjects of the Wesleyan Methodist Church, in our Province of Upper Canada, have represented to us that with the aid of private and voluntary contributions, they have erected certain buildings in the vicinity of the Town of Cobourg, in the Newcastle District of our said Province of Upper Canada, adapted for the purpose of an Academy of learning, with the intention of founding there an Academy for the general education of youth, in the various branches of literature and science on Christian principles, and that they have been advised that the said undertaking would be more successfully and effectually prosecuted, if it were protected by our Royal sanction, by means of a Royal Charter of incorporation, they have most humbly supplicated us to grant our Royal Charter of incorporation, for the purposes aforesaid under such regulations and restrictions as to us might seem right and expedient.

Now Know Ye that We, being desirous to maintain sound and useful learning in connexion with Christian principles, and highly approving the design of promoting the same in our said Province of Upper Canada, by means of the founding an Academy of learning, in our said Province, have by virtue of our Royal prerogative and of our especial grace, certain knowledge, and mere motion, granted, constituted, and declared, and by these Presents for us, our heirs, and successors, do grant, constitute, and declare that the Academy intended to be so founded shall be called "The Upper Canada Academy," and that for the purpose of establishing and maintaining the same, there shall be nine Trustees, three of whom shall go out of office annually in rotation, and whose places shall be supplied in manner hereinafter mentioned, and that our trusty and well-beloved subjects, the Reverend William Case, the Reverend John Beatty, Wesleyan Ministers of the City of Toronto, Home District, in our said Province ; Ebenezer Perry, Merchant, George Benjamin Spencer, Gentleman, John McCarthy, Merchant, of Cobourg, aforesaid ; James Rogers Armstrong, of the City of Toronto, Home District, Merchant ; John Counter, of Kingston, Midland District, in our said Province, Baker ; Billa Flint, jr., of Belleville, in the Midland District of our said Province, Merchant ; and the Reverend William Ryerson, of Hamilton, in the Gore District of our said Province, shall be and are hereby appointed and declared to be the first nine Trustees of the said Academy, and shall be and are hereby constituted one body politic and corporate, by the name of "The Trustees of the Upper Canada Academy," and shall by the same name and for the same purpose aforesaid, have perpetual succession, to be kept up in manner hereinafter directed, and shall have a common seal with power to break, alter, and renew the same at their discretion, and shall by the same name, sue and be sued, implead and be impleaded, answer and be answered unto, in any and every court of Us, our heirs and successors in any and every part of our Dominion.

And we do hereby will and ordain that by the same name, they and their successors shall be able and capable in law to take, purchase and hold to them and their successors, any goods, chattels, and personal property whatsoever, and shall also be able and capable in law to take, purchase, and hold to them and their successors, not only all such lands, buildings, hereditaments, and possessions, as may be from time to time exclusively used and occupied for the immediate purposes of the said Academy ; but also any other lands, buildings, hereditaments and possessions whatsoever, situate within our Dominions of North America, not exceeding the annual value of two thousand pounds, sterling money, such annual value, to be calculated, and ascertained at the time of taking, purchasing, and acquiring the same, and that they and their successors shall be able and capable in law, to grant, demise, alien, or otherwise dispose of all or any of the property, real or personal, belonging to the said Academy, also to do all other matters and things incidental or appertaining to a body corporate, and they and their successors shall have the custody of the common seal of the said Academy, with power to use the same for the affairs and concerns thereof. And the said Trustees shall have power to accept on behalf of the said Academy, gifts and endowments for promoting particular objects of education, science and literature, or otherwise in aid of the general purposes of the said Academy, on such terms and conditions as may be agreed on for the purpose between the Trustees and the persons bestowing any such gift or endowment.

And we do hereby will and ordain that the various branches of literature and science shall be taught on Christian principles in the said Academy, under the superintendence of a " Principal," or other " Head," Professors, and Tutors, or such other Masters or Instructors as shall from time to time be appointed in the manner hereinafter mentioned.

And we do hereby will and ordain, that there shall be five Visitors of the said Academy, with authority to do all those things which pertain to Visitors, as often as to them shall seem meet, and who shall go out of office annually.

And we will and ordain, that our trusty and well-beloved subjects, Charles Biggar, Esquire, Justice of the Peace, Murray, Newcastle District; Joseph A. Keeler, Esquire, Justice of the Peace, Colborne, Newcastle District; the Reverend John Ryerson, Wesleyan Minister, Hallowell, District of Prince Edward; the Reverend Joseph Stinson, Wesleyan Minister, Kingston, Midland District; and Alexander Davidson, Esquire, Port Hope, Newcastle District, shall be the first Visitors of the said Academy, and their successors shall be elected in manner hereinafter mentioned.

We further will and ordain, that there shall be a Treasurer and Secretary of the said Academy, who shall and may be chosen and displaced by the Trustees, as they shall think fit, at a meeting of the Trustees, at which not less than five of the Trustees shall be present; that a meeting of the Trustees, only, shall be called a " Trustee Meeting," of which five shall be a quorum, and a meeting of Visitors alone shall be called a " Visitors' Meeting," of which three shall be a quorum;

That the Trustees and Visitors together shall be called the "Board" of the said Academy, and a meeting of the Trustees and Visitors shall be called a "Board Meeting," of which eight shall be a quorum, and in all such meetings a Chairman shall be appointed by the members then present, from amongst themselves, and all questions which it shall be competent for any such meeting to decide, shall be decided by the majority of the members, being a quorum of such meeting then present, and the Chairman of every such meeting shall have a vote, and in case of an equality of votes, shall have a second or casting vote ;

That the Board, for the time being, shall have full power from time to time to appoint, and as they shall see occasion, to remove the "Principal," or other "Head," the professors, tutors and masters, and all officers, agents, and servants of the said Academy, and the said Board shall have full power, from time to time, to make and to alter or vary any by-Laws and regulations touching and concerning the time and place of holding ordinary Trustee meetings, Visitors' meetings and Board meetings, and for the good ordering and government of the said Academy, the performance of Divine service therein, the studies, lectures and exercises of the students, and all matters respecting the same ; the residence, duties, salary, provision, and emoluments of the professors, tutors, masters, officers, agents, and servants of the said Academy, respectively, and all other matters and things which to them may seem good, fit and useful for the well ordering, governing, and advancement of the said Academy ; and all such by-laws when reduced into writing, and after the common seal of the Academy hath been affixed thereto, shall be binding upon all persons, members thereof : Provided that no such by-law shall be repugnant to the laws and statutes of Great Britain and Ireland, or of our said Province of Upper Canada, or to this our Charter ; Provided also, that no religious test or qualification shall be required of or appointed for any person on his admission as a student or scholar into the said Academy ;

That any three Trustees shall, by notice in writing, to the other Trustees, be competent to call an extraordinary Trustee meeting, and any two of the Visitors shall be competent in like manner to call an extraordinary Visitors' meeting, and any five members of the Board shall be competent in like manner to call an extraordinary Board meeting at any time and place they may see fit, on any occasion which in their judgment may render it expedient for them so to do ;

That the Trustees, Visitors, and Board shall, respectively, cause records and minutes of all the proceedings, acts, and resolutions of all and every of their meetings, ordinary and extraordinary, to be entered and kept in books provided for that purpose, and which records and minutes shall, before the breaking up or adjournment of any such meeting, be read aloud by the Chairman in the presence of such meeting, and shall be signed by him, and being so signed, shall, until the contrary be shown, be deemed and taken to be the records and minutes of such meeting, and that the same meeting was duly convened and held. And the said Trustees shall keep a book or books of accounts of financial affairs of the said Academy, all which books of record, minutes and accounts shall be produced to and audited yearly at the annual meeting as hereinafter mentioned ;

That for making provision for filling up vacancies in the places of Trustees dying, resigning, or going out of office in manner hereinafter mentioned, and for appointing Visitors to the said Academy, there shall be holden in each year an annual meeting of the Ministers of the said Wesleyan Methodist Church in Upper Canada, and the first annual meeting of the said Ministers shall be holden at the City of Toronto, or the Town of Cobourg, in our said Province, on the Second Wednesday in the month of June, one thousand eight hundred and thirty-seven, and every subsequent annual meeting shall be holden at a place, and on some day in the month of June to be fixed and appointed at the said first and every subsequent annual meeting, for the then next annual meeting, and if no such day shall be fixed and appointed as aforesaid, and if the said annual meeting shall not be holden on the second Wednesday in the month of June, and if no place shall be fixed and appointed, as aforesaid, it shall be holden at the City of Toronto, aforesaid. Provided always, that every person who shall at the time of any such annual meeting, be duly authorized to solemnize the ceremony of matrimony in our said Province, by virtue of an Act of the Provincial Parliament of our said Province, made and passed the first year of our reign, and assented to by us, entitled: "An Act to make valid certain marriages heretofore contracted, and to provide for the future solemnization of matrimony in this Province," and who shall duly have obtained a certificate for that purpose as a Wesleyan Methodist Minister, according to the provisions of the said Act, and no other person whomsoever, shall be deemed and taken to be a Wesleyan Methodist Minister within the true intent and meaning of these presents.

That on the day on which the annual meeting in the year one thousand eight hundred and thirty-seven, one thousand eight hundred and thirty-eight, and one thousand eight hundred and thirty-nine, shall be holden, three of the said Trustees appointed, by this our Charter, to be determined by ballot, shall go out of office, and on the day on which every annual meeting shall be held after the year one thousand eight hundred and thirty-nine, three of the Trustees, who shall then have been longest in office, shall go out of office, calculating the period for which each of the Trustees for the time being shall have been in office, from the day of his last election, in case of his having been elected more than once; but the Trustees who on the day on which any annual meeting shall be held are to go out of office by ballot or rotation, as aforesaid, shall not be considered out of office until after such meeting shall have been broken up or adjourned.

That on the day on which the annual meeting in the year one thousand eight hundred and thirty-seven shall be holden, and on the day on which every succeeding annual meeting shall be holden, three Trustees shall be elected in the places of three, who are to go out by ballot or rotation as hereinbefore mentioned, but every Trustee going out of office, whether by ballot or rotation, shall be considered immediately re-eligible;

That in case there shall be any casual vacancy among the Trustees arising from death or any other cause except that of going out by ballot or rotation, as before mentioned, the annual meeting next after or during which any such casual vacancy shall occur, shall also elect a Trustee or Trustees, as the case may be, to fill every such casual vacancy, and any person who shall be elected a Trustee in consequence of, and to fill up such casual vacancy, shall be a substitute only for the person whose place he may supply, and shall continue in office only for the same period as the person whose place he may supply would have continued if such person had continued in office until such time as he must necessarily have gone out by ballot or rotation, as before mentioned.

That the said annual meeting, to be holden in the year one thousand eight hundred and thirty-seven, shall appoint five Visitors of the said Academy in the place of the five Visitors appointed by this our Charter, and every subsequent annual meeting shall appoint five Visitors in the places of the five who were in office during the preceding year, but any Visitor going out of office, shall be re-eligible to be immediately re-appointed to the office of Visitor; Provided, that no person shall at the same time be both a Trustee and Visitor of the said Academy;

That at the annual meeting in the year one thousand eight hundred and thirty-seven, and at the like meeting every succeeding year, the Trustees and Visitors shall report their proceedings during the preceding year, in the execution of their office and of the then existing state of the Academy, and shall cause the accounts to be balanced up to the thirty-first day of December in every year, or up to such other period as any annual meeting may from time to time appoint, and shall in every year produce, and lay all such accounts and proceedings before the said annual meeting, all which accounts and proceedings shall be examined in every year before the annual meeting, and so far as such accounts and proceedings shall be found to be correct, and shall not be found contrary and repugnant to this our Charter, nor to any such law, as aforesaid, the same shall be allowed and signed by the President and Secretary of the said annual meeting, and being so allowed and signed, shall, unless and until the same be shown to be incorrect, be binding and conclusive on all the members of the said corporation, and all persons claiming under them.

That the said annual meeting shall at any such meeting elect a Secretary and a President from among themselves, who shall continue in office unless sooner displaced by the said annual meeting, until a Secretary and President shall be in like manner elected at the then next subsequent Annual Meeting, and such Secretary and

President shall each have a vote, as other members of the meeting, and in case of an even division the President shall have and give an additional or casting vote ;

That no act in the premises shall be done at any such annual meeting, unless there be forty members thereof or upwards, present at the doing thereof, and the act of a majority of the members present shall be the act of the meeting ;

That, the election and appointment of all Trustees and Visitors of the said Academy by the said annual meeting, and all other their acts in the premises, shall be recorded in a book by the Secretary for the time being, and after being read aloud in the meeting by the Secretary for the time being, shall be signed by him and by the President for the time being, and being so signed, shall, so far as the same be not repugnant to this our Charter, or to any such law as aforesaid, be binding on the said Ministers, and on all the members of the said corporation, and all persons claiming under them.

That, in case the said Act of our said Province hereinbefore mentioned, shall be hereafter at any time, or from time to time, altered or repealed in whole or in part, and any other provision or enactment shall at any time or times hereafter be added to the said Act, or substituted for the same or any part thereof so repealed, and by which added or substituted enactment, the Ministers of the said Weslyan Methodist Church, in our said Province, shall be authorized to solemnize matrimony, this our Charter, shall for all and every the intents, purposes, and privileges of this our Charter, be held to have reference to, and shall have reference to every such added or substituted enactment as fully and effectually as the same now has to the said Act hereinbefore mentioned.

And lastly, we do hereby for Us, our heirs and successors, grant and declare that these our Letters Patent, or the enrolment or exemplification thereof, shall be in and by all things valid and effectual in the law according to the true intent and meaning of the same, and shall be construed and adjudged in the most favorable and beneficial sense for the best advantage of the said Academy, as well in all our Courts of every part of our Dominion as elsewhere, notwithstanding any non-recital, mis-recital, uncertainty, or imperfection in these Our Letters Patent.

In testimony whereof, we have caused these our Letters to be made Patent, and the Great Seal of our said Province to be hereunto affixed.

Witness, our trusty and well-beloved Sir Francis Bond Head, K. C. H., &c., &c., &c., Lieutenant-Governor of our said Province, at our City of Toronto, this twelfth day of October, in the year of our Lord one thousand eight hundred and thirty-six, and in the seventh year of our reign.

F. H. B.

By Command of His Excellency,
    D. CAMERON, Secretary.

APPENDIX H.

QUEEN'S COLLEGE CHARTER.

VICTORIA, by the Grace of God of the United Kingdom of Great Britain and Ireland, Queen, Defender of the Faith, &c., &c.

To all to whom these Presents shall come—GREETING :

Whereas the establishment of a College within the Province of Upper Canada, in North America, in connection with the Church of Scotland, for the education of youth in the principles of the Christian religion, and for their instruction in the various branches of science and literature, would greatly conduce to the welfare of our said Province; and whereas humble application hath been made to us by the Rev. Robert McGill, Moderator of the Synod of the Presbyterian Church of Canada, in connection with the Church of Scotland, and the Rev. Alexander Gale, Clerk of the said Synod, and the several other persons hereinafter named, to make them a body corporate and politic for the purposes aforesaid and hereinafter mentioned, by granting to them our Royal Charter of incorporation, and to permit them to use our Royal title in the name or style thereof ;

Now know ye that we, having taken the premises into our Royal consideration, and duly weighing the great utility and importance of such an institution, have, of our special grace, certain knowledge, and mere motion, granted, constituted, declared, and appointed, and by these presents for us, our heirs and successors, do grant, constitute, declare, and appoint the said Robert McGill and Alexander Gale, the Rev. John McKenzie, the Rev. William Rintoul, the Rev. William T. Leach, the Rev. James George, the Rev. John Machar, the Rev. Peter Colin Campbell, the Rev. John Cruikshank, the Rev. Alexander Mathieson (Doctor in Divinity the Rev. John Cook (Doctor in Divinity), and the Principal of th said college for the time being, Ministers of the Presbyterian Churc h of Canada in connection with the Church of Scotland ; the Honorable John Hamilton, the Honorable James Crooks, the Honorable William Morris, the Honorable Archibald McLean, the Honorable John McDonald, the Honorable Peter McGill, Edward W. Thompson, Thomas McKay, James Morris, John Ewart, John Steele, John Mowat, Alexander Pringle, John Nunn, and John Strang, Esquires, members of the said Church, and all and every such other person and persons as now is, or are, or shall or may at any time or times hereafter be Ministers of the Presbyterian Church of Canada in connection with the Church of Scotland, or members of the said Presbyterian Church in such connection and in full communion with the said Presbyterian Church, shall be and be called one body corporate and politic in deed and in law, by the name and style of " Queen's College at Kingston," and them by the name of " Queen's College at Kingston," we do for the purposes aforesaid and hereinafter mentioned, really and fully for us our heirs, and successors make, erect, create, ordain, constitute, establish, confirm, and declare by these presents to be one body politic and corporate in deed and in name : And that they and their successors by that name shall and may have perpetual succession as a College, with the style and privileges of an university, for the education and instruction of youth and students in arts and faculties ; and shall also have and may use a common seal, with power to break, change, alter, or make new the same seal, as often as they shall judge expedient, and that they and their successors by the name aforesaid shall and may forever hereafter be able in law and in equity to sue and be sued, inplead and be impleaded, answer and be answered unto, defend and be defended in all courts and places whatsoever, and also to have, take, receive, purchase, acquire, hold, possess, enjoy, and maintain in law to and for the use of the said College any messuages lands, tenements, and hereditaments of what kind, nature, or quality soever, so as that the same do not exceed in yearly value, above all charges, the sum of £15,000 sterling : and also that they and their successors shall have power to take, purchase, acquire, have, hold, enjoy, receive, possess, and retain all or any goods, chattels, moneys, stocks, charitable or other contributions, gifts, benefactions, or bequests whatsoever, and to give, grant, bargain, sell, demise, or otherwise dispose of all or any part of the same, or of any other property, real personal, or other, they may at any time or times possess or be entitled to, as to them shall seem best for the interest of the said College.

And we do further will, ordain, and grant, that the said College shall be deemed and taken to be an university; and that the students in the said College shall have liberty and faculty of taking the degrees of Bachelor, Master, and Doctor in the several arts and faculties at the appointed times, and shall have liberty within themselves of performing all scholastic exercises for conferring such degrees in such manner as shall be directed by the statutes, rules, and ordinances of the said College.

And we do further will, ordain, and appoint that no religious test or qualification shall be required of, or appointed for any persons admitted or matriculated as scholars within our said College, or of or for persons admitted to any degree in any art or faculty therein, save only that all persons admitted within our said College to any degree of Divinity shall make such and the same declarations and subscriptions as are required of persons admitted to any degree of Divinity in our University of Edinburgh.

And for the better execution of the purposes aforesaid, and for the more regular government of the said corporation, we do declare and grant that the said corporation and their successors shall forever have twenty-seven trustees, of whom twelve shall be Ministers of the said Presbyterian Church of Canada, and fifteen shall be laymen in full communion with the said Church; and that the said several persons hereinbefore named, and the Principal of the said College for the time being, shall be the first and present trustees of the said corporation, and shall respectively continue in such office until others shall be appointed in their stead, in pursuance of these our Letters Patent.

And we further will that the said trustees of the said corporation hereinbefore particularly named, shall continue in and hold the office of trustees until the several days and in the manner hereinafter mentioned, that is to say, three Ministers and four laymen, whose names stand lowest in these our Letters Patent, shall retire from the said Board of Trustees on the first day of the annual meeting of the said Synod in the year 1843, and their room be supplied by the addition of seven new members in manner hereinafter mentioned. Three other Ministers and four other laymen whose names stand next to those in these our Letters Patent, who shall have previously retired, shall retire from the said Board of Trustees on the first day of the annual meeting of the said Synod in the year 1844, and their room be supplied by the addition of seven new members in manner hereinafter mentioned. Three other Ministers and four other laymen, whose names stand next to those in these our Letters Patent who shall have previously retired, shall retire from the said Board of Trustees on the first day of the annual meeting of the said Synod in the year 1845, and their room be supplied by the addition of seven new members, in manner hereinafter mentioned; and the two remaining Ministers and the three remaining laymen whose names stand next to those in these our letters patent, who shall have previously retired, shall retire from the said Board of Trustees on the first day of the annual meeting of the said Synod in the year 1846, and their room be supplied by the addition of five new members in manner hereinafter mentioned. And in the first day of each succeeding annual meeting of the said Synod three Ministers and four laymen, whose names stand lowest in the future roll of Ministers and laymen composing the said Board of Trustees shall retire from the same, excepting in every fourth year, when two Ministers only, instead of three, and three laymen only, instead of four, shall so retire. And the new members of the Board to be appointed from time to time in succession to those who retire shall be appointed in manner following, that is to say: The three Ministers or two Ministers, as the case may be, shall be chosen by the said Synod on the first day of every annual meeting of the same in such manner as shall seem best to the said Synod; and the four laymen or three laymen, as the case may be, shall be chosen also on the first day of every annual meeting of the said Synod by the lay Trustees remaining after the others shall have retired and shall be so chosen from a list of persons made up in the following manner, that is to say: Each congregation admitted on the roll of the Synod and in regular connexion therewith shall, at a meeting to be specially called from the pulpit for that purpose in every third year, nominate one fit and discreet person, being a member in full communion with the said church, as eligible to fill the office of Trustee of the said College, and the persons' names so nominated being duly intimated by the several congregations to the Secretary of the Board of Trustees in such form as the said Board may direct, shall be enrolled by the said Board and cons'itute the list from which lay trustees shall be chosen to fill the vacancies occurring at the Board during each year, and the names of members thus added to the Board of Trustees shall be placed from time to time at the top of the roll of the Board, the names of the Ministers chosen as new trustees being first placed there in such order as the said Synod shall direct, and the names of the laymen chosen as new trustees being placed in such order as their electors shall direct, immediately after the names of the said Ministers: Provided, always, that the retiring trustees may be re-elected as heretofore provided, if the Synod and remaining lay trustees respectively see fit to do so ; and provided, always, that in case no election of new trustees shall be made on the said first day of the annual meeting of the said Synod, then and in such case the retiring members shall remain in office until their successors are appointed at some subsequent period ; and provided, always, that every trustee, whether Minister or layman, before entering on his duties as a member of the said Board, shall have solemnly declared his belief of the doctrines of the Westminster Confession of Faith and his adherence to the standards of the said Church in government, discipline, and worship, and subscribed such a formula to this effect as may be prescribed by the said Synod, and that such declaration and subscription shall in every case be recorded in the books of the said Board.

And we further will that the said trustees and their successors shall forever have full power and authority to elect and appoint for the said college a Principal, who shall be a Minister of the Church of Scoland, or of the Presbyterian Church of Canada in connexion with the Church of Scotland, and such professor or professors, master or masters, tutor or tutors, and such other officer or officers as to the said trustees shall seem meet, save and except only that the first Principal of the said College, who is also to be

Professor of Divinity, and likewise the first Professor of Morals in the said College, shall be nominated by the Committee of the General Assembly of the Church of Scotland : Provided always that such person or persons as may be appointed to the office of Principal or to any professorship or other office in the theological department in the said College, shall before discharging any of the duties or receiving any of the emoluments of such office or professorship, solemnly declare his belief of the doctrines of the Westminister Confession of Faith, and his adherence to the standards of the Church of Scotland, in government, discipline, and worship, and subscribe such a formula to this effect as may be prescribed by the Synod of the Presbyterian Church of Canada in connection with the Church of Scotland, and that such declaration and subscription be recorded in the books of the Board of Trustees ; and provided always that such persons as shall be appointed to professorships not in the theological department in the said College shall before discharging any of the duties or receiving any of the emoluments of such professorships subscribe such a formula declarative of their belief of the doctrines of the aforesaid Confession of Faith as the Synod may prescribe.

And we further will that if any complaint respecting the conduct of the Principal or any professor, master, tutor, or other officer of the said College be at any time made to the Board of Trustees, they may institute and enquire, and in the event of any impropriety of conduct being duly proved, they shall admonish, reprove, suspend, or remove the person offending as to them may seem good : Provided always that the grounds of such admonition, reproof, suspension, or removal be recorded at length in the books of the said Board.

And we further will that the said trustees and their successors shall have full power and authority to erect an edifice or edifices for the use of the said College ; Provided always that such edifice or edifices shall not be more than three miles distant from St. Andrew's Church in the Town of Kingston, in the Province of Upper Canada.

And we further will that the said trustees and their successors hall have power and authority to frame and make statutes, rules, and ordinances touching and concerning the good government of the said College ; the performance of Divine service therein ; the studies, lectures, exercises, and all matters regarding the same ; the number, residence, and duties of the professors thereof ; the management of the revenues and property of the said College ; the salaries, stipends, provision, and emoluments of and for the professors, officers, and servants thereof ; the number and duties of such officers and servants, and also touching and concerning any other matter or thing which to them shall seem necessary for the well-being and advancement of the said College ; and also from time to time by any new statutes, rules, or ordinances, to revoke, renew, augment, or alter, all, every, or any of the said statutes, rules, and ordinances as to them shall seem meet and expedient : Provided always that the said statutes, rules and ordinances, or any of them, shall not be repugnant to these presents, or to the laws and statutes of the said Province ; Provided also that the said statutes, rules, and ordinances, in so far as they regard the performance of Divine service in the said College, the duties of the professors in the theological department thereof, and the studies and exercises of the students of Divinity therein, shall be subject to the inspection of the said Synod of the Presbyterian Church, and shall forthwith be transmitted to the clerk of the said Synod and be by him laid before the same at their next meeting for their approval ; and until such approval, duly authenticated by the signatures of the Moderator and Clerk of the said Synod is obtained the same shall not be in force.

And we further will that so soon as there shall be a Principal and one professor in the said College the Board of Trustees shall have authority to constitute under their seal the said Principal and professor, together with three members of the Board of Trustees a court to be called "The College Senate," for the exercise of academical superintendence and discipline over the students and all other persons resident within the same, and with such powers for maintaining order and enforcing obedience to the statutes, rules, and ordinances of the said College as to the said Board may seem meet and necessary : Provided always that so soon as three additional professors shall be employed in the said College no trustee shall be a member of the said College Senate, but that such Principal and all the professors of the said College shall for ever constitute the College Senate with the powers just mentioned.

And we further will that whenever there shall be a Principal and four professors employed in the said College the College Senate shall have power and authority to confer the degrees of Bachelor, Master, and Doctor in the several arts and faculties.

And we further will that five of the said trustees lawfully convened, as is hereinafter directed, shall be a quorum for the dispatch of all business except for the disposal and purchase of real estate or for the choice or removal of the Principal or professors, for any of which purposes there shall be a meeting of at least thirteen trustees.

And we further will that the said trustees shall have full power and authority from time to time to choose a Secretary and Treasurer ; and also once in each year, or oftener, a Chairman, who shall preside at all meetings of the Board.

And we further will that the said trustees shall also have power by a majority of voices of the members present, to select and appoint in the event of a vacancy in the Board by death, resignation, or removal from the Province, a person whose name is on the list from which appointments are to be made, to fill such vacancy, choosing a Minister in the room of a Minister and a layman in the room of a layman, and inserting the name of the person so chosen in that place on the roll of the Board in which the name of the trustee in whose stead he may have been chosen stood ; so that the persons so chosen may be, as to continuance in office and in all other respects, as the persons would have been by whose death, resignation, or removal the vacancy was occasioned.

And we further will that the first general meeting of the said trustees shall be held at Kingston, upon such a day, within six calendar months after the date of these our Letters Patent, as shall be fixed for that purpose by the trustee first named in these presents, who shall be then living ; of which meeting thirty days' notice at least shall be given by notification in writing to each of the trustees for the time being, who shall be resident at the time within the Provinces of Upper and Lower Canada, and the same shall also be notified at the same time by advertisement in one or more of the public newspapers of the said Provinces. And the said trustees shall also afterwards have power to meet at Kingston aforesaid, or at such other place as they shall fix for that purpose upon their own adjournment, and likewise so often as they shall be summoned by the Chairman, or in his absence by the senior trustee, whose seniority shall be determined in the first instance by the order in which the said trustees are named in these presents, and afterwards by the order in which they shall be subsequently arranged pursuant to the powers hereinafter contained: Provided, always that the Chairman or senior trustee shall not summon a meeting of the trustees unless required so to do by a notice in writing from three members of the Board; and provided, also, that he cause notice of the time and place of the said meeting to be given in one or more of the public newspapers of the Provinces of Upper and Lower Canada, at least thirty days before such meeting, and that every member of the Board of Trustees resident within the said Provinces shall be notified in writing by the Secretary to the corporation of the time and place of such meeting.

And we will and by these presents for us, our heirs and successors, do grant and declare that these our Letters Patent, or the enrolment or exemplification thereof shall and may be good, firm, and valid, sufficient and effectual in the law according to the true intent and meaning of the same, and shall be taken, construed and adjudged in the most favourable and beneficial sense for the best advantage of our said College, as well in our courts of record as elsewhere; and by all and singular judges, justices, officers, ministers, and others subject whatsoever of us, our heirs, and successors, any unrecital, non-recital, omission, imperfection, defect, matter, cause, or anything whatsoever to the contrary thereof in any wise notwithstanding.

In witness whereof We have caused these, Our Letters, to be made Patent. Witness Ourself at our Palace, at Westminster, this sixteenth day of October, in the fifth year of our reign.

By Writ of Privy Seal.

EDMUNDS.

APPENDIX I.

TRINITY UNIVERSITY CHARTER.

VICTORIA, by the Grace of God of the United Kingdom of Great Britain and Ireland, Queen, Defender of the Faith, &c., &c.

To all to whom these Presents shall come—GREETING :

Whereas by an Act passed by the Legislature of our Province of Canada, in the fifteenth year of our reign, intituled, "An Act to incorporate Trinity College," there was constituted and established in the City of Toronto, within the Diocese of Toronto, in our said Province of Canada, a body corporate and politic, under the name of Trinity College, in connection with the United Church of England and Ireland, which Corporation is by the said Act made to consist of the Lord Bishop of Toronto, or in case of the division of the said Diocese, of the Bishops of the several Dioceses into which the Diocese of Toronto might be thereafter divided, and also of the Trustees of the said College, and of the members of the Council of the said College, not to be less than three in number, which said Trustees and the members of the said College Council, it was by the said Act provided, should be named in the first instance by the Lord Bishop of Toronto, and in the event of their death, removal from the Province, dismissal from office, or resignation, shall be replaced by other persons to be named in the like manner, or in such other manner as may from time to time be directed by any statute of the said College, to be passed for that purpose ;

And whereas it is by the said Act further provided that the said Corporation of Trinity College shall, besides other corporate powers and capacities necessary to the well ordering of their affairs, have full power to make and establish such rules, orders, and regulations (not being contrary to the laws of Canada, or to the said Act) as they shall deem useful or necessary, as well concerning the system of education in, as for the conduct and government of, the said College, and of a preparatory school to be connected with, or dependent on the same, and for the management of the property belonging to the said Corporation, and shall have power to hold for the said College real and personal estate and property, and to sell, alienate, convey, or lease the same, if need be ; provided that the total yearly income from the property so acquired shall not at any time exceed the sum of five thousand pounds of current money of our said Province ; and provided also, that no rule, order, or regulation, which shall be made and established by the said Corporation in manner aforesaid, shall be of any force or effect until the same shall have been sanctioned and confirmed by the said Lord Bishop or Bishops as aforesaid.

And whereas, since the passing of the said Act, the Council of the said College have, with the sanction of the Lord Bishop of Toronto, by their petition to us humbly set forth, that in pursuance of the provisions of the said Act, Trinity College hath been duly organized, by the appointment of trustees and of a College Council, and that certain statutes, rules, and ordinances have been made by the said Council, with the approval of the Lord Bishop of Toronto, and further, that a suitable building has been erected, and a Provost, and Professors in the faculties of Divinity and the Arts, and in Law and Medicine, have been duly appointed, and are now engaged in the education of a considerable number of scholars, duly admitted according to the statutes and ordinances of the said Corporation, and the said College being, according to the intention of the said Act of the Legislature of our Province of Canada, in strict connexion with the United Church of England and Ireland, and supported wholly from funds contributed by the members of that Church, and humble application hath been made to us by the said Corporation and many of our loving subjects in the said Province of Canada, that we would be pleased to grant our Royal Charter for the more perfect establishment of the said College, by granting to it the privileges hereinafter mentioned ;

Now know ye that We, having taken the premises into our Royal consideration, and being willing to promote the more perfect establishment within the Diocese of Toronto of a College in connexion within the United Church of England and Ireland, for the education of youth in the doctrines and duties of the Christian religion as inculcated by that Church, and for their instruction in the variour branches of science and literature which are taught in the Universities of this Kingdom, have of our special grace, certain knowledge, and mere motion, willed, ordained, and granted, and do by these presents, for us, our heirs, and successors, will, ordain, and grant, that the said College shall be deemed and taken to be a University, and shall have and enjoy all such and the like privileges as are enjoyed by our Universities of our United Kingdom of Great Britain and Ireland, as far as the same are capable of being had or enjoyed by virtue of these our Letters Patent; and that the students in the said College shall have liberty and faculty of taking the degrees of Bachelor, Master, and Doctor in the several arts and faculties, at the appointed times, and shall have liberty within themselves of performing all scholastic exercises, for the conferring such degrees, in such manner as shall be directed by the statutes, rules, and ordinances of the said College.

And, in order that such degrees may be in due form granted in the said College, we do further will, and direct, and ordain that there shall be at all times a Chancellor of the said University to be chosen at and for such periods of time, and under such rules and regulations as the College Council, by and with the sanction and approbation of the Lord Bishop or Bishops, aforesaid, may, by their statutes, rules, or ordinances, to be from time to time passed for that purpose, think fit to appoint.

And that the Chancellor, Provost, and Professors of the said College, and all persons admitted therein to the Degree of Master of Arts, or to any Degree in Divinity, Law, or Medicine, and who from the time of such their admission to such Degree shall pay the annual sum of twenty shillings of sterling money for and towards the support and maintenance of the said College, shall be, and be deemed, taken, and reputed to be members of the Convocation of the said University, and as such members of the said Convocation, shall have, exercise, and enjoy all such powers and privileges in regard to conferring degrees, and in any other matters, as may be provided for by any rules, orders, or regulations of the said College

Council, sanctioned and confirmed by the Lord Bishop or Bishops as aforesaid, so far as the same are capable of being had and enjoyed by virtue of these our Letters Patent, and consistently with the provisions thereof, and with the said Act of the Legislature of our Province of Canada.

And we will, and by these presents for us, our heirs and successors, do grant and declare, that these our Letters Patent, or the enrolment or exemplification thereof, shall and may be good, firm, valid, sufficient, and effectual in the law, according to the true intent and meaning of the same, and shall be taken, construed, and adjudged in the most favourable and beneficial sense, and to the best advantage of our said College, as well in our courts of record as elsewhere, and by all and singular judges, justices, officers, ministers, and other subjects whatsoever of us, our heirs and successors, any mis-recital, non-recital, omission, imperfection, defect, matter, cause, or thing whatsoever to the contrary notwithstanding.

> In witness whereof, We have caused these Our Letters to be made Patent. Witness Ourself, at our Palace at Westminster, the sixteenth day of July, in the sixteenth year of our reign.

{ L.S. }

By Her Majesty's Command.

EDMUNDS.

APPENDIX J.

McGILL UNIVERSITY CHARTER.

VICTORIA, by the Grace of God, of the United Kingdom of Great Britain and Ireland, Queen, Defender of the Faith, &c., &c.

To all to whom these Presents shall come—GREETING :—

Whereas the Honourable James McGill, late of the City of Montreal, in that part of the Province of Canada heretofore constituting the Province of Lower Canada, by his last will and testament, bearing date at Montreal aforesaid, the eighth day of January, in the year of our Lord one thousand eight hundred and eleven, did give and bequeath a certain tract of land near the said City of Montreal, with the dwelling house and other buildings thereon erected, to trustees in trust to convey and assure the same to the Royal Institution for the Advancement of Learning, established by virtue of an Act of the Provincial Parliament of the said then Province of Lower Canada, made and passed in the forty-first year of the reign of our late Royal Predecessor King George the Third, intituled "An Act for the establishment of Free Schools and the Advancement of Learning in this Province," upon condition that the said institution should within ten years from the decease of the said James McGill, erect and establish, or cause to be erected and established, upon the said land, an University or College, for the purposes of education and the advancement of learning in the said then Province, with a competent number of professors and teachers to render such establishment effectual and beneficial for the purpose intended, and also upon condition that one of the colleges to be comprised in the said university should be called "McGill College;" and whereas the said James McGill, Esquire, by his said will, did further give and bequeath to the said Trustees, the sum of ten thousand pounds in trust, to pay the same with interest to accrue thereon from and after the expiration of three years from his decease to the said Royal Institution for the Advancement of Learning, to be applied as soon as the said institution should have erected an university or college on the said land, towards defraying the expenses thereby incurred, and towards maintaining the said university or college so erected and established; and whereas our late Royal Predecessor King George the Fourth, upon the humble petition to that effect of the said Royal Institution for the Advancement of Learning, was pleased by his Letters Patent, bearing date at Westminster the thirty-first day of March in the second year of his reign, to will and ordain in manner following, that is to say :—

"Whereas the Honorable James McGill, late of the City of Montreal, in the Province of Lower Canada, now deceased, by his last will and testament, bearing date at Montreal the eighth day of January, in the year of our Lord one thousand eight hundred and eleven, did give and bequeath a certain tract of land near the said City of Montreal, with the dwelling house and other buildings thereon erected, to Trustees in trust to convey and assure the same to the Royal Institution for the Advancement of Learning, established by virtue of an Act of the Provincial Parliament of Lower Canada, made and passed in the forty-first year of the Reign of His late Majesty, intituled 'An Act for the establishment of Free Schools and the Advancement of Learning in this Province,' upon condition that the said Institution should, within ten years from the decease of the said James McGill, erect and establish, or cause to be erected and established, upon the said land, an University or College, for the purposes of education and the advancement of learning in the said Province, with a competent number of professors and teachers to render such establishment effectual and beneficial for the purpose intended, and also upon condition that one of the Colleges to be comprised in the said University should be called 'McGill College'; and Whereas the said James McGill, Esquire, by his last will, did further give and bequeath to the said Trustees the sum of £10,000 in trust to pay the same, with interest to accrue thereon from and after the expiration of three years from his decease, to the said Royal Institution for the Advancement of

Learning, to be applied as soon as the said Royal Institution should have erected an University or College on the said land, towards defraying the expenses thereby incurred, and towards maintaining the said University or College so erected and established ; and Whereas, We have been humbly petitioned by the said Royal Institution for the Advancement of Learning, that We would be pleased to grant our Royal Charter for the more perfect erection and establishment of the said College, and for incorporating the members thereof for the purposes aforesaid, and for such further endowment thereof as to Us should seem meet, We, having taken the premises into our Royal consideration, and being desirous that an University or College should be established for the education of youth in the principles of true religion, and for their instruction in the different branches of science and literature, are willing to comply with the prayer of the said petition, and to afford every assistance towards carrying the intentions of the said James McGill into execution ;

"Therefore, know ye that We, of our special grace, certain knowledge, and mere motion, have willed, ordained, and granted, and do by these presents for Us, our heirs, and successors, will, ordain, and grant, that upon the said land and in the said buildings thereon erected, or to be erected, there shall be established from this time one College at the least, for the education of youth and students in the arts and faculties, to continue forever, and that the first College to be erected thereon shall be called 'McGill College,' and that our trusty and well beloved, the Governor of Lower Canada, Lieutenant-Governor of Lower Canada, Lieutenant-Governor of Upper Canada, the Bishop of Quebec, the Chief Justice of Montreal, and the Chief Justice of Upper Canada, for the time being, shall be Governors of the said McGill College, and that the said McGill College shall consist of one Principal, to be elected in manner hereinafter mentioned, and who shall be during his continuance in the said office, a Governor of the said College, of four Professors to be also elected in manner hereinafter mentioned, and of Fellows, Tutors, and Scholars in such numbers, and at such salaries and subject to such provisions, rules, and regulations as shall hereafter be appointed by the statutes, rules, and ordinances of the said College ;

And we do, by these Presents, for Us, our heirs and successors, will, ordain, and grant that the Principal and Professors of the said College shall be from time to time elected by the said Governors or the major part of them as shall be present at any meeting to be holden for such election ; and in case of an equality of votes, the officer present at such meeting whose office is first described in order in these presents shall have a double and casting vote ; provided always, that the persons by whom such election shall be made shall notify the same respectively to Us, our heirs and successors, through one of our or their principal Secretaries of State, by the first opportunity, and in case that We, our heirs or successors, shall disapprove of any person so elected, and shall cause such disapprobation to be notified to him under the Royal signet and sign manual, or through one of the principal Secretaries of State, the person so elected as aforesaid shall immediately upon such notification, cease to hold the office of Principal or Professor to which he shall have been elected as aforesaid, and the said Governors shall thereupon proceed to the election of another person to fill the office of such Principal or Professor respectively, and so, from time to time, as often as the case shall happen.

" And We do by these presents, for Us, our heirs and successors, will, ordain, and grant that the said Governors, Principal, and Fellows, and their successors for ever, shall be one distinct and separate body politic and corporate in deed and in word, by the name and style of ' The Governors, Principal, and Fellows of McGill College, at Montreal, in the said Province of Lower Canada,' and that by the same name they shall have perpetual succession and a common seal, and that they and their successors shall, from time to time, have full power to break, alter, make new, or change such common seal at their will and pleasure, and as shall be found expedient, and that by the said name the said Governors, Principal, and Fellows, and their successors, from time to time, and at all times hereafter, shall be a body politic and corporate in deed and in law, and be able and capable to have, take, receive, purchase, acquire, hold, possess, enjoy, and retain.

" And We do hereby, for Us, our heirs and successors, give and grant full authority and free license to them and their successors, by the name aforesaid, to have, take, receive, purchase, acquire, hold, possess, enjoy, and retain to and for the use of the said College, notwithstanding any statutes or statute of mortmain, any manors, rectories, advowsons, messuages, lands, tenements, rents, hereditaments of what kind, nature, or quality soever, so as that the same do not exceed in yearly value the sum of £6,000 above all charges ; and moreover, to take, purchase, acquire, have, hold, enjoy, receive, possess, and retain, notwithstanding any such statutes or statute to the contrary, all or any goods, chattels, charitable or other contributions, gifts and benefactions whatsoever ; and that the said Governors, Principal, and Fellows, and their successors, by the same name, shall and may be able and capable in law to sue and be sued, implead and be impleaded, answer and be answered in all and every Court or Courts of record or places of judicature within our United Kingdom of Great Britain and Ireland, and our said Province of Lower Canada, and other our dominions, and in all and singular actions, causes, pleas, suits, matters, and demands whatsoever, of what kind and nature and sort soever, in as large, ample, and beneficial manner and form as any other body politic and corporate, or any other our liege subjects being persons able and capable in law may or can have, take, purchase, receive, hold, possess, enjoy, retain, sue, implead, or answer, or be sued, impleaded, or answered, in any manner whatsoever.

"And We do by these presents, for Us, our heirs, and successors, will, ordain, and grant, that the Governors of the said College, or the major part of them, shall have power and authority to frame and make statutes, rules, and ordinances touching and concerning the good government of the said College, the performance of Divine service therein, the studies, lectures, exercises, and degrees in arts and faculties and all matters regarding the same, the election, qualification, and residence of the Principal, Professors, Fellows, and Scholars, the salaries, stipends, and provisions for the Principal, Professors, Fellows, and Scholars, and Officers of the said College, and touching and concerning other matter or thing which to them shalll seem good, fit, useful, and agreeable to this our Charter, provided that no such statutes, rules, and ordinances shall have any force or effect until allowed and confirmed by Us, our heirs, and successors ; and also from time to time to revoke, augment, or alter the same as to them, or the major part of them, shall seem expedient, subject always to our allowance and confirmation as aforesaid, provided that the said statutes, rules, and ordinances, or any of them, shall not be repugnant to the laws and statutes of this our realm, and of our said Province of Lower Canada ; and we do hereby for Us, our heirs, and successors, charge and command that the statutes, rules, and ordinances as aforesaid, subject to the said provisions, shall be strictly and inviolably observed, kept, and performed, so long as they shall respectively remain in force and effect, under the penalties to be thereby or therein inflicted or contained ;

And we do by these presents, for Us, our heirs, and successors, will, ordain, direct, and appoint, that the members of the Royal Institution aforesaid, for the time being, shall be visitors of the said College ;

And we do further will, ordain, and grant, that the said College shall be deemed and taken to be an University, and that the Students in the said College shall have liberty and faculty of taking the degrees of Bachelor, Master, and Doctor in the several arts and faculties, at the appointed time, and shall have liberty within themselves of performing scholastic exercises, for the conferring of such degrees, in such manner as shall be directed by the statutes, rules, and ordinances of the said College ;

And We do by these presents for Us, our heirs, and successors, grant and declare that these our Letters Patent, or the enrolments or exemplifications thereof shall and may be good, firm, and valid, sufficient and effectual in the law according to the true intent and meaning of the same, and shall be taken, and construed, and adjudged in the most favourable and beneficial sense for the best advantage of the said Governors, Principal, Fellows, and Scholars of the said College at Montreal aforesaid, as well in our Courts of Record, as elsewhere, and by all and singular judges, justices, officers, ministers, and other subjects whatsoever, of Us, our heirs, and successors, any misrecital, nonrecital, omission, imperfection, defect, matter, cause, or thing whatsoever to the contrary thereof, in anywise notwithstanding, without fine or fee, great or small, to be for the same in any manner rendered, done, or paid to Us in our hanaper or elsewhere to our use."

And whereas it is deemed expedient for the interests of the said College, and for the augmentation of its funds, and the better and more easy management of its affairs and the government of the said College, to make certain alterations in the provisions of the said hereinbefore recited and existing Letters Patent, which said alterations are and have been assented to by the said Royal Institution for the Advancement of Learning and by the said Corporation of the said College :

Now Know Ye, that We, of our special grace, certain knowledge, and mere motion, have willed, ordained, and granted, and by these presents do, for Us, our heirs, and successors, will, ordain and grant, that henceforth from the date hereof, the members of the Royal Institution aforesaid for the time being shall be and remain Governors of the said College, and shall have and exercise all and every the powers, authority, and jurisdiction given and granted unto the Governors nominated and appointed in and by the said Letters Patent, save only in so far as the provisions of the said Letters Patent in that behalf are or may be by these presents altered ; and shall also have and exercise all and every the powers, authority, and jurisdiction given and granted under and by virtue of these presents ;

And We do further by these presents for Us, our heirs, and successors, will and ordain, that henceforth from the date hereof, the Governor of Lower Canada, the Lieutenant Governor of Lower Canada, the Lieutenant Governor of Upper Canada, the Bishop of Quebec, the Chief Justice of Montreal, the Chief Justice of Upper Canada, and the Principal of the said College, shall not, nor shall any or either of them, as such Governor of Lower Canada, Lieutenant Governor of Lower Canada, Lieutenant Governor of Upper Canada, Bishop of Quebec, Chief Justice of Montreal, Chief Justice of Upper Canada, and Principal of the said College, be Governor of the said College, or use or exercise any power, authority or jurisdiction in or over the same in any manner or way whatsoever ;

And We do further, by these presents, for Us, our heirs, and successors, will, ordain, and grant, that the said College shall consist of one Principal, of such and so many Professors in the various arts and faculties as from time to time may be judged necessary and expedient by the said Governors, and of Fellows, Tutors, and Scholars, in such numbers and at such salaries, and subject to such provisions, rules, and regulations as shall be appointed by the statutes, rules, and ordinances of the said College; that save and except for the purposes hereinafter specially mentioned and excepted, three of the said Governors shall be a sufficient number to be present at any meeting for the transaction of the ordinary business of the said College; that the determination of all questions, matters, and things submitted to the said Governors at their meetings, shall be made by the votes of the majority of those present, including the vote of the Governor presiding at such meeting, who shall have a double or casting vote in the case of an equality of votes thereat; that the President or Principal for the time being of the said Royal Institution, in all cases when present, shall preside at the said meetings, and in his absence the member of the said Royal Institution first or senior in order of appointment of those present at the meeting, shall preside thereat; that the Principal and all the professors of the said College shall from time to time be elected by the said Governors or the major part of them present at a meeting specially convened and holden for the purpose of such election, and shall and may hold their respective offices subject to the right and power of amotion by the said Governors for the time being, at a meeting specially convened and holden for the said purpose: Provided always that no less than five of the said Governors shall be present at such special meeting for the purpose of election or amotion, and that special notice in writing of the time, place, and object of every such special meeting, by the Secretary of the said College, addressed to each of the said Governors, shall have been delivered by the said Secretary into the Post Office of the said City of Montreal at least fifteen days before the time appointed for such meeting; that within forty-eight hours after every such election or amotion, notice thereof in writing, sealed with the College Seal, signed by the Secretary of the said College, or in his absence by the Governor who shall have presided at the meeting whereat such election or amotion shall have been voted, and addressed to our Visitor of the said College hereinafter mentioned, for the time being, shall be delivered into the Post

Office of the said City of Montreal; that every such election or amotion shall be subject to the review of our said Visitor, whose determination thereon being signified in writing to the said Governors within sixty days after such delivery as aforesaid at the said Post Office of the City of Montreal, of the said notice of such election or amotion, shall be final and conclusive unless the same by any order or orders to be by Us, our heirs or successors made in our or their Privy Council shall be altered, revoked, or disallowed as hereinafter is provided; that during the said last mentioned period of sixty days the said election or amotion, as the case may be, shall have no force or effect; and that failing such signification within the said last mentioned period, such election or amotion shall be and be held and taken to be by him approved and confirmed;

And We do further by these presents for Us, our heirs and successors, will and ordain, that henceforth from the date hereof such election shall not be required to be notified to Us, our heirs, and successors, in the manner provided and required in and by the said Letters Patent, or in any other manner whatsoever;

And We do further by these presents, for Us, our heirs and successors, will, ordain, and grant, that the said Governors, Principal, and Fellows, and their successors for ever, shall be one body politic and corporate, by the name of "The Governors, Principal, and Fellows of McGill College," and by the said name shall have perpetual succession, and a common seal, and shall by the same name sue and be sued, implead and be impleaded, and answer and be answered unto, in every Court of Us, our heirs and successors, henceforth from the date hereof, and shall no longer be known by the name in the said Letters Patent mentioned, and shall retain all and every the property, franchises, rights, and privileges granted under and by virtue of the said Letters Patent, and belonging to the said Corporation immediately before the date hereof, and shall be and remain liable to all claims and duties to which immediately before the date hereof they were subject, save only in so far as by these presents may be otherwise specially provided;

And We do further by these presents, for Us, our heirs, and successors, will, ordain, and grant, to the said Governors, Principal, and Fellows, and their successors, by the name aforesaid, full authority and free license to have, take, purchase, and hold, to them and their successors to and for the use of the said College, any goods, chattels, or personal property whatsoever ; and also that by the name aforesaid they shall be able and capable in law, notwithstanding any statutes or statute of mortmain, law, usage, or custom whatsoever to the contrary, to have, take, purchase, and hold to them and their successors to and for the use of said College, any other manors, rectories, advowsons, messuages, lands, tenements, rents, and hereditaments of what kind, nature, or quality soever, over and above the manors, rectories, advowsons, messuages, lands, tenements, rents, and hereditaments in the said Letters Patent mentioned of the yearly value of Six thousand pounds above all charges as in the said Letters Patent is set forth, but not for the purpose or with the view of re-selling the same ; provided always, that the whole shall not exceed the yearly value of Twelve thousand pounds above all charges, such annual value to be calculated and ascertained at the period of taking, purchasing, or acquiring the same ;

And We do further by these presents, for Us, our heirs and successors, appoint as our Visitor in and over and for the said College, our Governor General of our said Province of Canada, for the time being, or in his absence the Administrator of the Government for the time being ; who shall exercise, use, and enjoy all and every the powers and authority of a Visitor, for and in the name and behalf of Us, our heirs and successors, of the said College in all matters and things connected with the said College, as to him shall seem meet, according to the tenor and effect of these presents, and of the laws in force in our realm of England in relation to such powers and authority.

And We do further by these presents, for Us, our heirs and successors, revoke and annul the power and authority in and by the said Letters Patent given and granted to the members for the time being of the Royal Institution for the Advancement of Learning, to be Visitors of the said College ; and do will and ordain that henceforth from the date of these presents the power and authority so given and granted to the said members of the said royal institution to be such Visitors, shall absolutely cease and determine, and shall not be exercised or used by them or any of them.

And We do further by these presents, for Us, our heirs and successors, will, ordain, and declare that the statutes, rules and ordinances from time to time framed and made by the said Governors of the said College, touching the matters and things in the said Letters Patent and in these presents enumerated, or any thereof, or for the revoking, augmenting, or altering of any statutes, rules, or ordinances theretofore framed and made, so always as the same be not repugnant to the laws of Our realm or of Our said Province of Canada, or to the objects and provisions of this Our Charter, shall have full force and effect, without the allowance and confirmation of Us, Our heirs and successors, as ordained in and by the said Letters Patent; provided always, that a certified Copy of all such statutes, rules and ordinances, sealed with the College seal and addressed to Our said Visitor of the said College for the time being, shall have been delivered into the Post Office of the said City of Montreal, and that the same shall not have been disallowed by Our said Visitor, and such disallowance signified in writing to the said Governors, within sixty days after such delivery of such copy into the said Post Office.

And We do by these presents, for Us, our heirs and successors, expressly save and reserve to Us, our heirs and successors, the power of receiving, and by any order or orders to be by Us, or Them, made in Our or their Privy Council revising, confirming, altering, revoking or disallowing, all or any of the decisions, sentences, or orders so as aforesaid from time to time by the said Visitor to be made and rendered in reference to any such statutes, rules and ordinances, or the disallowing thereof, or in reference to any matter or thing whatsoever, as to which any power or authority is by these presents given and granted to him;

And We do by these presents, for Us, Our heirs and successors, will, ordain, and grant, that nothing herein contained shall be held, construed, or considered to have in any manner or way whatsoever revoked, cancelled, abrogated, or altered the provisions, powers, authorities, and grants in and by the said Letters Patent ordained and granted, or any thereof, save and except in the particulars hereinbefore specially and expressly set forth; but that all and every the said provisions, powers, authorities, and grants in and by the said Letters Patent ordained and granted, shall subsist and continue in full force and effect, save and except in the particulars aforesaid, in the same manner as if these Our Letters Patent had never been made, ordained, or granted; and We do further by these presents for Us, our Heirs and Successors, grant and declare that these our Letters Patent, or the enrolment or exemplification thereof, shall be in all things valid and effectual in the law according to the true intent and meaning of the same, and shall be taken, construed, and adjudged in the most favourable and beneficial sense for the best advantage of the said College, and of the said Governors, Principal, Fellows, and Scholars thereof, as well in our Courts of Record as elsewhere, and by all and singular judges, justices, officers, ministers and other subjects whatsoever of Us, our heirs and successors, any misrecital, non-recital, omission, imperfection, defect, matter, cause, or thing whatsoever to the contrary thereof in any wise notwithstanding.

> In witness whereof We have caused these Our Letters to be made Patent. Witness Ourself at Our Palace at Westminster, this sixth day of July, in the sixteenth year of Our Reign.
>
> By Her Majesty's command,
>
> (Signed) EDMUNDS.

BISHOP'S UNIVERSITY CHARTER.

VICTORIA, by the Grace of God of the United Kingdom of Great Britain and Ireland, Queen, Defender of the Faith, &c., &c

To all to whom these Presents shall come—GREETING:

Whereas, by an Act passed by the Legislature of our Province of Canada, in the seventh year of our reign, intituled, "An Act to incorporate Bishop's College in the Diocese of Quebec," there was constituted and established at Lennoxville, in the Township of

Ascot, in the District of Saint Francis, and within the Diocese of Quebec, in our said Province of Canada, a body corporate and politic, under the name of Bishop's College, in connection with the United Church of England and Ireland, which said Corporation is, by the said Act, made to consist of : First, the Lord Bishop of Quebec, or other superior ecclesiastical functionary of the United Church of England and Ireland, in the said Diocese of Quebec ; Secondly, the Trustees of the said Bishop's College, not less than three in number ; and Thirdly, the College Council of the said Bishop's College, not less than three in number ; which said Trustees and the members of the said College Council shall be named by the said Lord Bishop of Quebec, or other superior ecclesiastical functionary as aforesaid, and shall, in the event of their death, removal from the Province, dismissal from their office, or resignation, be replaced by other persons to be named in like manner, and so on continually forever ;

And whereas it is by the said Act further provided that the said Corporation of Bishop's College shall, besides other corporate powers and capacities necessary to the well ordering of their affairs, have full power to make and establish such and so many rules, orders, and regulations (not being contrary to the laws of Canada or to the said Act) as they shall deem useful and necessary, as well concerning the system of education in, as for the conduct and government of, the said College, and of any other institution or school connected with or dependent on the same, and of the corporation thereof, and for the superintendence, advantage, and improvement of all the property, movable or immovable, belonging to, or which shall hereafter belong to the said Corporation, and shall have power to take under any legal title whatsoever, and to hold for the said College, without any further authority, license, or letters of mortmain, all land and property, movable or immovable, which may hereafter be sold, ceded, exchanged, given, bequeathed, or granted to the said Corporation, or to sell, alienate, convey, let, or lease the same, if need be : Provided always, that the net rents, issues, and profits arising from the immovable property of the said Corporation shall not at any time exceed the annual sum of three thousand pounds current money of the Province of Canada; Provided, also, that no rule, order, or regulation, which shall be made and established by the said Corporation in the manner aforesaid, shall be of any force or effect, until the same shall have been sanctioned and confirmed by the said Lord Bishop or other ecclesiastical functionary, as aforesaid ;

And whereas, by another Act passed by the Legislature of the Province of Canada, at a Session held in the fifteenth and sixteenth years of our reign, intituled "An Act to amend the Act incorporating Bishop's College," it is enacted that the Bishop of Montreal, as well as any other Bishop or Bishops who may be appointed for any diocese of the United Church of England and Ireland which may hereafter be constituted in Lower Canada, together with the Bishop of Quebec, shall hereafter constitute the first branch of the Corporation of Bishop's College ;

And whereas since the passing of the said first mentioned Act, the Corporation of the said College have, with the sanction of the Lord Bishop of Quebec, by their petition to us, humbly set forth that in pursuance of the provisions of the said Act, Bishop's College has been duly organized by the appointment of Trustees and of a College Council, and that certain statutes, rules, and ordinances have been made by the said Corporation, with the approval of the Lord Bishop of Quebec ; and, further, that a suitable building has been erected, and a Principal and professors in the faculties of Divinity and of the Arts have been duly appointed, and are now engaged in the education of a number of scholars duly admitted, according to the statutes and ordinances of the said Corporation ; and the said College being, according to the said Act of Legislature of our Province of Canada, in strict connection with the Church of England and Ireland, and supported by an endowment provided by the bounty of members of that Church and otherwise, an humble application has been made to us by the said Corporation, that we would be pleased to grant our Royal Charter for the more perfect establishment of the said College, by granting to it the privileges hereinafter mentioned :

Now know ye that We, having taken the premises into our Royal consideration, and being willing to promote the more perfect establishment within that part of our Province of Canada called Lower

Canada, of a College in connection with the United Church of England and Ireland, for the education of youth in the doctrines and duties of the Christian religion, as inculcated by that Church, and for their instruction in the various branches of science and literature, which are taught in the Universities of this Kingdom, have, of our special grace, certain knowledge, and mere motion, willed, ordained and granted, and do by these presents, for us, our heirs and successors, will, ordain, and grant, that the said College shall be deemed and taken to be a University, and shall have and enjoy all such and the like privileges as are enjoyed by our Universities of our United Kingdom of Great Britain and Ireland, as far as the same are capable of being had or enjoyed by virtue of these our Letters Patent ; and that the students at the said College shall have liberty and faculty of taking the Degrees of Bachelor, Master, and Doctor, in the several arts and the faculties of Divinity, Law and Medicine, at the appointed times, and shall have liberty within themselves of performing all scholastic exercises for the conferring of such degrees, in such manner as shall be directed by the statutes, rules, and ordinances of the said College ;

And in order that such degrees may in due form be granted in the said College, We do further will and direct, and ordain, that there shall be at all times a Chancellor and Vice-Chancellor of the said University, to be chosen at and for such periods of time, and under such rules and regulations as the Corporation of the said College may, by their statutes, rules, and ordinances, to be from time to time passed for that purpose, think fit to appoint, and that the Chancellor, Vice-Chancellor, Principal and professors of the said College, and all persons admitted therein to the degree of Master of Arts, or to any degree in Divinity, Law, or Medicine, who, from the time of such their admission to such degree, shall pay the annual sum of twenty shillings of current money for and towards the support and maintenance of the said College, shall be and be deemed, taken, and reputed to be members of the Convocation of the said University, and as such members of the said Convocation shall have, exercise, and enjoy all such powers and privileges, in regard to conferring degrees and in any other matters, as may be provided for by any rules, orders, and regulations of the said College, duly sanctioned and confirmed, as far as the same are capable of being had and enjoyed by virtue of these our Letters Patent, and consistently with the provisions thereof. And we will and by these presents for us, our heirs, and successors, do grant and declare that these our Letters Patent, or the enrolment or exemplification thereof, shall and may be good, firm, valid, sufficient, and effectual in the law, according to the true intent and meaning of the same, and shall be taken, construed, and and adjudged in the most favourable and beneficial sense, and to the best advantage of our said College, as well in our Courts of Record as elsewhere, and by all and singular judges, justices, officers, ministers, and other subjects whatsoever, of us, our heirs and successors, any misrecital, non-recital, omission, imperfection, defect, matter, cause or thing, whatsoever, to the contrary notwithstanding.

> In witness whereof We have caused these Our Letters to be made Patent. Witness Ourself at Our Palace at Westminster, this twenty-eighth day of January, in the sixteenth year of Our reign.

> > By Her Majesty's Command,

> > > EDMUNDS.

APPENDIX K.

LAVAL UNIVERSITY CHARTER.

VICTORIA, by the Grace of God of the United Kingdom of Great Britain and Ireland, Queen, Defender of the Faith, &c., &c.

To all to whom these Presents shall come—GREETING :

Whereas it hath been represented unto us that there has existed during the last two hundred years, and does now exist in that part of our Province of Canada called Lower Canada, a Seminary established for the education and instruction of youth and known by and under the corporate style and title of " Le Seminaire de Quebec ;" that the said Seminary comprises a school of divinity and classes of instruction in science and literature, at present frequented by more than four hundred pupils ; that the said corporation is amply endowed, being provided with abundant means for carrying out its objects without assistance from the Provincial Legislature ; that it possesses extensive and valuable libraries, rich and costly collections of all kinds of philosophical and other apparatus requisite for assisting in imparting a knowledge of the sciences; and Whereas humble application hath been made unto us by the very Reverend Louis Jacques Casault, Superior of the said Seminary, and the Reverend Antoine Parant, Joseph Aubry, John Holmes, Leon Gingras, Louis Gingras, Michel Forgues Elzear, Alexandre Taschereau, and Edward John Horan, directors of the said Seminary, that We would be pleased to grant our Royal Charter for the purpose of authorising the said corporation to confer degrees, and granting unto the said corporation all other privileges usually granted to and enjoyed by universities :

Now know ye that, having taken the premises into our Royal consideration, and duly appreciating the great utility and importance of the enjoyment of these privileges by the said "Seminaire de Quebec," We, of our especial grace, certain knowledge, and mere motion have ordained and granted, and by these presents do for us, our heirs, and successors, ordain and grant that the said Louis Jacques Casault, Antoine Parant, Joseph Aubrey, John Holmes, Leon Gingras, Louis Gingras, Michel Forgues Elzear, Alexandre Taschereau, and Edward John Horan, and their successors in their offices aforesaid shall be and be called as heretofore one body corporate and politic, and shall in addition to the powers and privileges by them hitherto possessed and enjoyed in their said corporate capacity, have, possess, and enjoy the rights, powers, and privileges of an University as hereinafter directed for the education and instruction of youth and students in arts and faculties, and that in each and every act or deed done and performed under and in virtue of this charter, the said " Seminaire de Quebec " shall be named, called, and known as the " Université Laval " (Laval University).

And We do hereby, for us, our heirs, and successors, declare, ordain, and grant that our trusty and well-beloved the most Reverend Pierre-Flavien Turgeon, Roman Catholic Archbishop for the time being of the said Diocese, or the person administering the said Diocese, shall by virtue of his office be Visitor of the said University.

And We do hereby for us, our heirs, and successors, declare, ordain, and grant that there shall be at all times one Rector of the said University, and that the said office of Rector shall be held by the Superior of the said Seminaire de Quebec for the time being.

And We do hereby for us, our heirs, and successors, declare, ordain, and grant that there shall be such and so many professors in the different arts and faculties in our said University as from time to time shall be deemed necessary or expedient, and as shall be regulated by the Visitor of our said University, by and with the advice of the University Council hereinafter established.

And We do hereby for us, our heirs, and successors, declare, ordain, and grant that the said Rector and the said professors of our said University, and all persons who shall be duly matriculated into and admitted as members of our said University and their successors forever shall be one distinct and separate body politic in deed and in name, by the name and style of " the Rector and members of L'Université Laval (Laval University), at Quebec, in the Province of Canada," and that by the same name they shall have perpetual succession and a common seal, and that they and their successors shall from time to time, have full power to break, change, alter, or renew such common seal at their will and pleasure, and as often as they shall judge expedient, and that by the same name, they, the said Rector and members of the said University and their successors from time to time and at all times hereafter, shall be able and capable in law to sue and be sued, implead and be impleaded, answer and be answered in all or any court or courts of record within our United Kingdom of Great Britain and Ireland and our said Province of Canada and other our dominions, and in all singular actions, causes, pleas, suits, matters, and demands whatsoever, of what nature or kind soever, in as large, ample, and beneficial a manner as any other body corporate and politic, or any other our liege subjects, being persons able and capable in law, may or can sue, implead, or answer, or be sued, impleaded, or answered in any manner whatsoever.

And We do hereby, for us, our heirs, and successors declare and ordain that there shall be within our said University a Council, to be called and known by the name of the "Université Laval (Laval University) Council."

And We do for us, our heirs, and successors, will and ordain that the said Council shall consist and be composed of the Rector of the said University, of the directors of the said Seminaire de Quebec, to wit the Reverand Antoine Parant, Joseph Aubry, John Holmes, Leon Gingras, Louis Gingras, Michel Forgues, Elzear Alexandre Taschereau, and Edward John Horan, by virtue of their office as such directors, and their successors, whether the said directors be or be not professors in the said University, and of the three senior professors of the several Faculties of Divinity, Law, Medicine, and Arts in the said University.

And We do hereby for us, our heirs, and successors, further will and ordain that by the term "director" shall be understood any and every person considered as such by the said Seminaire de Quebec.

And We do hereby, for us, our heirs, and successors, further will and ordain that all the powers and privileges granted by this our Charter shall be vested in and exercised by the said Council.

And We do hereby, for us, our heirs, and successors, will and ordain that the members of the said University Council shall hold their seats in the said Council so long only as they and each of them shall retain their respective offices as aforesaid, by and in virtue of which they become members thereof.

And We do hereby, for us, our heirs, and successors, will and ordain that the Rector, for the time being, of the said University, shall preside at all meetings of the said University Council, at which he may be present, and that in his absence from any such meeting it shall be presided over by such member thereof who may then be first Assistant Superior of the said Seminaire de Quebec, or in the absence of this latter by the second Assistant Superior thereof, and in the absence of all three of the above functionaries, by the member of the said Council who shall be the senior director of the said Seminaire then present.

And We do hereby, for us, our heirs, and successors, declare and ordain that no meeting of the said Council shall be or be held to be a lawful meeting thereof, unless a majority of the members thereof be present during the whole of every such meeting; and that all questions and resolutions proposed for the decision of the said University Council shall be determined by the majority of the votes of the members of Council present, including the vote of the Rector or other presiding members; and that in case of an equal division of such votes, the Rector or other member presiding at any such meeting shall give an additional or casting vote.

And We do by these presents for us, our heirs and successors will, ordain, and grant that the said Council of our said University shall have full power and authority to frame and make statutes, rules, and ordinances touching and concerning the good government of the said University, the studies, lectures, exercises, degrees in arts and faculties, and all matters regarding the same; and also touching and concerning any other matter or thing which to them shall seem good, fit, and useful for the well being and advancement of our said University and agreeable to this our Royal Charter; and also from time to time by any new statutes, rules, or ordinances, to revoke, renew, augment, or alter all, every or any of the said statutes, rules, and ordinances as to them shall seem fit and expedient : Provided always that the said statutes, rules, and ordinances or any of them shall not be repugnant to the laws and statutes of the United Kingdom of Great Britain and Ireland or of our said Province of Canada, nor repugnant to or inconsistent with this our Charter or any of the provisions thereof; provided, also, that a copy of all statutes, rules, and ordinances so to be made as aforesaid under and in virtue of this our Charter shall be furnished with all convenient speed after the making thereof to the Visitor of our said University for the time being, who shall have authority within two years from the day of the receipt of such copy to disallow any such statute, rule, or ordinance or any part thereof and such disallowance shall without delay be signified in writing under the hand of our said Visitor to the Rector of our said University, and thenceforward such statute, rule, or ordinance, or any part thereof so disallowed, shall be void and of no effect, but otherwise shall be and remain in full force and virtue ; provided also that all statutes, rules, or ordinances repugnant to law as aforesaid or to this our Charter or inconsistent therewith shall be *ipso facto* null and void. And we do hereby for us, our heirs and successors will, ordain, and declare that the said University Council shall have full power and authority to nominate and appoint the various professors for the several faculties of law, medicine, and arts, and of revoking and cancelling all such nominations and appointments whenever they shall find just and sufficient cause ; and the said Council shall also have and possess the right and privilege of presenting and submitting the names of candidates for the professorships of divinity to the Visitor of the said University, by whom alone the appointment of the professors of divinity shall be made and confirmed ; but the said Council shall have no power or authority to revoke or annul the nomination or appointment of the said professors of divinity without the previous consent of the said Visitor.

And whereas it is necessary to make provision for the completion and fitting up of the said Council at the first institution of our said University and previously to the appointment of any professors, now We do for us, our heirs and successors further ordain, and declare that until such professors be named the Rector and directors of the said Seminaire shall be deemed to constitute the said council and shall be to all intents and purposes capable of performing and exercising all and every the duties, powers, authority, and privileges hereby granted to and vested in the said Council.

And We do hereby for us, our heirs and successors, charge and command that the statutes, rules, and ordinances aforesaid, subject to the said provisions, shall be strictly and inviolably observed, kept, and performed from time to time under the penalties to be thereby or therein imposed or contained.

And we do for us, our heirs and successors further will, ordain, and grant that the said Université Laval (Laval University) shall, as such University hereby constituted, have, possess, and enjoy all such and the like privileges as are now enjoyed by our Universities of our United Kingdom of Great Britain and Ireland, so far as the same are capable of being had, possessed, or enjoyed under and by virtue of this our Royal Charter, and that the said University Council shall have power and liberty to grant and confer on all students, whether they be or be not students in the said Seminary or University, or in any other college or seminary within our said Province which shall be affiliated to and connected with the said University as hereinafter provided, who shall be found duly qualified according to the statutes, rules, and ordinances aforesaid, to receive the same, the degrees of Bachelor, Master, and Doctor in the several of arts and faculties, and the said University Council shall have power and liberty within itself of causing to be performed all scholastic duties for the conferring of such degrees in such manner as shall be directed by the statutes, rules, and ordinances aforesaid.

And We do further for us, our heirs and successors, will, ordain, and grant that the said University Council shall for the purposes of this our Royal Charter have, possess, and enjoy the right and power to affiliate to and connect with the said University any one or more college or colleges, seminary or seminaries, public institution or institutions of education within our said Province as to the said Council may seem fit, subject nevertheless to the statutes, rules, and ordinances aforesaid.

And We for us, our heirs and successors, do further will and ordain that no religious test or qualification shall be required of or appointed for any person to be admitted or matriculated as students within our said University, provided, nevertheless, that all persons admitted to any degree in any art or faculty therein shall make such declarations and subscriptions as by the statutes, rules, and ordinances aforesaid, shall be fixed and appointed : Provided always, and this our Royal Charter is granted upon the express terms and conditions, that the powers, authorities, privileges, and rights hereby granted shall not in the exercise of them by the said University Council in any manner or way interfere with, diminish, or otherwise affect the powers, rights, and privileges of the said Seminaire de Quebec, as now enjoyed and exercised by the Superior and directors of the said Seminaire, but that all and every the said rights, powers, authorities, and privileges of the said corporation of " Le Seminaire de Quebec," shall in the administration of the affairs of the said Seminaire de Quebec remain the same as heretofore.

And We will, and by these presents for us, our heirs and successors do ordain and declare that these our Letters Patent, or an exemplification thereof, shall and may be good, firm, valid, sufficient, and effectual in law, according to the true intent and meaning of the same, and shall be taken, construed, and adjudged in the most favorable and beneficial sense, and to the best advantage of the said "Rector and members of our said University," as well in our courts of record as elsewhere, and by all and singular judges, justices, officers and other subjects whatsoever, of us, our heirs and successors, any mis-recital, non-recital, omission, imperfection, defect, matter, cause, or thing whatsoever to the contrary thereof in any wise, notwithstanding.

> In witness whereof We have caused these Our Letters to be made patent. Witness Ourself at our Palace at Westminster, this eighth day of December, in the sixteenth year of Our reign.

www.ingramcontent.com/pod-product-compliance
Lightning Source LLC
Chambersburg PA
CBHW021233300426
44111CB00007B/528